Framing Silence

In the Hills of Haiti. . . . *(Photo: M.J.A. Chancy)*

Framing Silence

REVOLUTIONARY NOVELS BY HAITIAN WOMEN

MYRIAM J. A. CHANCY

Rutgers University Press
New Brunswick, New Jersey

Library of Congress Cataloging-in-Publication Data

Chancy, Myriam J. A., 1970–
    Framing silence : revolutionary novels by Haitian women / Myriam
J. A. Chancy.
       p.   cm.
    Includes bibliographical references and index.
    ISBN 0-8135-2339-7 (cloth : alk. paper). — ISBN 0-8135-2340-0
(pbk. : alk. paper)
    1. Haitian fiction—Women authors—History and criticism.
2. Haitian fiction—20th century—History and criticism. 3. Women
and literature—Haiti—History—20th century. I. Title.
PQ3944.C43   1997
843—dc20   96-2697
                                                CIP

British Cataloging-in-Publication information available

Manufactured in the United States of America

For the women of my family, whose strength, perseverance, and capacity for love never ceases to amaze and sustain me; and for my father, Wilbert Chancy, who, in singing the beauty of Haiti, held fast the memories.

CONTENTS

ACKNOWLEDGMENTS

I wish to thank Adeline L. Chancy for her assistance with the numerous translations needed to produce this text, for proofreading and assisting with the preparation of the index, and, mostly, for many enlightening discussions on the literature itself; Florence S. Boos for her meticulous readings of the introduction, chapter three, and chapter four as the project took its initial form and for her faith in my work; A. Manette Ansay for reading and providing generous comments on an early draft of chapter four; Leslie Mitchner and Marilyn Campbell for their care in seeing the project through the Press; and the University Research Council of Vanderbilt University for providing a subvention to offset the cost of reproducing the photographs included in this publication.

"Dahomey" and "A Woman Speaks," from *The Black Unicorn* by Audre Lorde, copyright © 1978 by Audre Lorde, are reprinted by permission of W. W. Norton & Company Inc. An excerpt from *Cahier d'un Retour au Pays Natal* by Aimé Césaire, copyright © 1944, is reprinted by persmission of Présence Africaine.

Framing Silence

Paròl gin pié–zèl

—◦—➤═◄—◦—

Let Me Tell You a Story

*I*n front of the Palais National, in the
capital of Haiti, Port-au-Prince, a square is alight with dreams. The nights
in Port-au-Prince are unusually cool for the visitor, past resident, or tourist,
who imagines that the Caribbean is perpetually hot, sweltering, always
scorching below a tropical, yellowish orange orb of sunlight. The nights
here betray such myths. The coolness offers a respite from days filled not
with the make-believe world of the Club-Meds, which populate the Third
World like parasites upon a dying host, but from days filled with work hard
beyond imagining and the horrors of civil strife: the country is at war with
itself at the same time that it is exploited by its too near neocolonial neighbors within the Caribbean basin as well as on the "mainland." Poverty, as
we well know, is rampant in Haiti. Yet, there are lights burning in the piazza
in front of the Palais, white like snow in the incandescent moonlight. They
blaze as they should in front of any official government building in the
Americas, as they do elsewhere in capitals around the world.

The piazza is not empty. As in any large city, stragglers are making
their way to and from the watering holes on the main street; some are returning home after a long day of lacing baseballs, others are just arriving.
Among the arrivals are children who have come late after supper with
dingy tote bags hung from their thin shoulders. They say that over 90 percent of the population on this island is illiterate; this is not for lack of trying. The children beneath the lights in the piazza are dream-seekers of the
purest kind; they hope to work their way into the world that has kept them
at arm's length, coded each among them as undesirables.

As you imagine this scene—the backs of children curved over hesitant pencil markings upon yellowed, lined paper; the shuffling of bare feet
in the dust of the broken cobbles of what was once the pride of a new nation; the slow murmur of one child reading to another, who writes each

1

word painstakingly as if it were a *dictée*—see one little girl apart from the rest. At first glance, she does not seem unique in any way. Her name: let it be Solange. She is named for an ancestor, perhaps, whose photograph you will never have the occasion to finger, to contemplate.

Solange is small for her eleven years. You may wonder if she does not get enough to eat at home. Her family does well enough; her mother allows her to go to school, to do her homework once she has completed each of her chores. She is one of the lucky ones who will have choices someday, or so she hopes. As far back as she can remember, Solange's chores have involved cleaning the bedrooms and taking care of her two younger brothers by making sure they are bathed and dressed every morning. At night, she helps with the preparation of the meal, usually a portion of rice for each of them, *bananes pesées,* and sometimes *grillot* or chicken necks. She cleans the dishes after her father leaves the table to go to bed. He rises early to set off for the factory. Solange can't remember the last time she has seen him in the morning. But she does not think of these things as she studies; these hours enveloped beneath the unnatural light of her favorite lamp are precious. She is here simply because electricity does not flow to their home and oil must be used only in great need. This is her alternative, her hope. At least she has this option: something she can count on that she has made her own.

On this night, Solange is dreaming of revolution. She is reading her textbook, *L'histoire d'Haïti,* for her morning class. The stories—for this is what they seem to her, no different from fairy tales, bedtime lullabies— fascinate her. Here she reads of a world she has never known and can only imagine. She reads about the five kingdoms of the Tainos, the Arawak tribes decimated by the arrival of the *fameux* Christophe Colomb. She imagines the hills of Haiti as they once were, lush-green, bursting with potential. (Even in the dark, you can see the country is not as it once was: the rivers no longer run, are filled with rocks; the hills are bald, burned beyond recognition as the result of deforestation.) Solange reads on and encounters the African rebels who fought against their enslavement, the *marrons.* She knows some of them have survived, are referred to as *cacos,* and are feared, benevolently, unlike the *macoutes* who are thought of only as evil incarnate—werewolves—and seldom as men and women made of pliant flesh and brittle bone. She fashions for herself visions of Boukman, of Toussaint, the liberators as they were known then, in the years just preceding independence in 1804. It must have been an exciting time. It must have been so very difficult.

Solange is filled with a sense of possibility. Can she dare to dream a place for herself in this record of the passage of time? Could she display such courage? Had any Haitian women before her taken up arms? She does not know. The book on her lap answers her with silence, save for dates, battle scenes. Solange plays with the edge of her slip, which protrudes slightly from beneath her flowered skirt. She chews on a wisp of her hair, which has flown free from the braid lying across the nape of her neck.

The air is growing cooler. Solange is torn between the impulse to continue looking for images of herself in her history book and to close it like a door against the past so that she can return home before the night is lost without the weight of the questions in her mind. She does not have much time to decide. The curfew is in effect for all the school-aged. They say it is to keep the calm, to eliminate chaos. In fact, the opposite has occurred: she, like the others, find any way they can to be in the streets, hiding in the shadows of the police. Ironically, it is only at night that she feels that there is hope, that fewer eyes are upon her. There is freedom in living in the shadows, although it means that there can be no real life—not one, in any case, that can be recognized and flourish unheeded in the clear light of day.

In the shadows, things go on that seem to have no meaning. Gun shots echo like whistles. Pavements ring out with the sound of fleeing feet, and it is impossible to tell in which direction those feet go. Eventually, the sounds are carried away on the wings of the sea breeze. Solange listens and listens, trying to make sense of it all. Could these sounds be remainders, fragments of the Revolution? How different can they be except that there is pavement now? Those feet are the same, running away from terror, poverty, impossible hopes, towards . . . Solange wonders. Why all this running? A gun sounds so close to her she can smell the powder. Like fireworks on days of celebration. The fireworks are in her head. So colorful. So painful. The book falls out of her hand. She wants to reach for it but cannot move. There is simply too much pain. Solange closes her eyes, and soon she can feel nothing. She hears her mother's voice screaming so loudly "*Anmoé!! Anmoé!!*," calling for help. The year is 1990 and it has been four years since Bébé Doc fled the capital with his wife and young children. No one will ever admit to having killed Solange.

This story is only true in spirit. It is inspired by accounts of childhood in Haiti told me by my father who remembers well years in the country's history when the emerging working, middle classes petitioned for electricity, and roads were beginning to be built to join the metropolis,

Port-au-Prince, to smaller cities, like the burgeoning Pétion-Ville. In the absence of modern conveniences, those who had gained access to education, but not to privileges of class that would guarantee the means to sustain such thirst for knowledge, would do all that it took to obtain books, or light by which to read—the latter most often found in public spaces. Knowledge was not, as it often is in elitist institutions of the West, equated with privacy, with the curved walls of the ivory tower of intellectual endeavor.

Solange's story is also inspired by Paul Farmer's account of the death of Roseline Vaval, who, killed by the army in the small town of Petit Goâve at eleven years of age (and yes, while she was reading her history of Haiti), became the catalyst for grassroots uprising throughout the provinces. Her death became symbolic of the repression perpetuated by the army under General Prosper Avril, from 1988 to 1990, through the same dictatorial means established so thoroughly by the Duvalier patriarchs. According to Farmer, Roseline Vaval's memorial services "turned into anti-Avril demonstrations" which resulted in Avril's resignation. Roseline Vaval had been killed on March 5, 1990. Avril fled the nation on March 12 (149–150).

Farmer relates two other incidences in his most recent historical-political text, *The Uses of Haiti,* in which Haitian girls and women figure prominently; like his relation of the first, however, neither of these are recounted with any particular attention to the fact that the actors presented are women. The first incident tells of the carnage that took place during the 1987 elections. In one voting center, three generations of women were gunned down. This is especially significant when one considers that Haitian women had only been able to vote once before, *as women,* in any *open* election in the country's history.[1] In a second incident during the summer of 1988, in the midst of a raid on a church, women banded together in order to resist: "A group of young women were in the front courtyard and were attempting to resist the onslaught, attempting to resist, with our own kind of arms, the heavy weapons that the men were using against us from the street—this was a prophetic, historic resistance that we will never forget" (Romélus, qtd. Farmer 146). As in the case of Roseline Vaval, this latter event precipitated a wave of protest from the grassroots level. In presenting these three cases, Farmer never provides a gendered analysis of each. This, to me, is disturbing for two reasons. The first is that, by failing to do so, Farmer perpetuates the monolithizing of Haitians as a group within which differences of class, color, race, and gender are said not to exist. Secondly, all three of the aforementioned incidents demonstrate that women have been and continue to be an important part of the revolutionary undercurrents that have enabled generation upon generation of Haitians, following the independence of 1804, to survive an endless succession of dictatorial governments. Because, in this context, women are not normally discussed in terms of how their gendered identities affect the ways in which they express their resistance to modes of oppression, the absence of anti-female, sexist oppression in the Haitian context is often touted in both academic and political circles.

Although Farmer's account of Roseline Vaval's death ensures that her name will be a part of the historical record, it does not reveal the inherent irony of this young girl's death; in my mind, she is representative of an entire generation of children whose lives are continuously at risk. Furthermore, she represents, for me, a symbol of Haitian girlhood, spent in dreams, lived in the imagination, and extinguished before *croissance.* I have attempted above to recreate the essence of the last moments of Roseline Vaval's life to demonstrate how the story of this girl's life reverberates on levels not analyzed in Farmer's text, or even in general reports describing the civil unrest that has plagued Haiti of late. At the beginning of each chapter of literary analysis to follow, I will return to this story, rewriting it continuously, in order to remind myself and the reader of the connection between history and storytelling, between Haitian women's lives and the ways in which narrative enables Haitian women writers to preserve those lives.

Narratology: The Novel as Revolutionary Tool

The underlying assumption in this critical undertaking is that the study of narrative implies an awareness of the cultural modes of production, that it delineates the ways in which we both understand ourselves within culture and transmit our knowledge of codes of (self)representation. As comparativist Didier Coste writes in *Narrative as Communication:* "narratology has an anthropological scope: it is concerned with the production, transmission, and exchange of information on change and simulacra of change." Coste thus discusses narrative, both textual and verbal, as a form of communication whereby meaning is derived from the interaction of "participants and witnesses" with the mode of transmission and writes "I measure meaning in order to measure myself" (5). One of the questions this book aims to answer is to what extent we can arrive at a narratological reading of Haitian women's literature from which can be extracted a measure of meaning. In other words, do Haitian women writers rely on a unified understanding of Haitian culture on which to base their narratives or do they redefine it? If, as I claim, the latter is the case, then how might we reconceive approaches to literatures arising out of the feminine Caribbean? Or to "postcolonial" theory in general? Might there be a *distinct* Haitian woman's literary tradition?

Since a codified history of Haitian women has yet to be written, the project of recovering the roots of Haitian women's self-definition is made possible only through the evaluation of narrative forms. In fact, the writings by women of color in the United States as well as in the Third World reveal that the creation of identity in the face of imperialist and colonial oppression begins with the transmutation of the personal into the creative, into modes of self-empowerment that in and of themselves create a theory of self-definition. In this book, I posit that Haitian women writers have— since the publication of the first known Haitian women's novel, Mme. Virgile Valcin's *Cruelle destinée* (1929)—created a vision of Haitian women in fictional form that corresponds to a feminized reading of the history of our country. Many of the novels with which I will be dealing are narratives told in the first person. This reflects a political strategy used not only to create a sense of extra-textual intimacy, but also to create a space within the parameters of the genre that redefines national identity in terms of the personal. Given that women have too few avenues for self-expression in Haiti, a discussion of this approach is crucial to a thorough analysis of texts which formulate distinct images of Haitian women's lived lives. The fictional is therefore a conduit for a historical narrative that is elsewhere denied existence. The earliest novels written during the U.S. Occupation, which make use of traditional, French sentimentalism, are also in the service of this politicized discourse, since they present, within what appears to be a detached and "objective" perspective, complex representations of the sexual dimensions of Haitian women's lives. Traditional forms are thus, at times, invoked to critique social mores that have denied women control over their lives within rigid class and gendered social stratifications.

I posit first that much of Haitian women's literature should be read as a literature of revolution. My definition of revolution emerges from a radical feminist perspective in which the search for an irrevocable alteration of the status quo, not only between women and men, but among women themselves, in a context of oppression, is demanded. Here, I am aligning myself with the editors of *This Bridge Called My Back,* Cherríe Moraga and Gloria Anzaldúa, who, along with the contributors to their anthology, cogently articulate the tenets of radical feminism for women of color—tenets grounded in an awareness and open defiance of the forces of multiple oppression as lived under U.S. imperialism—by making visible the effects of that oppression on the lives of Third World women. Consequently, my choice of texts in the present study reflects this feminist ideology—I have purposefully brought together novels whose authors contest the regimented view of Haitian history that has denied female existence, and who do so by addressing more than only gender as a point of oppression for Haitian women, whether those points of oppression be color, class, sexuality, or nationality. My own analysis is thus rooted in a radical re-reading of Haitian culture that re-draws the parameters of current "postcolonial" criticism—which, by and large, stifles any claims to the presence of feminism in the Third World—in order to forge a distinct space for Haitian women's voices within feminist discourse.

My text is also actively double-voiced, echoing the critical writings of other scholars or writers of African descent like Derrick Bell and Patricia J. Williams, who incorporate storytelling and autobiographical resonance in addressing issues like those of race, class, and gender. I thus echo Williams who writes in *The Alchemy of Race and Rights:* "I am trying to challenge the usual limits of commercial discourse by using an intentionally double-voiced and relational . . . vocabulary" (6). In this context, the "commercial discourse" I am contesting is critical-literary rhetoric itself. I am more interested, for the purposes of this book, to chart ideological innovation than aesthetic or linguistic ones. This interest has led me to exclude some writers and their texts—in particular, the novels of Liliane Dévieux-Dehoux and Marie-Thérèse Colimon-Hall, which can be considered well at the forefront of Haitian women's literature, even in the absence of any formal agreement on a "canon." As Adrienne Gouraige has noted, however, Colimon-Hall's heroines "do not accomplish spectacular action" and her novels resist psychological explorations in order to depict Haitian women primarily as martyrs (36); the same can be said of Dévieux-Dehoux's heroine in *L'amour, oui, la mort, non* (1976). Clearly, such works fall outside of the purview of a study focusing on literary attempts to produce empowering images of Haitian women or critiques of the cultural norms that have so disempowered us. Neither is the following a survey of Haitian women's novels. In order both to illustrate as accurately as possible the ways in which Haitian women novelists have transhistorically brought a pluralistic feminist lens to bear on representations of Haitian women and to provide a cross-section of what I perceive to be a visible strain of revolutionary narrativism in Haitian women's literature, I have chosen to balance discussions of well-known Francophone texts (by Mme. Virgile Valcin, Nadine Magloire, Jan J. Dominique, and Marie Chauvet) with less well-known ones (by Annie Desroy and Ghislaine Charlier), including two Anglophone texts (by Edwidge Danticat and Anne-christine d'Adesky).

The reader will note that the novels of Marie Chauvet have no central place in this study, though they are by far the best-known works by a Haitian woman novelist (and some of the writers included in this study, such as Ghislaine Charlier, have gained inspiration from her writings). I have deliberately chosen not to foreground them for two crucial reasons. First, in order to avoid repeating studies (my own included) focusing on Marie Chauvet's *Amour, colère, folie* (1968) and other novels, I have opted to analyze her final novel, *Les rapaces* (1986), which has not been critically assessed and which, further, provides a productive contrast to d'Adesky's recent novel, *Under the Bone* (1994), in light of current discussions of apocalyptic rhetoric as we near the end of this century. Secondly, what this book offers is a *conceptual and theoretical framework* in which Chauvet's work might be placed rather than a showcase for it; it is the framework of the tradition of women's writing in Haiti that is the main focus of this text and it is the revolutionary scope of this tradition which interests me most.[2] This said, it is also my belief that Chauvet's work is deserving of its own book-length study, which my present work cannot hope to encompass. Thus, I have made the difficult but conscious choice to foreground those Haitian women writers whose voices have been the most silenced. I do believe that there is much to be gained by coming to terms with these silenced texts, the further marginalized voices. For, as the creole saying goes, *paròl gin pié—zèl* (words have feet, wings), and their words will carry us far toward a better understanding of the Haitian woman.

As might be surmised, this text resists, rather than participates in, current trends to canonize the "postcolonial." I mean to go beyond the current terminology of "resistance literature" that is affixed to literatures arising out of colonial and/or postcolonial contexts; in so doing, however, I do not eliminate the categorization of Haitian women's literature as one engaged in counter-colonial (or counter-hegemonic) discourse. In her *Resistance Literature,* Barbara Harlow defines literature of resistance as follows: "Whereas the social and the personal have tended to displace the political in western literary and cultural studies, the emphasis in the literature of resistance is on the political as the power to change the world. The theory of resistance literature is in its politics" (30). Resistance literature thus implicitly and explicitly removes itself from Western modes of theorizing by deploying its own cultural and literary theory, which is one of "political and politicized activity" (Harlow 28). Literature thus becomes "an arena of struggle" (Harlow 2) in which history, culture, and their modes of reproduction are contested and reformulated. By necessity, the cultural or literary critic must engage such texts not as empty artistic vessels standing outside of time, but as political manifestoes emerging from distinct spatial and geographical locations and from distinct cultural and historical periods, and articulated from differing positions within those locations and periods.[3] In keeping with this perspective, then, the absolute demand made by resistance literature is to displace Western ideology, to move beyond discourses, such as histories of colonialism ("what the white man did") and nationalist historiography ("legend of . . . resistance which omits the uncomfortable fact of collaboration" [Worsley, qtd. Harlow 5]), as well as theories of postcolonialism and postmodernism, that deny the complexities of cultures that have undergone constant disruptions, but which have also, despite continued subjugation, reconstituted themselves as distinct from the West in important ways. My own study will refuse to participate in the Western critical practice of co-optation by contesting theories of postcolonialism and postmodernism and displacing them through the theories the texts themselves unleash.

All of the works I analyze here are novels: this is not incidental. That I have chosen to focus on novels is not to deny that there is a rich poetic legacy, but, as Christophe Charles's anthology of Haitian women's poetry attests,[4] that poetry is primarily romantic and nostalgic in nature and almost entirely devoid of politics. Although few novels by Haitian women have been published since 1934, the constancy of their themes—from memory to sexual freedom to women's solidarity—provides a clear historical progression from one text to the next that makes them suited to the kind of enterprise I am most interested in here: a politicized reading of the historiographic purposes of Haitian women's literature. As Harlow notes, the novel as narrative lends itself more clearly to the political project of analyzing and redefining social norms than does poetry: "The use by Third World resistance writers of the novel form as it has developed within the western literary tradition both appropriates and challenges the historical and historicizing presuppositions, the narrative conclusions, implicated within the western tradition and its development" (78). In the Haitian context, the "woman's novel" appropriates and challenges not only the Western tradition but also the counter-discourse established by Haitian male resistance writers. As such, the Haitian woman's novel as resistance narrative "is not only a document, [but] . . . also an indictment" (Harlow 96) of both Western literariness and Haitian literariness. Furthermore, the novel genre enables these visionary women to go beyond the formal components of resistance poetry where, as Harlow points out, "the symbols and images often fail to elucidate the implicit power structure of a given historical conjuncture [while] the discourse of narrative is capable of exposing these structures, even, eventually, of realigning them, of redressing the imbalance" (85). Along these lines, it becomes necessary to define the novelistic literary tradition of Haitian women as one that transgresses nationalistic ideologies and reformulates nation and identity through the lens of personal and communal exile.

History Revisited

"Storytelling," writes Trinh T. Minh-ha, "the oldest form of building historical consciousness in community, constitutes a rich oral legacy, whose values have regained all importance recently, especially in the context of writings by women of color." She continues:

> She who works at un-learning the dominant language of "civilized" missionaries also has to learn how to un-write and write anew. And she often does so by re-establishing the contact with her foremothers, so that living tradition can never congeal into fixed forms, so that life keeps on nurturing life, so that what is understood as the Past continues to provide the link for the Present and the Future. (148–149)

Trinh speaks of women attempting to emerge from the bind of "postcolonial" erasure. As an anthropologist and a filmmaker, Trinh contends that women whose cultural identities have been plundered by imperialism and colonialism may reclaim the past by connecting themselves to a communal consciousness, the origin of which is the voice of their foremothers. Not surprisingly, given the historical, academic devaluation of theories produced by women of color whose politics are invested in foregrounding the lived realities of women,[5] Trinh's concern with the recuperation of women's lives in the Third World has been negatively criticized.

Sara Suleri, in her article "Woman Skin Deep: Feminism and the Postcolonial Condition," for example, charges that "[w]hen feminism turns to lived experience as an alternative mode of radical subjectivity, it only re-hearses the objectification of its proper subject. . . . neither should such data serve as the evacuating principle for both historical and theoretical contexts alike" (248). Suleri attempts to prove her point by referring us to Trinh's final chapter in *Woman, Native, Other,* "Grandma's Story," which begins:

> Let me tell you a story. For all I have is a story. Story passed on from generation to generation, named Joy. Told for the joy it gives the storyteller and the listener. Joy inherent in the process of storytelling. Whoever understands it also understands that a story, as distressing as it can be in its joy, never takes anything away from anybody. Its name, remember, is Joy. Its double, Woe Morrow Show. (119)

Suleri, who leaves out the last two sentences when she quotes these lines in her essay, contends that Trinh's presentation of "lived experience" is both objectifying and ahistorical. She calls it a "fallacious allegory for the re-constitution of gendered race [that] bespeaks a transcendence—and an at-tendant evasion—of the crucial cultural issues at hand" (248). What is particulary disingeneous about this criticism is that it fails to take into ac-count the fact that the concepts Trinh presents are an essential component of identity construction for the forgotten women of the (post)colonial world. In the above passage, Trinh is reclaiming the voice of the storyteller and supplanting the objectifying voice of Western History that mystifies popular knowledge of oppressed groups. This voice is her source of "joy," a celebration of lives reclaimed; Trinh impels her readers to "remember" through and with that voice. Memory, then, serves as the paradigm for sur-vival transhistorically: it is not a claim to an evasion of history but, rather, a challenge to remember that cultures are shaped by what survives from one generation to the next.

Trinh follows her opening words in "Grandma's Story" with a quota-tion from Korean writer Theresa Hak Kyung Cha's text, *Dictée,* thus locat-ing the context of her words within a culture that parallels her own, complex identity—it is a context that encompasses the meeting of at least three differing cultural groups. Suleri ignores this context in order to deny Trinh (and women like her) her polyphonic discourse, a discourse that re-flects the lived realities of those who must speak through more than one language/culture at once. Hence, Trinh writes: "Something must be said. Must be said that has not been *and* has been said before." She continues:

The story of a people. Of us, peoples. Story, history, literature (or religion, philosophy, natural science, ethics)—all in one. They call it the tool of primitive man, the simplest vehicle of truth. When history separated itself from story, it started indulging in accumulation and facts. Or thought it could. It thought it could build up to History because the Past, unrelated to the Present and the Future, is lying there in its entirety, waiting to be revealed and related. (120)

Trinh's model of storytelling is simply one intent on revealing a continuum denied by History. Her work describes the ways in which the voices of *griots,* of elders, in various eras, in various societies, have been denigrated: "Imagination is . . . equated with falsification" (121). Reclaiming the stories of submerged worlds is one way in which the totalization of the Third World can be circumvented. Through them, History (Suleri's lower-case history) can be displaced in order to make room for an alternative remembrance of the erosion of time, of the formation of previously invisible cultures.

In Haitian women's literature, the novel most often serves as the vehicle through which identity is articulated and affirmed. Counter to Western ideology, imagination is rendered factual rather than false, a key to the real rather than its mere shadow. Still, the context from which this literature emerges is one bound to illiteracy, and limited access to the means by which to textualize the imagination; in a country in which literacy is rare, it is not surprising, therefore, to find that there exists a limited female literary tradition.

In 1987, Pierrette Frickey, in her study of the production of literature by Afro-Caribbean women, found that only fifteen women writers had been published in Haiti, as opposed to over four hundred male writers (cited in Campbell, 119).[6] In her analytical survey of Caribbean women's literature, Maryse Condé further shows the disparity between women and men's history of publication in Haiti when she writes that "in a recent anthology entitled *Contemporary Haitian Poetry* . . . among the 61 authors cited, only 4 are women."[7] But in her careful analysis of novels by Adeline Moravia, Marie Chauvet, and Liliane Dévieux-Dehoux, Condé also shows that these writers reveal through their writings aspects of the roles played by women in Haitian society and the ways in which traditional mores are perceived by different Haitian women as either contestable or unbreachable. Creative textual expressions thus function as a repository of images of women that exists nowhere else, or in few places. Condé cites, for instance, the presence of literary figures such as Jamaica's Nanny and Guadeloupe's "'mulâtresse Solitude'" in the barren landscape of the historization of women's role in insurrections across the islands. Condé warns readers against an overinvestment in ethnological and political discourses within literature, but she nonetheless concludes that "through literature ["elle"], it is possible to capture the image of a community. . . . The novel, if it represents the intimate world to which an author gives us access, is also a witnessing of society."[8] Here, the feminine pronoun "elle," which refers to literature, a "female" noun in French, moves me to extend Condé's statement to take into account the authors' gendered identities, that is, to point out that "through [woman]" it is possible to extract a sense of women's place in Caribbean society, to extract from the text moments in time which reflect lived experience, and finally, that her writings provide witness to a suppressed historical presence.

La Marabout: The Paradoxical Haitian Woman

Haitian women writers have been forced to articulate their marginalization on multiple fronts: the experience of the Haitian woman is defined by exile within her own country, for she is alienated from the means to assert at once feminine and feminist identities at the same time that she undergoes the same colonial experiences of her male counterparts. Because women have consistently been written out of both the historical and literary records of Haiti, it is necessary to scrutinize the representation of women's roles in the texts under discussion.

Traditionally, Haitian women have been subsumed under an overtly male-identified national identity. What Haitian women writers demonstrate is that the project of recovering Haitian women's lives must begin with the re-composition of history and nationality. In this, they participate in the re-visioning of the ongoing debate over the features of pan-African nationalism as historically debated by fellow Haitian René Depestre and Martiniquan Aimé Césaire. Depestre, in 1955, wrote of the difficulty of creating a unique voice and style without denying his double heritage (Huannou 97). He defined his double heritage in literary terms as a "patrimoine culturel d'Afrique [African cultural patrimony]" joined to a "héritage prosodique français [French prosodic heritage]" (Huannou 97). Depestre, in affirming the uniqueness of Haitian culture in its syncretic constitution, concluded that "the national character of a culture, of a literature, is not a function of the language of its expression."[9] Unlike Césaire, Depestre refused to endorse an ideology of pan-Africanism, which later became known as *négritude,* because he could not hierarchize disparate features of African cultures. For him, there was no unique or transcendent African culture that could be easily defined (Huannou 105). As these debates raged on, one thing remained constant: the debaters were men and they assumed a literary tradition that was also male. Depestre may have believed in the inclusivity of racio-cultural markers, but he neglected the role gender plays in the development and perception of these markers.

As I will demonstrate, the representation of Haitian women in women's literature invokes visions drawn from folk traditions. Specifically, the authors reformulate the image of the *marabout* eternalized in Oswald Durand's still popular folksong "Choucoune" of 1883.[10] Most literary analyses dealing with representations of women in Haitian literature insist on narrowly linking this image to that of the *vodou* mulatta goddess Erzulie. This insistence suggests that images of women in popular culture have not been explored fully. Allusions to Erzulie only perpetuate the marginalization of Haitian women, in my opinion, since, as goddess, she occupies a spiritual realm and remains largely inaccessible. The *marabout,* on the other hand, has become a part of communal consciousness through song and through her physically distinctive attributes, which include her striking beauty, dark skin, and long, Arawak-straight hair.

In "Choucoune," the *marabout* is a woman about to be wed to a Haitian man who is the singer of the song. At the last minute, Choucoune falls in love with a "petit blanc [poor white male]" and leaves her betrothed behind. Writes Maximilien Laroche: "the speaker in the poem represents himself five times as agent, in the grammatical function of subject and ten times as victim, in the grammatical function of object."[11] Thus, the speaker assumes a subject/object duality, while Choucoune is cast as a traitor who responds to neocolonialism by rejecting the Haitian man who idolizes her, and hence Haitian culture itself.

Although "Choucoune" tells the story of lost love, the song is traditionally sung in a cheerful tone and quick tempo. The resulting effect is one that celebrates Choucoune even as it articulates her loss: she represents a lost, colonized Haiti. I will be suggesting, then, that Haitian women writers respond to this implicit image of betrayal/loss by *reconstituting* the *marabout* figure in their works. She becomes a woman to be pursued, desired, emulated and, ultimately, *retrieved by women,* thus subverting Durand's male voice within the song by replacing it with their own; some writers, notably Annie Desroy, go so far as to use the same language to describe their *marabout* characters. This intertextuality is in keeping with the idea of creole encoding. As Laroche writes, "the actual literature written in Haitian pushes itself to maroon the dominant literature written in French through the oraliture of the dominated."[12] The underlying orality of Haitian literature is rooted for Laroche in folksongs like "Choucoune"[13] (hence his use of the neologism "oraliture") that began the project of Haitian literary creolism. Haitian women writers continue in this tradition, adding to it an analysis and a political revisioning of the image of the strikingly beautiful women of Haiti, the *marabout,* as one of empowerment rather than shame. In more recent writings, the image of the Haitian woman as *marabout* is additionally reconfigured through the trope of the *marassa,* or the *vodou* cult of twinship, by which women's solidarity is envisioned as a crucial component of ideological revolution. And, strikingly, choice in sexuality is also articulated through this paradigm in the embodiment of bisexual/lesbian characters and women-identified women who make up yet another aspect of revolution in this (literary) context.

Thus, social and literary "History" are both revealed as "man"-made artifacts in Haitian women's literature that are meant to make sense of the "incomprehensible" sequence of events populating the cultural life of nations but fail to do so; these histories are not, therefore, infallible, for all these "facts" must bear the weight of interpretation, that of one particular power which controls the coloring of the storytelling. When a population is considered so insignificant that its existence goes undocumented, storytelling becomes, necessarily, a source of retrieval; a story must be imagined, a fiction created, that will stand the stress of devaluation. Not surprisingly, Haitian women's literature is marked, as is most women's literature of the Caribbean, by "the sense of history—and personal fate—as incomplete, unfinished" (Paravisini-Gebert and Webb 129). Going beyond this sense of "incompleteness," novelists such as Mme. Virgile Valcin, Annie Desroy, Nadine Magloire, Edwidge Danticat, Anne-christine d'Adesky, Ghislaine Rey Charlier, Marie Chauvet, and Jan J. Dominique create heroines who retell the salient events of Haitian history beginning with the revolution of 1786–1804 and ending with the current U.S. occupation.

Both Marie-Denise Shelton and Léon-François Hoffmann contend that the U.S. Occupation of 1915–1934 has left an indelible mark upon the Haitian psyche that is memorialized in Haitian literature (Shelton 771; Hoffmann 46). It is my feeling that the current presence of U.S. soldiers in Haiti constitutes a second invasion, one that has reopened the wounds of the former. Haitian women writers solidify the connections between these moments in history at the same time that they articulate women's absence at each of these junctures within the historical record; the "gaps" they uncover are specifically gendered and seen not merely as absences but as sites of affirmation. It is through the consciousness of absence, then, that identity is recovered and preciously defended. Crucial to my study is this sense of feminist/feminized doubleness: the preservation of absence is, as I will explain in more detail below, as important as the awareness of its constitution.

Culture-lacune: A Theory of Revolution

As a Haitian woman who has resided in Port-au-Prince, in the Canadian cities of Quebec, Winnipeg, and Halifax, and more recently in the United States, I have spent a great deal of energy negotiating my identity in cultures that have excluded me on the basis of my "differences." These differences are multiple, along the lines of race, class, sex/gender, sexuality, nationality. Still, it is through language that I have found myself most alienated. My consciousness lives against a backdrop of Haitian creole, a language I was never taught, have barely spoken, yet understand; it informs the way I think, feel, and position myself in various contexts and is translated through French, my first language. Since I live in worlds in which it is perceived as an anomaly to be of African descent and be fluent in French, my thoughts undergo a further translation as I decode my self to make "me" intelligible to the Anglophone world in which I now reside. For most of my life, I have not seen this process of negotiation as positive: it has often hampered my ability to access what I felt to be my "true" self, my *Haitiennité.* As a woman, I lacked the tools to voice this silence. Eventually, I came to understand that even though I was constantly engaged in acts of translation, of a removal from self, I did not subscribe to a total and ultimately, annihilating assimilation. I ask the simple question: why not? The answer is as clear as my need to survive.

I have survived annihilation, both cultural and personal, by clinging to the vestiges of creole that lie dormant in my mind and by preserving a sense of self in an area of my consciousness that seems untranslatable. Where I once thought of myself as having no identity, or as having one filled with holes, with what in French are referred to as *lacunes,* I have come to understand myself as operating out of a *culture-lacune.* This phrase comes to me from my analysis of the novels I have chosen for this study. In each of these, absence is palpable in the form of marginalization.

But from this marginalization emerges a sense of a women's culture that defines itself *through its silencing.* The doubling of identity in this manner is what I find to be the revolutionary dimension of Haitian women's literature: it defies easy categorization and defines a distinct literary tradition.

In French, the word *lacune* usually connotes a negative absence. By joining the word to *culture,* which connotes the positive presence of social, collective existence, I am implying that *lacune* can be read into the texts as a space of "nothingness" that is transformed and affirmed through the politics of representation revealed in each. The French *Petit larousse* dictionary defines *lacune* in four distinct ways: 1) as an empty space within a body; 2) a textual interruption; 3) that which is missing to complete a person, thing, or place; and 4) the absence of a level of soil in a stratigraphic sample. In my use of the term, I connect all four meanings in studying the presence of absence in each of the eight novels I analyze. All of the texts use textual ellipsis to reveal the presence of a subsumed, secret, or silenced aspect of Haitian women's history and/or culture. Further, since my study incorporates questions of sexuality, I have found it important to image the role of the female body in acts of representation: how is the body made invisible within society? how is it exploited? More specifically, how is sexual desire presented with respect to the female body? Finally, Haitian women's lives should be understood as embodying that absent "level of soil" in the Haitian landscape with which Haitian women are often metaphorically conflated. In their absence from historical and literary documents, Haitian women represent the ultimate *lacune* in Haitian society: they are the absence that completes the whole. Working with these various definitions of *lacune* simultaneously, it becomes possible to apprehend the diverse levels of Haitian women writers' visions: these visions describe a culture within a culture, one that embraces its own silencing even as it contests it. This is the essence of *culture-lacune,* a theory that positions the margin as its own center and, paradoxically, as a tool not only for subversion but also for self-expression.

It is thus possible to distinguish Haitian women writers from what has become an overpopulated geography of exclusion, here and there tokenly referred to as "borderland" culture. José David Saldívar, for one, in his *The Dialectics of Our America,* describes his own project as one that "charts an array of oppositional critical and creative processes that aims to articulate a new, transgeographical conception of American culture—one more responsive to the hemisphere's geographical ties and political crosscurrents than to narrow national ideologies" (xi). Although this approach participates in deconstructing the Western myth of homogeneity, it unself-consciously subcribes to the new theoretical hegemony, prescribed by the "center," which views the multiplicity of cultures within the Americas (and elsewhere) only in terms of oppositionality.

Saldívar's allegiance to postcolonial/postmodern theory and his use of the "borderlands" ideology within those theoretical paradigms has the effect of divorcing the latter term from its original inception as articulated by Chicana theorist Gloria Anzaldúa, who sees the "center" as not only displaced or decentered but also as replaced and recentered. As critic Mary DeShazer writes in *A Poetics of Resistance:* "Revolutionary efforts are not locked into binary structures. . . . to define resistance solely as oppositional . . . suggests that resisters are always victims and that struggles for a just society can be viewed only in terms of inverting the current paradigm" (2). As I will show throughout the chapters to follow, it is critical to view literatures of resistance and/or revolution as establishing their own paradigms that refuse, even as they "write back" to the colonizing powers (be these defined as patriarchal or imperial), to be entirely subsumed by the cultures that have denied their existence. Thus, to define resistance literature as merely oppositional within the realm of postcolonial/postmodern theory is to define it in terms invented by the "center" that is being resisted and so to define it in ways that can only serve to perpetuate marginality rather than displace it.

In her essay "Haitian Women Writers," Marie-Denise Shelton suggests that there is a link between the "potential power of the creative act of women writers," and Anzaldúa's borderlands consciousness which aims to "make a home out of the cracks" (777). Shelton, however, speaks of Haitian women's literary efforts as embryonic. "The literary quality," she claims, "is in some instances limited; the voice at times utters unclear paroles," although she also asserts that the "critic interested in defining the complexion of Haitian literature must recognize the contribution of women authors" (776). My aim is not, in fact, to simply recognize or describe how Haitian women's writing "fits into" the broader context of Haitian literature (which is by default defined as supremely male by most critics in the field of Caribbean studies) but to demonstrate that, taken as a corpus spanning several decades, this literature has its own internal codes that formulate a unique tradition. Thus, if a cross-cultural connection need be made between Haitian women writers and Chicana writers, it is this: that Haitian women writers, like Chicana writers, do indeed make "a home out of the cracks." They show that "home"—that is, the center of cultural production—can reside where it is said that nothing exists, that out of invisibility and marginality, a culture can be articulated. Haitian women writers adopt the following position, as articulated by Anzaldúa in *Borderlands/La Frontera:* "if going home is denied me then I will have to stand and claim my space, making a new culture . . . with my own lumber, my own bricks and mortar and my own feminist architecture" (22). What is "owned" differs from one culture to the next, however, and my study will reveal how Haitian women writers stand to claim their space, as well as how and when that space is defined as a feminist one.

Thus, though cross-cultural connections can be made between Haitian women writers and contemporary women writers within other cultural groups (and I will make those connections when warranted), Haitian women's literature must be distinguished from that of other groups through its own cultural, social, and political aims. It is important to resist the subsuming of this literature under the rubric of "Black women's literature,"[14] which literary and cultural critics have largely defined in terms of African-American women's writings, even as they acknowledge the cross-cultural links forged by women of African descent across the diaspora. For instance, bell hooks, like Anzaldúa, cites "home" or "homeplace" as a site of transformation, and writes that "throughout our history, African-Americans have recognized the subversive value of homeplace, of having access to private space where we do not directly encounter white racist aggression" (47). Writing out of a Caribbean "homeplace," Haitian women writers are less invested in defining that space as oppositional to white racism; their works describe a complex history of sexist oppression at the hands of white and black, at the hands of French, Haitian, and American men whose identities cross racial lines. They themselves occupy more than one racial category since, as we know, the Caribbean is made up of various cultures, of races that have been intermingled by the force of rape and historical domination since imperial colonization. As hooks writes in her essay "Choosing the Margin," home can mean many things: it "changes with experience of decolonization, of radicalization. At times, home is nowhere. At times, one knows only extreme estrangement and alienation. Then home is no longer just one place. It is locations" (148). Likewise, for Haitian women writers home is never "just one place" but many places at once; in this way, their words reflect the African diasporic experience hooks theorizes, yet, at the same time, this experience can never be defined as the positionality of "blackness," which hooks invokes, because it tends to be singular rather than pluralistic. "Blackness" in the Haitian context is complicated by the continuous presence of "whiteness," which is not seen as something "out there" to be opposed, but a part of the culture, of the self.

Parameters

The first chapter of the text arises out of my own personal history: as a descendent of Toussaint L'Ouverture's oft-forgotten sister, Geneviève Affiba, I have sought to come to terms with the tactile absence of women's names and images in historical reconstructions of the Haitian Revolution (1786–1804) and of all the major periods of colonialism that took place following Independence. At the same time that women have not been memorialized in the country's historical record (records written both within and without the island), they have also consistently been sexually objectified and violently attacked in their homes and in the streets. For this reason, I attempt to uncover the history of Haitian women's feminism as it arose during the U.S. Occupation, in light of contemporary discussions of female subalternity and essentialism. It is my contention that Haitian feminism strives to overcome the bipolarized discourses of essentialism and anti-essentialism, of oppressor/oppressed, in order to foreground and contextualize the very physical harms suffered by Haitian women, as well as to find solutions to these violations. In this, they echo the efforts made by African-American women in the 1800s who strove to speak the truth of their oppressions in the service of transforming the ideological underpinnings of the colonial world. In this chapter, I also consider whether Haitian women merely participate in the construction of a Third World feminist ideology, or instead provide their own unique perspective. Ultimately, I demonstrate that current theoretical discourses are neither adequate to nor cognizant of the "real" lives of "subaltern" women.

In chapter two, I analyze Mme. Virgile Valcin's *La blanche négresse,* and Annie Desroy's *Le joug,* both published in Port-au-Prince in 1934, the last year of the U.S. Occupation, as artifacts of a distinct period in modern Haitian history. Both novels seek to vindicate Haitian women from their image as "savages" perpetuated in part by William Seabrook in his pseudo-ethnographic tome *The Magic Island,* which utilizes the Haitian woman as the primary vehicle for colonial phantasm. In so doing, the authors draw a clear link between imperialism and patriarchal domination. Women are thus portrayed as quintessential Haitians at the same time as they are denied this national identification. In Valcin's work, the exploration of the link between imperialism and patriarchal domination is complicated by the author's own resistance to the growth of the Afrocentric *indigénisme* movement that would deny her mulatta heroine a role in the Haitian nationalism of the time. As might be expected, the heroines of both novels perpetuate their own oppression by clinging to the caste system that has provided them a measure of power as members of the privileged upper classes. Race thus plays a paramount role in these Occupation tales in that the influx of white Americans throws the culture into racial shock: at the same time that the caste system inherited from French colonialism remains in place, racial stereotypes rooted in Anglo-imperialism buoyed by denigrating images of African women (such as the Venus Hottentot) are introduced and reinforced. Consequently, women of the working classes are imaged here as *marabouts* at once demonized and desired by the American occupants. The Haitian heroines, on the other hand, persist in purifying the American image of Haitian women in order to resist the pull of American assimilation. They ultimately defy assimilation by assuming roles of respectability, though they do not attain any measure of power within this historical time-frame.[15]

The third chapter expands upon the second by focusing on the role of women in Haitian political and social history. I argue that memory is a dominant theme in Haitian women writer's works and posit that these works contest the "nation-state" construct that has long dominated the overtly male ways in which texts emerging from the Caribbean have been analyzed. Through this contestation, writers like Ghislaine Rey Charlier and Jan J. Dominique critique the faulty collective memory on which Haitian women have had to rely in order to position themselves within a society that implicitly rejects them. Memory therefore takes on a double purpose in both Charlier's *Mémoire d'une affranchie* (1989) and Dominique's *Mémoire d'une amnésique* (1984)—a doubleness reflected in the very mirror of their titles. Charlier and Dominique introduce a new sense of collective memory that is rooted in women's personal interaction with each other as well as with the world beyond them. Because these authors take liberties with the relationship between chronology and voice in order to articulate memory, their works might be labeled "postmodern"; their works are, in fact, the only Haitian women's novels published to date that make such explicit use of postmodern textual strategies. But in keeping with my contestation of postcolonial discourse, I demonstrate in this chapter that postmodernism is also an ideology that robs texts emerging from the Third World of their cultural and political matrices, and show how both *Mémoire d'une affranchie* and *Mémoire d'une amnésique* position themselves outside of current postmodern/postcolonial discourse, engaging instead in discourses tied to Haitian folklore, memory, and women's *culture-lacune*. Dominique's text is particularly transgressive in its compelling presentation of a heroine whose bisexuality becomes one part of the submerged reality of Haitian women's identities; in this, the novel succeeds in its attempt to present an all-encompassing vision of women's lives in the Haitian context.

In my fourth and penultimate chapter, I focus specifically on the contestation of women's sexual roles in Haitian society. The novels I analyze here are Nadine Magloire's *Le mal de vivre* (1967) and Edwidge Danticat's *Breath, Eyes, Memory* (1994), which directly confront the potential for women's autonomous identification with one another. Separated by almost three decades, the novels come together in their depiction of Haitian women's loss, and reconfiguration, of sexual identity. In both, the retrieval of sexual autonomy is made possible through textuality: the novel and literacy, respectively, are posited as vehicles through which women might achieve the means to make sexual choices. Yet, traditional narrative is revealed in both as inadequate to the fulfillment of sexual freedom for women: in *Le mal de vivre,* the traditional novel genre is ultimately dismantled and abandoned as a mode of self-actualization; likewise, in *Breath, Eyes, Memory,* the traditional form of the novel is undermined through a doubling of language in which female desire—directed towards other women (or their *marassa*)—and identity are simultaneously reclaimed with literacy. In both plots, a realized female agency around sexuality is specifically refused formal encoding. Magloire and Danticat's texts are thus also examples of Haitian women's *culture-lacune,* as they divulge implicitly homoerotic themes that are otherwise articulated with difficulty.

In connecting Marie Chauvet's posthumously published work, *Les rapaces* (1986), with Anne-christine d'Adesky's *Under the Bone* (1994), in the fifth chapter, I mean to emphasize the constancy of women's encounters with violence in the political arena in Haiti and to show how that violence serves to undermine previous and contemporary efforts on the part of women authors to express a feminist and women-identified politics. Specifically, I draw a parallel between the two authors' overtly political agendas, through which each seeks to reveal the destruction of women's lives under, and immediately after, the Duvalier regime. Moreover, I explore how each author counters current apocalyptic rhetoric, which silences Third World visions of a regenerative future in which justice will prevail, by revisiting Haiti's recent neocolonial history. In this revisitation, both authors stress the need for women to regain the power of their own discourse, that is, of the imagination. Both use the subconscious, or dreams, as symbols for women's subversive potential, as visions that can transform their claustrophobic and often violent worlds. In the end, Chauvet's and d'Adesky's novels are an evaluation of U.S. neocolonialism and its effect upon women's ability to participate in Haiti's independence, as well as to advocate for their own within Haiti. They demonstrate that women's political consciousness, which subsists along with their actual bodies in the spaces to which those bodies have been relegated, is the medium through which the hope that will lead to visibility and emancipation is continually voiced.

In the final analysis, my study seeks to unravel the reasons behind the censoring of Haitian women's literary voices by making use of an explicitly feminist methodological approach. In this, I urge readers to adopt, if they have not already, feminized Third World frames of reference, which necessarily impact upon the reading process and influence the nature of the analytical conclusions that can be drawn from each of the texts. Foremost, the study focuses on ways in which those few women writers who have been published have themselves sought to represent at once communal and individual visions of the Haitian woman. I am cognizant of the fact that, since this study will be among the first devoted entirely to Haitian women's literature, it may face critical expectations based on criteria other than those outlined above. It is my hope that this text will raise as many questions—ranging perhaps from aesthetic ones to ones concerning the comparative analyses of Haitian female and male writers—as it answers. Concurrently, the findings of this text should foster further study of Haitian women's literature. The Haitian woman has a voice that must be heard. *Nou là:* we are here. *Our* time has arrived.

CHAPTER 1

Nou Là!

HAITIAN FEMINISM AS THE CROSSROADS POLITICS
OF THEORY AND ACTION

＊＋ ≡◆≡ ＋＊

*Chers amis, je ne veux pas vous faire un discours sur la Femme
avec un grand (F). Vous me reprocheriez, avec raison d'ailleurs,
un féminisme outré, que pour ma part je trouve un peu désuet.
Mais puisqu'il m'est donné aujourd'hui de vous parler au nom
de l'Etudiante, permettez-moi de vous dire en passant que la
femme qui entre à l'Université, que la jeune femme qui entre à
la Faculté de Droit ne démissionne pas de son rôle de femme,
que la femme qui ouvre les yeux sur les champs du savoir n'en
est que plus humaine, puisque pensant elle se rend plus digne de
sa qualité d'être humain, j'allais dire de sa qualité d'homme. A
quelqu'un qui me demandait mon avis sur le droit de vote
accordé à la Femme et particulièrement à la femme haïtienne, je
voudrais qu'aujourd'hui vous puissiez tous répondre avec moi:
la femme haïtienne doit pouvoir voter puisqu'en somme elle
peut. . . elle peut être aussi préparée que l'homme haïtien.—
Mais insister davantage sur un problème actuellement dépassé
serait vous faire injure. Il est inutile en effet de vouloir prouver
ce que personne, du moins je l'espère, ne conteste plus, ce qu'il
suffit de constater si l'on est de bonne foi: et je veux croire que
tous ici vous êtes de bonne foi.*

*[Dear friends, I do not want to preach to you about Woman with
a capital "W." You would accuse me, with good reason, of an
emboldened feminism, which, for my part, I find somewhat ob-
solete. But since it is my task to speak to you today in the name
of the Female Student, allow me to tell you in passing that the
woman who enters the university, that the young woman who
enters the Faculty of Law, does not abandon her role as a
woman, that the woman who opens her sights onto vast fields of
knowledge is but the more human for it, since, thinking, she becomes more worthy of herself as human being, I was going to
say as man. To someone who asked me my opinion on the right
of Woman and particularly of the Haitian woman, to vote, I
would wish that today you could all answer along with me: the*

*Haitian woman must be able to vote since in the final analysis
she has the skills to do so . . . and she can be as well-prepared
as the Haitian man.—But to insist any more on a problem we
have already tackled would be to insult you all. It is useless, in
fact, to want to prove what no one, I hope, contests, what can
easily be discerned by those of good will: and I would like to
believe that all of you are of good will.]*
—Adeline Lamour, Valedictorian Address, Centennial Commemoration
(1860–1960) of the Haitian National School of Law

Speech as Revolutionary Praxis

*I*magine yourself to be the first wo-
man to graduate at the head of the class from a law school in a small, increasingly lawless, Caribbean country. It is the hundredth anniversary of
the School of Law where women have been allowed to study alongside men
for only about forty years of its history. You are giving the Valedictory
speech—the first woman to ever do so—before your fellow students, es-
teemed professors, and the despot who has turned the laws you have been
studying for the past three years into mere shadows of policing, into vessels
of justice as empty as wooden hunting decoys. That despot is François
Duvalier himself, in power only for as long as the three years you have
been studying, but already feared, an emblem of terror.

Only those who have lived in nation-states where extreme abuses of
human rights are the order of the day will grasp the temerity of this Valedictorian who read her speech in 1960, the year in which Duvalier declared
himself President-for-Life and began the thirty-year dynasty that would advance at a snail-pace crawl through violent bloodshed. Ten years earlier,
Haitian women had earned themselves the right to vote, after years of activism. Ironically, the presidential "election," which marked Duvalier's ascension in 1957, with the U.S.-trained Haitian army standing at the ballot
boxes in their fatigues and guns, was the first in which women could exercise the new constitutional right to present their marked ballots. Duvalier's
government brought to an end the overt feminist movement that had flowered by 1934, the final year of the first large-scale U.S. occupation of
Haiti.

I chose to open this chapter with words from a speech because the
speech, as a genre, encapsulates the praxis of reflection and action—that is,

the politicized activation of language. The speech act thus serves as a tool for the dissemination of revolutionary thought for one woman seeking to represent many women in the field of civil rights. The covert and overt feminist discourse of the passage above reflects the necessity of creating a new, yet unobtrusive, woman's space in the everyday civil life of a nation-state that had only very recently recognized women as having their own agency as human beings, independent of men, as having their own intellectual integrity and personal will. This is a pattern repeated over and over again, as I will show, in Haitian women's writing. The speaker makes ironic reference to the good will of her audience, a reference undermined by the historical context in which such words of good faith have been expressed. The presence of Duvalier in that room signifies rather starkly the disintegration of a progressive social order.

By 1960, the year in which the opening words of this chapter were spoken, speech had become an endangered activity, one fraught with political danger. With Duvalier as master of propaganda, words became ready tools of oppression. Using Haitian folklore, he invoked the most feared of *vodou* myths to create an atmosphere of paranoia and violence in which he himself became Baron Samedi, the revengeful god of death. Although both men and women suffered violence at the hands of the new ruler's secret police—the *Tontons macoutes*—women, by virtue of their sex, were given fewer avenues to access the power of the word.[1] The language of the speech is correspondingly double-coded; it adopts an apologetic tone to pacify a hostile audience at the same time that it asserts a feminist outlook demanding women's equal access to a politicized education. More striking is the fact that as daring as the speech I have cited is, it was altered before its printing in the commemorative booklet. The speaker had not originally stated that women "could be as prepared as the Haitian man" but that "men are not any more prepared than women to exercise their voting privileges," adding that "Let us hope that one day both groups will be as prepared as each other." Though seemingly slight, these alterations of the text are significant in that they undermine the author's intent to underscore the presence of corrupt voting practices in the nation, by which groups of men (often said to be illiterate) would be made to vote two or three times in different localities in exchange for bribes of food, alcohol, or money. The text thus continues in its doubleness, exposing the argument that women cannot vote because they are not as knowledgeable as men as false, since corrupt political practices prevent the exercise of suffrage on the part of men as well. This piece of the speech has been excised not only because it alludes to such corruption but also because it deflates a misogynistic argument that provides a convenient smoke screen for the illusion that men have rights, which they exercise on behalf of themselves and their families, and that women are cared for in the French tradition of *femme couverte*—meaning covered by the legal rights extended to them as minors or wives.[2] Haitian women's demand for equal rights thus not only defies the society's traditional sexism but also presents a challenge to the colonial tradition of exclusion: the demand for women's equal rights exposes the non-existence of civil rights for most of the country's inhabitants.

The speech follows in the tradition established by the feminist movement of the two to three decades preceding the ascension of the Duvaliers. I reproduce it here as a manifesto—albeit one resisting its own forthright political agenda—of Haitian women's feminism during the Duvalier regime. It survives as a significant document of a woman's voice in the first years of despotic suppression in the area of freedom of speech; it is part of the legacy of Haitian women's efforts to present and support a feminist politics within a social atmosphere opposed to the advancement of women in academic, professional, market, and social spheres. It is all the more important to me because its author is my mother; it is thus not only part of a broader national legacy of women's activism but also a part of my familial legacy.

In this chapter, I will seek to demonstrate the ways in which a speech such as this one, typical in many respects of the enthusiastic Valedictory speeches made year in and year out at any number of college graduations, distinguishes itself from other such declarations in its revolutionary content. The speech is revolutionary not simply in its lobbying on behalf of women's rights but also in its tenacious persistence at a time when free speech was submerged beneath the morass of Duvalerian terror and anti-woman politics. It reveals the necessity of articulating that women be integrated into the political apparatus that for so long denied their existence. Furthermore, it exemplifies a pattern in Haitian feminism, which progresses from *speech activation* to *dialogue integration,* to the paradoxical *creation of an imperceptible woman's space,* to the *enforced implementation of women's rights* beyond a closed sphere of women's interactions as revolutionary consciousness is developed and honed.

This chapter also aims to demonstrate that literature produced by Haitian women over the last sixty years is rooted in a long tradition of feminist organizing and theorizing of women's condition in the Haitian context. I will also show that Haitian women, along with Third World women in and outside of the West—most specifically African-American women—actively take part in feminist politics, a participation that has all but been denied in recent postcolonial feminist scholarship produced in the West.[3] Haitian feminism stands as a model of Third World feminist politics in that it is articulated through a critical praxis that eludes the pitfalls of the theory/practice split that has been created by mainstream white academicians (see Toril Moi's *Sexual/Textual Politics,* for example) to marginalize feminists of color and/or lesbian feminists.[4] In the most crude of explanations, "minority" women are stereotyped as uneducated, sheltered, or unable to relate to men; no matter what these women might do to better their condition (as women) they are said to be acting on a base survival instinct. This denigration of marginalized feminists—whom one might define as the oppressed within an oppressed class—is simply another form of what Paulo Freire has termed the "absolutizing of ignorance" whereby an oppressed group is kept disempowered relative to the dominant group, which insists on the former's ignorance and thus denies its claims for self-governance. This self-serving accusation results in the denial of the agency of the oppressed, that is, of their consciousness, their introspections, their solution-solving processes; such bias is especially damaging to women whose feminism is enacted through *masking strategies of doubleness* meant to protect female participants from often violent political and social reprisals, resulting, at times, in death.

Refuting the Rhetoric of Subalternity

It is a miracle that even edited, my mother's words survived as an indictment of the Duvaliers' "brave new world." Duvalier's regime was, in fact, an artful deception in an era of unimaginable terror (which has resurfaced more explicitly in the last five years as various political factions have warred against each other openly and violently in the daylit streets of Haiti) that hid itself behind a vast and colorful tapestry of the fulfillment of *noirisme* "intellectualism" (the moral right of Haitian "blacks"—a difficult to define racial/class category—to rule) and the promise of U.S.-supported industrial "development" and economic gain. Chillingly, the words of the speech reveal that the speaker had been effectively disempowered. Her word-acts are uttered but go unheard. In a manner of speaking, the author-speaker is not perceived by the governing audience as an actor, and therefore, her tempered yet bold statements voiced on behalf of female emancipation are emptied of their revolutionary impact. In true hegemonic form, the oppressive powers render revolution impossible in denying the existence of the oppressed as an *active* participant in the world around them. If the revolutionary speaker is not perceived by the dominant powers to be involved in the act of speaking, the potential of counter-hegemonic discourse is neutralized for all practical, political purposes. How, then, does the speaker circumvent erasure?

On one level, the speaker and her words escape erasure through the existence of the document. But of what importance is a written document to the group it seeks to represents if most of its members cannot decipher it, that is, cannot read the words on the page meant to unlock facets of their oppressive world? The survival of such words, and the revolution they reflect, will depend in part on the creation of effective alliances across barriers of dominant and dominated, oppressed and oppressor. In short, the oppressed must be unified. The Haitian feminist movement, prior to the Duvalier regime, in fact demonstrated a willingness to try to overcome obstacles of class in order to achieve this empowering unification; it was one dedicated to revolution. It is certain that elitism plagued the movement in many ways, but it is elitism of another sort that has kept Western feminists from recognizing the strides achieved by Haitian feminists along with other Third World women over several decades.

In the final words of her pivotal essay, "Can the Subaltern Speak?" postcolonial theorist Gayatri Spivak succinctly summarizes the general attitude of mainstream feminist academics with regard to their female counterparts in the non-academic and/or Third World: "The subaltern cannot speak. There is no virtue in global laundry lists with 'woman' as a pious item. Representation has not withered away. The female intellectual as intellectual has a circumscribed task which she must not disown with a flourish" (104). Since Spivak is commonly seen in academic circles as a speaker for the Third World woman (wherever she may be), her words are of particular importance to my present discussion. Although it is possible to interpret these words as an attempt at self-reflexivity, they nonetheless reinforce the view that Third World women, or those who have not had access to Western/European educations, cannot participate in forming their own representations: even as they speak—whether through words or physical acts—they are silent. The Third World woman does not exist unless the well-meaning academic takes up her cause, renders her visible. Spivak's views here have made acceptable the co-optation of Third World women's feminist agendas on the premise that such women have no way of speaking *for* themselves or of controlling *how* they are represented on the world stage. In actuality, Third World women articulate themselves through daily acts of resistance, organized political activism, and written manifestoes. Spivak's approach, developed in the belief "that the possibility of collectivity itself is persistently foreclosed through the manipulation of female agency" (78), is complicit with hegemonic discourses that chain the identity of the oppressed to their position as subjugated objects.

Spivak's primary case study in her essay revolves around the Western demonization of the practice of *satí*. She argues that the practice of immolating oneself after the death of one's spouse must be placed in its cultural-historical context in order to be properly understood. The question of origins is, of course, paramount to accessing Indian women's understanding of, and participation in, a tradition that, despite Spivak's claim to gender neutral etymological origins (100), has not been considered a male prerogative. Spivak would have us consider the historical colonization of India as evidence of the cultural corruption, and hence, of the creation of, the subaltern female object. She writes that

> what interests me is that the protection of woman (today the "third-world woman") becomes a signifier for the establishment of a *good* society which must, at such inaugurative moments, transgress mere legality, or equity of legal policy. In this particular case, the process also allowed the redefinition as a crime of what had been tolerated, known, or adulated as ritual. (94)

Spivak goes on to suggest that Hindi women were robbed of their free will in taking part in the ritual if they so chose (98) when the British, in imposing their concepts of "good society" upon India, outlawed the practice and pronounced it barbaric. One cannot (and, in my view, should not) defend British imperialism, but Spivak's logic begs an important question, namely, the extent to which cultural practices that oppress women should be lauded on the basis that others outside the practice have denigrated it to serve their own oppressive aims. In other words, had the British not imposed an anti-*satí* law during their colonization of India, would Spivak and other postcolonial feminists support the practice of self-immolation, given that it is limited mostly to women? Spivak would appear to suggest that choice is not the issue and neither are the terms of Indian/Third World women's oppression. Regardless of their motivations, aims, and politics, the "subaltern" woman has no existential dimensions other than her role as object. Thus, Spivak ends her essay with the example of a woman who is claimed to have committed suicide through self-immolation in order to save her honor when she could not perform a political assassination in the struggle for Indian independence (103). The woman's act is posthumously reread by her family as "a case of delirium rather than sanity" (104) and her effort to save face is erased through the assumption that she killed herself *out of shame* because of an illicit love affair. Spivak concludes that since the woman's actions are misread and thus misremembered that "the subaltern as female cannot be heard or read" (104). In order to accept fully Spivak's argument we would have to believe first that Indian women in general had no agency before or after the British invasion and, secondly, that no Indian women ever objected then or since to the practice of *satí* as it became gendered.

As Ania Loomba asserts in her article "Overworlding the Third World," Spivak's approach in itself *leads* to the silencing of Indian and other Third World women: "[Spivak's] two positions—the deconstructive one detecting methodological and epistemological problems with charting subject positions, and the second one emphasizing epistemic and other violence of colonialism—so slide into each other that the force of the first one is borne entirely by the subaltern alone: she alone is silenced" (317). It is an approach that denies the existence of indigenous women's modes of resistance. As Loomba points out, "other women who are trying, precisely, to record such voices within colonial and postcolonial history do not indicate the epistemic wasteland Spivak implies" (318). Loomba cites Vandana Shiva's book *Staying Alive: Women, Ecology, and Survival in India* as an example of a text that has sought out and documented Indian women's history of feminism under shifting contexts of suppression. Both Spivak and Loomba, however, are leary of studies that make use of nostalgic revisionism in order to demonstrate women's attempts at agency. For my part, it would seem that to label Shiva's work, as well as other women's efforts to reclaim the silenced past of women in the Third World, as empty nostalgia is to greatly threaten the possibility of hearing Third World women's speech in Western contexts: it implies that the revisionist, poststructuralist approach of postcolonial theory is more "truthful" than other forms of revisionism and, therefore, that it is the only approach that counts.

The "truth" of women's lives cannot be arrived at by proposing from the outset that silence is an inevitable side effect of living in various Third World contexts. Theoretical proposals that refuse to accept that women have agency (it is a different matter altogether to understand when, how, and why that agency has been co-opted or negated) are counter-revolutionary in nature and constitutionally oppressive rather than transformative.

Paulo Freire rightly claims that "to speak a true word is to transform the world," for, as he explains, dialogue is enacted linguistically through the interrelationship of reflection and action spoken between human beings to move the world (69). "Consequently," he continues, "no one can say a true word alone—nor can she say it *for* another, in a prescriptive act which robs others of their words" (69). Spivak's understanding of subalternity preempts dialogue since its initial question presupposes an absence of the ability to communicate. And, even as she moves towards it, she negates self-reflexivity by refusing to surrender the privileged label of "intellectual" that she applies to herself. Thus she is able to assert that "[i]n seeking to learn to speak to (rather than listen to or speak for) the historically muted subject of the subaltern woman, the postcolonial intellectual *systematically* 'unlearns' female privilege" (91). This assertion reflects a deeply-rooted elitism, whereby privilege is feminized in function of the author who cannot help but universalize her own identity position, summarily dismissing female disenfranchisement in a refusal to speak as one of the disenfranchised—that is, *with* the "subaltern" woman rather than *to* her dispassionately. Here we should recall Freire's statement that in order for revolutionary transformation to take place, leaders (self-appointed or recognized) must speak *with* the oppressed, not *for* the oppressed, or else fall into the trap of repeating the model of oppression they pretend to be attempting to disassemble:

> Organizing the people is the process in which the revolutionary leaders, who are also prevented from saying their own word, initiate the experience of learning how to *name* the world. This is true learning experience, and therefore dialogical. So it is that the leaders cannot say their word alone; they must say it *with* the people. Leaders who do not act dialogically, but insist on imposing their decisions, do not organize the people—they manipulate them. They do not liberate, nor are they liberated: they oppress. (159)

In order to participate in the creation of revolutionary discourse in the realm of academia, the intellectual must first renounce the title of intellectual, which suggests that the disprivileged have no intellect or are unprepared to tackle the challenges of introspection, interrogation, and problem-solving. One cannot enter into dialogue with another if one believes that the other is incapable of logical thought.

The very use of the term "subaltern" by academics binds the individual labeled as such to her/his state of oppression because it implies that her/his identity is primarily constituted by her/his oppression. Thus, in using the term, academics occlude representation from the start: the subaltern has no face but the face of oppression. If the academic refuses to unburden her/his own terminology from the weight of binarism, then, truly, the subjugated individual or group can never be accurately represented by her/him. This does not mean that the academic must disinvest herself/himself entirely of an inadequate critical language or invent language anew; what it means, rather, is that those words that fail to encompass the humanity of various individuals must be interrogated, discarded, or redefined.

In keeping with this line of thought, I am conscious of the implications that my own use of the diad oppressor/oppressed throughout my study and of my use of the phrase "Third World" to describe Haitian women as well as women residing in economically depressed, formerly colonized and/or neocolonized countries throughout the world may suggest. As will become evident, however, I use the words "oppressor" and "oppressed" to describe unequal power relationships in ever shifting socio-historical contexts; I do not use them as, nor should they be taken for, blanket terms that elide specificity. I use the term "Third World" in concert with other women in countries such as Haiti who do so in order to bring into relief the very real dependency relationship the First World has created in order to render invisible its exploitation of countries populated by people of other than European descent.

In refusing the terminology of subalternity, I am simply making the claim that oppression should not be conflated with identity. In other words, I do not mean to imply that agency frees the oppressed individual from her/his status of enslavement (for all oppressed peoples are in one way or another prevented from achieving freedom in the societies that make their existence marginal to begin with). As Ania Loomba puts it, "To say that if the subaltern could speak she/he would not be a subaltern is a neat enough formulation, but somewhat inadequate if the 'Third World' is not to be, yet again, theorized into silence" (320). Loomba's resistance to the notion that speech=freedom=privilege readily negates Spivak's assertion that the subaltern cannot speak. Since oppression continues to exist even as we persist in exposing the power structures that bring that oppression into being, it is facile to conclude that it is lack of speech that keeps the oppressed in their positions of subjugation. Since my supposition remains that the "subaltern" is always speaking, and since oppression still exists, it follows then, of course, that the "subaltern" continues to exist in her/his state of oppression even as she/he speaks. It is the fact that such speech is suppressed that renders the oppressed the identifiable "subaltern" in any given society. Those who dominate have full knowledge of the speech they are occluding, silencing, and marginalizing, if indeed they permit it free circulation.

The Necessity of Collective Action: Third World Women in the West

The rupture between oppressed and oppressee can only be repaired through unity, that is, through collective action. In turn, collectivity can only be achieved by recognizing class differences and by working to bridge the alienation that unequal power relationships create. Failure to recognize power inequity among women (which mirrors inequities between racial groups, between men and women, between nation-states) *can only result* in the token inclusion of marginalized feminists in feminist movements—that is, in an inclusion that neutralizes the need to address multiple fronts of oppression. This is a form of "cultural invasion." As Freire writes:

> [C]ultural invasion is . . . always an act of violence against the persons of the invaded culture, who lose their originality or face the threat of losing it. In cultural invasion . . . the invaders are the authors of, and actors in, the process; those they invade are the objects. The invaders mold; those they invade are molded. The invaders choose; those they invade follow that choice—or are expected to follow it. The invaders act; those they invade have only the illusion of acting, through the action of the invaders. (133)

The token inclusion of Third World women in Western feminist discourse has long resulted in a homogenization of women's experiences cross-culturally and globally. This is a harm that only serves to undermine each woman's ability to proceed with a political agenda consonant with her own social and cultural exigencies, exigencies that will differ from country to country and that, further, will be mediated within any particular social context by issues of race, sex, sexuality, and class.

For example, token inclusion in the mainstream U.S. women's movement in the early to mid-1900s led African-American women to disavow the label of "feminist" and create a counter designation, that of "womanist." They did so to assert their cultural differences and to preserve their historic involvement in the movement for women's emancipation prior to what has commonly been referred to as the second wave of the U.S. women's movement. The need to self-define is an important one, indeed often necessary in order to reclaim a dismissed culture and to fend off acts of cultural invasion. Cultural invaders are, however, by definition, persistent in their labeling of the othered group as inferior. In the case of African-American women's struggles to be recognized as participants in the formulation and execution of feminist theory, the move out of the women's movement was perceived as anti-feminist. In other words, feminism was a white woman's thing—Black women were seen as incapable of participating in the mainstream women's movement, not because of the racism the movement itself perpetuated, but because they were perceived as having to "displace" their identities as women (as if such a displacement were possible) in order to contend with issues such as race, poverty, and children's rights. Such perceptions of Black women only fueled the long-standing misconception that women of the Third World find feminism anathema to other struggles they face in everyday life, when in fact what African-American women were objecting to was the cooptation of a term that increasingly denoted a specific group of women, namely, white, middle- to upper-class heterosexual women.

African-American women and other women of color globally are not any more (or less) likely than are white American women to refuse to be associated with feminist politics; they refuse this "membership" only when organized feminist groups use race, class, and/or sexuality to exclude whole groups of women. Contrary to Western feminist myths about feminism in the Third World, Third World feminists do not engage in an isolated effort focused only on issues of access for women (to wealth, health, and legal rights); rather, Third World feminists attempt to disrupt patterns of hegemony that bind whole groups of people to poverty, illiteracy, and lives filled with violence. We need only to think of the Combahee River Collective Statement of 1977, which spelled out the need for the recognition of multiple oppression in Third World women's lives in the United States to recognize Third World women's tacit understanding that the liberation of women on multiple fronts will result in the emancipation of all. The expression of feminist politics can thus take on as varied configurations as exist in the West, including lesbian feminist politics and organizations based on religious and geographic particularities. These particularities must be at the forefront of any attempts at global feminism. As feminist theorist Chandra Mohanty writes, "Sisterhood cannot be assumed on the basis of gender; it must be forged in concrete historical and political praxis" (201). Thus, the ignorance usually attributed to the oppressed is in reality a basic feature of the constricted vision of the oppressing group.

It is important to note, as Mohanty points out, that the Western feminist universalization of women's lot is detrimental to potential cross-cultural coalitions, for it creates distinctions "on the basis of the privileging of a particular group as the norm or referent" (199). Mohanty specifies that the "homogeneity of women as a group is produced not on the basis of biological essentials, but rather on the basis of secondary sociological and anthropological universals. . . . in any given piece of feminist analysis, women are characterized as a singular group on the basis of secondary sociological and anthropological universals" (200). For Mohanty, the homogenizing of women as a global, oppressed class, wherein women are defined "primarily in terms of their *object status* . . . needs to be named and challenged" (201). The revolutionary potential of feminism in its Western incarnations is undercut by the refusal on the part of Western feminists to "un-house," to paraphrase Freire, the oppressor within. It is the inability of women of privileged classes to recognize their capacity to oppress other women who do not occupy the same positions of relative power that extinguishes the transformative potential of feminist politics.

Because of the ability to communicate (and here let me underscore that communication need not be limited to the act of speaking, of making "sound"), very few human beings are completely powerless. Language, in whatever form, is the vehicle through which power is enunciated as transformative or as destructive. It can be used to forge alliances or prevent them; it can be used to enlighten or to blind. Every individual capable of communicating with another, regardless of social standing, has the choice to use speech to broaden humanity or to narrow the scope of human progress. Thus, those who are themselves oppressed because a dominant but minority group has chosen to exclude them from what is considered the "norm"—inclusion in the "race" of "mankind"—are never as disempowered as their oppressors would have them believe. The oppressed can use tools of communication to transform their own perceptions of self as well as those of their captors. Hence the habitual process of self-definition that occurs at the onset of revolutionary action.

Here, I invoke the Third World feminist legacy of one woman *who changed her name* to reflect her revolutionary purpose: Sojourner Truth. Sojourner Truth named herself thus because, as she traveled through the United States to speak out against the disenfranchisement of Black women, men, and children, she endeavored *to speak the truth* on behalf of the African-American community, and most specifically, on behalf of its female community. When Truth rose and spoke at the women's rights convention of 1851, she asserted—through a doubly-encoded speech—the fullness of her as yet denied humanity as a Black woman:

> And a'n't I a woman? Look at me! Look at my arm! (and she bared her right arm to the shoulder, showing her tremendous muscular power). I have ploughed, and planted, and gathered into barns, and no man could head me! And a'n't I a woman? I could work as much and eat as much as a man—when I could get it—and bear de lash as well: And a'n't I a woman? I have borne thirteen chilern, and seen 'em most all sold off to slavery, and when I cried out with my mother's grief, none but Jesus heard me! And a'n't I a woman? (qtd. Ruth, 490)

Truth, untutored, considered illiterate, flexed not only her physical muscles but also the muscle of her intellect in order to transform both body and soul into the very subject of woman denied her in the pre–Civil War United States. Truth's insights are the product of lived experience and self-reflection. Her rhetorical question, phrased as a negation, is, as feminist theorist Tania Modleski suggests, an assertion of a complex sense of identity. Modleski writes of Truth that she "contests ideology by an appeal to experience, and experience by appeal to ideology, and in the very space of this negation affirms herself *as a woman*" (21). As a witness to her own oppression, which mirrors that of her ancestors and fellow African-American sisters, she boldly affirms her humanity by *embodying the power of speech.*

The fact that Truth's truth was uttered within this specific historical moment serves to question the essentialist/anti-essentialist opposition invoked in current prostructuralist, postcolonial feminist theorizing. Denise Riley, for one, resists the possibility that this fissure can be reconciled when she proposes that had Sojourner Truth lived in the late 1980s she would have risen to utter the following anti-essentialist question: "Ain't I a fluctuating identity?" According to Riley, the future of feminism (one assumes that "feminism" here is defined as mainstream feminist thought) will depend on preserving the tensions between the shedding of the label of "woman" and the constant reformulation of that label. For Riley, the category of "woman" flies in the face of what she esteems to be feminism's goal, that is, "the ideal of a non-sexed Humanity" (9), since "anyone's body is . . . *only periodically either lived or treated as sexed* . . . the gendered division of human life into bodily life cannot be adequate or absolute" (103, emphasis mine). It is only possible to accept this anti-essentialist point of view if one perceives of identity as hinging *solely* upon social *interactions,* as if individuals are not born into very specific cultures and historical modalities that determine their identities before they are even aware of the social constructs they will have to contend with as their bodies move through the world. In other words, a woman like Sojourner Truth, born to an enslaved African woman, had *no choice* but to be a slave at the time in history in which she came into the world: her heritage and physical body determined her initial fate and her race and sex determined the hardships she endured in that socio-historical context. Thus, I join with Modleski in flying to Sojourner Truth's defense for the reason that, as Modleski puts its, "excluding women from a contested category on the grounds that there *is no category* may well be the latest ruse of white middle-class feminism" (21). "The position of female anti-essentialism as it is being theorized by some feminists today," Modleski further notes, "is a luxury open only to the most privileged of women" (22). Though Sojourner's speech is timeless in its affirmation of African-American women's humanity, the positionality evoked by her corporeal identity is not; the historical temporality of her life had no periodizing effect that would have enabled her to escape her marginalized identity. By locating the impetus for her revolutionary praxis in the journeying of her Black female body through a particular moment in time, we can, in hindsight, witness the emergence of a pluralistic vision of women's rights that I term *syncretic feminism*. This syncretism is ironically born of differing cultural matrices brought into conflict through the domination of one culture by another. The oppressed culture survives by resisting the co-optation of its own values at the same time that it adopts a mask of conformity (a mask not to be confused with the Fanonesque internalization of the oppressor's norms that all but destroy the oppressed's sense of self). When that mask is removed, revolutionary praxis is born.

Haitian Feminism Unmasked

Haitian feminism distinguishes itself from mainstream Western feminism in its refusal to acknowledge *lack of consciousness*. In opposition to the widespread myth that those who are members of oppressed groups are not conscious of their lot and must be "educated" before they can rise to oppose their oppressors, the history of Haitian women suggests quite another approach, one that *presupposes* that the consciousness of the oppressed is a given and that considers the paramount issue to be the *communication* of that consciousness. Haitian feminists speak on behalf of themselves individualistically in order to take part in the *dialogic expres-*

sion of a feminist agenda articulated by Haitian women as a socio-political group. In their unrelenting press for advancement, Haitian feminists of the early 1900s created a revolutionary movement that went underground as a result of the anti-revolutionary activities of Duvalier despotism. The strides made by Haitian feminists in the early decades of the twentieth century were achieved largely through the accession to language and the means by which to publish and hone an emerging dialogue between Haitian women and men in elite circles, between Haitian women and feminists globally, and between Haitian women of varying social classes within Haiti.

Perhaps one of the reasons why the existence of feminism in the Third World has been contested is that women's lives generally and women's political activity specifically have gone largely undocumented. Nationalist agendas, focusing as they do on "the people," have, by and large, been gendered as male even as they espouse gender-neutral politics. In Haiti, the neuterizing of nationalism from the onset of Independence contributed to the general exclusion of women from the nation's historical record—if women were involved at all in revolutionary acts they were re-membered not as having taken part in them as women but as members of the faceless mass. Reconstructing the forging of a feminist politics in Haiti is thus always a piece-meal endeavor, filled with gaps. Nonetheless, what evidence survives points to the ongoing involvement of women in Haiti's internal struggles to rid itself of the remnants of colonialism. For example, the grassroots movement of 1844 known as the "Piquet Revolt" is credited to a woman, Louise Nicolas (Bellegarde-Smith 71). The "suffering army," as it was otherwise known because of the participants' poverty and lack of weapons other than picks, proceeded to battle the mulatto elite (later to be kept in place by U.S. forces) at Les Cayes, Jérémie, and L'Anse-à-Veau. Although the revolt failed and solidified class antagonisms, it is nonetheless striking to me that a woman headed a movement of *armed* resistance.

According to Haitian historian Patrick Bellegarde-Smith, women had also been instrumental in organizing against the U.S. Occupation, using their mobility as market women to "[smuggle] ammunition and intelligence on U.S. troop movements to insurgents throughout the countryside" (Bellegarde-Smith 83). A report made in 1927 by the U.N. Women's International League for Peace and Freedom revealed further that U.S. troops had been responsible for innumerable "war crimes" against women, including execution by machine gun, beatings, torture, and burnings at the pyre. The indiscriminate use of violence on the part of the U.S. troops made it impossible for women not to take an active part in the country's affairs. But since the resistance movement that took place during the years of the Occupation was largely nationalistic in its aims, women could not easily divorce themselves from the larger dissident group to pursue women's independence as a separate issue. It is not surprising, then, that an active women's movement arose at the end of the Occupation, as the U.S. hold on Haiti diminished.

In 1934, the Ligue féminine d'action sociale was formed by women of the upper classes, who chose to abandon their usual appoach of individualized patronage and to adopt instead a more communal approach that would attack Haiti's greater social problems (Bouchereau 86). The Ligue founded the Association des femmes Haitiennes pour l'organisation du travail/Association of Haitian Women for the Organization of Work in 1935, a foundation for homemakers in 1937, and an organization to work on behalf of children's rights in 1939. The children's rights organization pursued legislation for the protection of children as well as published a journal entitled *L'aube* (*Sunrise*). A fund for social assistance was also brought into being in 1939 with the support of Résia Vincent, the then-president's wife. The Ligue's two most prominent achievements were the passing of constitutional amendments that validated and protected women as fully emancipated citizens of the State and protected their children's rights, and the promotion of cross-class unity through the literary/political journal *Voix des femmes*. The Ligue took seriously its mandate to disseminate information on the realities of woman's lot in Haiti and to perpetuate an overtly feminist politic. Its motto was advanced on the front page of every issue with a quotation authored by Mustapha Kémal who, in 1929, supported and legislated women's rights in the Turkish empire through a new civil code: "A nation which divides itself into two categories of people each living their separate lives—on one side the men, on the other the women—will always be a weak nation. We must arrive at a collaboration of the two sexes for the good of the country."[5] The journal was used to clarion women's rights and to advance a progressive feminist agenda calling for women's suffrage, among many other rights, such as women's independence within marriage and children's equity.

An article in the December 1939–January 1940 issue of *Voix des femmes,* by Denyse Guillaume, adroitly challenged the commonly held view that Haitian women, under what was then French law, were protected through the marriage contract: "Married or not, women possess no political rights; less favored than her illiterate brothers, she cannot elect a deputy or give her opinion on a theoretical text. Certain functions which necessitate the enjoyment and exercise of political rights such as being a judge, a member of a jury or a notary are inaccessible to her. Such is the legal status of the Haitian woman."[6] The journal also exhorted those of the privileged class to become conscious of their responsibilities as citizens to the impoverished classes. Articles published in it dealing with the subject of poverty, though tainted with elitist jargon exalting the nobility of the poor peasant, severely criticize the members of the upper class for their "avarice" (Metzger-Theard 5). Reports also appeared in the journal summarizing the activities of international women's meetings and lending support to resistance movements around the world (Sylvain 2).

In effect, the Ligue's main purpose was to act as a bridge between the global and the local. It did so more or less successfully in its first ten years of activism. In 1934, the Ligue participated in lobbying for legislation to provide an equal minimum wage for men and women and three weeks paid maternity leave for women. In 1943, their efforts resulted in the opening of a high school for young women in Port-au-Prince; by 1944, girls were admitted to traditionally male high schools in the capital. Women's access to education was also pursued in the countryside, as branches of the Ligue were started in outlying areas and run by women from these communities. In the country, literacy was perhaps the most dominant educational issue and, statistically, it appears that the Ligue's efforts contributed to the growth in functional literacy among the general Haitian populace, which rose from 12 percent in 1920 to 44 percent in 1980–1986 (Miller 76).

By 1944, the Ligue's efforts to have women's political rights recognized in the Constitution had resulted in women being granted the right to be elected to political office. This limited recognition led to a student revolt in 1946, the hero of which again was a woman, Léonie Madiou, who was injured and arrested during her participation (Bouchereau 92). The revolt itself backfired, as elected officials declared that "women were responsible for all the ills of Haiti" (Bouchereau 92, translation mine) and proceeded to revoke the right of elligibility and deny women suffrage.

But the Ligue, which included writers such as Cléanthe Desgraves (also known as Mme. Virgile Valcin), fought back by increasing the rate of publication of their journal and by also publishing political manifestoes. Their activism led to the declaration *Voeux du premier Congrès national des femmes Haitiennes* in 1950, which demanded a revision of the civil and penal code "en vue d'y établir l'égalité des Droits entre l'Homme et la Femme [in view of establishing the equality of Rights between Man and Woman]" (3). The list of demands enumerated in the document include the reform of laws pertaining to marriage, the creation of maternity rights, laws enforcing paternal responsibility, the closure of brothels, the admission of women to juries, women's right to vote, modifications to divorce laws that favored husbands, laws to protect children's rights, and the improvement of women's prison facilities. The document elicited vitriolic rebuttals, such as W.A. Rochemont's *Du féminisme national,* that attacked Haitian feminists for "abandoning" their roles as mothers and wives to censure male politicians "par le truchement de leur vilaine et insinuante petite bouche [by the vehicle of their ugly and insinuating little mouth]" (9). Despite opposition, a petition signed by thousands demanding equal civil and political rights for women was carried before the Constitutional Assembly by a group of over one thousand women of all social classes and geographical areas (Bouchereau 96), and in 1950, article nine of the Haitian Constitution recognized women as fully emancipated human beings with equal rights.

Because of its undercutting, the Haitian feminist movement has been largely unrecognized until its recent resurrection in the post-Duvalier years, following the military coup of 1986. A recent article on Haitian feminism today by Carolle Charles contributes to the misconception that Haitian women, as Third World feminists, cannot bridge class differences in order to assert a revolutionary agenda. In the article—"Gender and Politics in Contemporary Haiti: Transnationalism and the Emergence of a New Feminism (1980–1990)"—Charles gives short thrift to the activities of the Ligue Feminine d'Action Sociale of the 1930s, stating that it emerged from the organizing of a small group of "female intellectuals," which "suffered from its narrow class perspectives and from conflicting interests within the organization," and that the Ligue itself was "a modest program" (146–147). As I outlined above, this "modest program" led to women's suffrage, the legal recognition of women in the penal code, and access to broad education. Charles further argues that suffrage led to Haitian women's political suicide under the Duvalier regime, since women were treated as "political subjects," that is, as individuals or citizens of the state who would suffer the same violent reprisals as their male counterparts. "The Duvalierist state," Charles claims, "targeted women in a systematic way, redefining forms of gender oppression . . . [focusing] on a 'patriotic woman' whose allegiance was first to Duvalier's nation and state. . . . the gendered politics and ideology of the Duvalierist state created a paradox, the increased politicization and raised consciousness of women and their transformation into political agents of social change." The indoctrination of women under a despotic regime is, in fact, nothing new or particular to the Duvaliers; one need only think of the missing and tortured women of Argentina, of women's participation in the Cuban revolution that brought Castro to power, of the women forced to adhere to Mao's "Cultural Revolution" in China. Women under Duvalier were to serve the State in a singularly *depoliticized* manner: to serve the State meant to renounce the advancements made by women in the years just preceding the 1957 presidential election, to be good, dependent wives, mothers, and even productive market women. There was no need for Duvalier to "appeal to the image of the suffering, self-sacrificing, patriotic mother who has no place in the political arena" (Charles 139) because the Duvalier philosophy was not based in socialist or communist dogmas of sacrifice for the nation but in the promise of long-awaited capitalistic prosperity opposed to the mulatto elite only to the extent that it could remove that elite from the seat of political power. Women of the mulatto classes became the target of a violence that had been reserved in the past—during the early 1900s in particular—for women of the working classes or of the white, colonial classes. The decrease of feminist activity post-1957 can be directly linked to the fact that women were actively discouraged from participating in the politics of the country in any way that would promote feminist principles; Duvalierism resulted in the destruction of any feminist political outlets.

Charles believes that before the Duvalier years, women's position as "femme couverte" kept them protected from such institutionalized violence: "they had the 'privilege' of not being subjected to state violence" (139). In my opinion, nothing could be further from the truth. Throughout its history, Haiti's women have been a part of the political apparatus, taking up arms in various revolutions over the years and suffering the consequences accordingly. To believe that women were "protected" by laws under which they were not recognized as full human beings is to accede to the full weight of hegemonic discourse whereby one is forced to believe in the powerlessness of the subjugated and the "freedom" of false consciousness in order to explain away the inefficacy of revolutionary thought and practice. This condescension is best understood as symptomatic of U.S. racist attitudes instituted during the Occupation and sustained by the misogynist practices of the Duvalier government. Finally, Charles declares that under Duvalier, "state violence created, for the first time, gender equality" (140). This statement is disturbing on many fronts. For one, it completely alters the feminist definition of "equal rights." If we follow Charles' logic, then we must believe that gender equality is defined simply as equal *treatment* under any form of government. For another, leaving aside the fact that Haitian women have never been free from politically motivated violence, it would be foolish to believe that the violence inflicted on women is "the same" as that inflicted upon men. The use of rape, for instance, as an instrument of state-instituted violence has increased massively over the last ten years, which is not to say that the same form of violence was not used under Duvalier (Marie Chauvet's novels disabuse us of such naiveté). Women have always been used as political pawns between male-dominated political factions, and the violence against them has only increased with the departure of the Duvaliers. Says one spokeswoman for the contemporary feminist organization SOPHA: "Before, the military didn't kill women. They raped them and humiliated them. They humiliated them in all forms. . . . They humiliated the women who are more organized than others. In the last few weeks, they have killed many women. You find the body in the street without the head. They separate the body and the head and the arms and the legs" (*oob* 16). Suffrage did not give women the human face that Duvalier could then see fit to desecrate (Charles' line of thought also assumes that Haitian feminists can only be of the middle and upper classes), as the opening quote to this chapter demonstrates; it was a right, which hard-won, was denied in order to exploit a vast labor force.

What is essential to the proper evaluation of Haitian feminism on the global scale is to recognize that the category of "oppressed" is not a static one. As in most Third World countries, race, for example, is not simply a question of white versus black, but a complex interrelation of economics and lineage not necessarily dictated by racial characteristics—this, of course, results from the colonial process, which leads to syncretism of the oppressing and oppressed cultures, normally understood to be in constant and polarized conflict. As a Third World movement, Haitian feminism counters rather than follows the Western models of French and North American mainstream feminism, at the same time that it finds parallels with the enunciation of feminist politics by Third World women in the West, most notably by their African-American counterparts. Faced with finding solutions to poverty, illiteracy, limited education, inaccessible careers, voting rights, and protection under the law, Haitian feminists could not afford to be narrow in their vision. On the other hand, within Haiti, the debilitating class structure (which pits Haitians against Haitians) resulted in an increasingly condescending approach to the needs of women of the working and impoverished classes. Nonetheless, keeping such contradictions in mind, Haitian feminism, successful at times, a failure at others, presents itself as a defiant strain of Third World feminism in the West, hinging on socialist reform, a belief in the universalization of human rights, and a steadfast dedication to the uplift of woman in nationalist and global agendas.

CHAPTER 2

Ayiti çé tè glissé:

THE U.S. OCCUPATION OF HAITI AND THE EMERGENCE OF HAITIAN WOMEN'S LITERARY VOICES

⊷ ⊨⧫⊨ ⊶

We had to kill a few times at first, for various reasons. But that is all fortunately ended. Our attitude now in Haiti is superior, but kindly.
    —William B. Seabrook, *The Magic Island*

Dear me, think of it! Niggers speaking French.
    —U.S. Secretary of State William Jennings Bryan

Être américains en Haïti, depuis 1915 . . . c'est se promener en pleine paix avec des machines-guns braquées sur de pauvres étudiants en grève; être américains, enfin, c'est vivre d'abondance, mourir d'indigestion à côté de l'haïtien dont les tripes se sont rapetissées à force de privations.

[To be American in Haiti, since 1915 . . . is to walk about in an atmosphere of peace with machine guns pointed on defenseless students on strike; to be American, finally, is to live extravagantly, to die of indigestion beside the Haitian whose intestines have shrunk from deprivation.]
    —Mme. Virgile Valcin, *La Blanche Négresse*

Solange's mother tries to warn her about the dangers she will have to face. She tells her incredible stories about evils lurking in the shadows that can manifest themselves in the shape of the closest friend one has or even the benevolent traffic comptroller who helps her cross the street on her way to school. Sometimes, the stories tell of the good things that can come from learning about the world around her—which herbs to harvest to curb a child's croup, which to avoid. Solange believes that her mother has a story for every conceivable occasion. She counts on them the way one expects the sun to rise in the morning or fall at night. Her mother has answers to all the questions she can think to ask. Solange understands that her mother is afraid for her but she is not certain exactly why.

Solange would like to take her mother's face in her small hands and look into her mother's eyes and take away the fear that lurks there. But she is still a child and children do not look into their mother's eyes. It would be to show a lack of respect, possibly to insult. Solange would not want to hurt her mother in any way. At times, Solange sees her mother flinch for no reason at all. Once, she remembers, she asked her mother for some *chewing gum* and her mother snapped at her to speak proper creole. Then her mother went about her work in the kitchen slamming pots and pans in the cupboards talking to herself about *yankiez* and how everything had changed because of them. Solange could not understand the relationship between her request for the chewy candies and the people she saw carrying on in the television box she sometimes watched on the neighbors' porch. She watches her mother bustling around the kitchen in her cloud of anger and she is suddenly ashamed. She will wait until after dinner to ask her mother for the story that will explain everything, that will take away the shame.

When her mother tells her story, it is an incredible tale of *blancs* armed with shotguns, wearing long-sleeved shirts and long pants, climbing through the vined mountainsides to round up country people they accuse of conspiracy against the U.S. government. The *blancs* take over the best pieces of land and the largest houses by the side of the sea. They despise anyone who stands in their way. They condescend to speak only to Haitians with the lightest skins who they mistake for French citizens even when they speak only a quick and witty creole.

Solange's mother has heard all of this from her own mother who was herself a child when the Americans came to tell their family that they would have to give over their farm's produce to feed the sickly soldiers on the base nearby. The boys had to stop going to school and her mother—Solange's grandmother—who had been promised at least her first three years of elementary schooling once the boys had finished their studies, had to learn at home in between shifts of feeding the goats or harvesting small ears of corn. Solange's mother sighs: *It took ten years after the Americans left for girls like you to get the chance to go to school.* And even then, it was a difficult thing for all of them since they were poorer than before the Occupation and still as dark, and the schools, which were moving away from the French system toward the American one, dissuaded poor children from attending classes. Solange's mother turns to Solange without a smile and hands her her history book. *This is why you must do the best you can and know where you came from,* she says.

Solange takes the book from her mother and turns to the page with the picture of the big, grey battleship standing in the still green-blue waters of the harbor between l'Ile de la Gonâve and Port-au-Prince. She wants to make her mother proud and so she begins to read.

To Occupy Is to Possess

The U.S. Occupation of Haiti lasted almost twenty years, from 1915 to 1934, and had a severe impact on the country. For one, the Occupation changed the face of Haitian letters, which until then had never textually engaged its looming northern neighbor. Censorship, imposed by the American occupants, made it difficult, if not impossible, for writers to express freely their political views, especially with regard to the U.S. occupants; the task of presenting political views in literature was all the more difficult for female writers who had not yet begun to forge their own distinct literary voice. As critic Michael Dash notes, the American as character "does not explicitly emerge in Haitian writing . . . until the 1930s when censorship was less rigidly enforced" (51). Haitian writers such as Stephen Alexis, F. Morisseau-Leroy, Jean F. Brierre, Edris Saint-Amant, Maurice Casséus, René Bélance, René Depestre, Léon Laleau, Mme. Virgile Valcin, and Duraciné Vaval (Dash 52; Bellegarde-Smith 235) were nonetheless radicalized by the experience of neocolonialism, which forcibly sought to invalidate Haitian culture and identity. The radicalization of the entire country in response to the invasion—the rise of Haitian nationalism in particular—allowed for the relatively unopposed involvement of women in politics, and with it, the evolution of Haitian feminism. It makes sense, then, that the first women novelists would pen their novels at this time and that their work, which openly addressed nationality, class, and gender issues in Haiti during the Occupation, would appear no earlier than 1929 with Mme. Virgile Valcin's *Cruelle destinée.* The two novels that will be the focus of this chapter appeared five years later, in 1934, the final year of the Occupation, and both texts—Mme. Virgile Valcin's *La blanche négresse* and Annie Desroy's *Le joug*—sought to come to terms with the effects of the United States on the Haitian (female) psyche.

Very different in their execution, the novels reflect the steady progression of Haitian women's literary aesthetics from French sentimentalist modes to a syncretic Haitian form using modernist experimentation and psychological drama to represent the merest beginnings of the politicization of women's literary voices. Both authors seek to redefine Haitian society from a female point of view at the same time that they find themselves unable to present compelling female characters. Strikingly, the image of the Haitian woman in both works emerges not as a function of characterization but as a result of a dialectic struggle between American representations of Haitians through the female subject and the refutation of that image via plot and allegory. Thus, the Haitian woman is imaged through a textual absence—a feature of Haitian women's *culture-lacune.*

Mme. Virgile Valcin, also known as Cléante Desgraves, one of the founders of the Ligue féminine nationale d'Haiti and the journal *Voix des femmes,* is best known for her sentimental novels. Of course, Valcin holds the distinction of having published the first woman's novel in Haiti, which was quickly followed by *La blanche négresse,* the story of a French-Haitian woman whose reluntant marriage to an American during the Occupation results in disaster when the couple discover that she is, despite outward appearances, of African heritage. The literary and cultural merits of Valcin's works are often overlooked by contemporary scholars of Haitian literature who find her melodramatic tales outdated and politically vacuous: in them, class mores are always depicted as tragically unbreachable, sexuality is prudishly excised, and violence is but a murmur of reality. Given the turmoil of Haitian politics, most scholars have found Valcin's tales unrealistic and amateurish. In my opinion, it is the very simplicity of Valcin's plots that provides her readers with a template from which to draw broader conclusions than her plots, on first appearance, seem capable of suggesting. Valcin was adroit in exploiting the sentimental genre, which meant that her characters were sympathetic, engaging, and their real or imagined plights realistically portrayed. To support her characters, Valcin took care to provide a structural frame drawn from the social milieu of the middle to upper classes. The fictive society of her characters mirrored real life and provided the source of each character's motivation. *La blanche négresse,* which, at first glance, appears to be nothing more than a tragic mulatta tale, provides literary evidence of the ways in which race matters were irrevocably altered by the American presence. It also attempts to explain the rise of feminism in the context of American-based racism and critiques the *indigéniste* movement's creation of an image of the "true" Haitian woman that Valcin appears to believe conflicts with the country's complex (that is, neither completely white nor black) racial make-up.

Annie Desroy's only published novel, *Le joug,* has received even less attention than Valcin's works even though she had already produced two plays in Haiti—*Et l'amour vint!* in 1921 and *La cendre du passé* in 1931. Desroy, an active participant in Haiti's cultural and literary milieux, presents a much more complex treatment of the effects of the Occupation upon the Haitian psyche in her novel than does Valcin in *La blanche négresse.* The latter opened with a remarkably laudatory preface written by Jean Price-Mars in which the famed anthropologist/ethnologist remarked: "[Valcin's] novel is . . . a slice of contemporary history and the reader will not be surprised to confront in the course of the narrative a critical viewpoint on men and issues which occupy the public in its most immediate context."[1] But Desroy's novel, which appeared in an edition of only fifty copies, is much more overtly political and far less devoted to the features of sentimentalism or romance in the tradition of the pre-twentieth century Franco-Anglo European women's novel that Valcin exploited. Desroy makes use of two couples—one American, the other Haitian—to examine, at a purely psychological level, the dynamics of race, sex, and class during the Occupation. Desroy also anticipates the eroticism engendered in the writings of her later counterpart, Marie Chauvet (who is now, with good reason, considered Haiti's foremost woman writer), and unflinchingly makes use of the novel as a political forum in which to question the mores of two colliding societies in a modernist context.

Haitian literary critic Yvette Tardieu Feldman suggests that Desroy's novel has been intentionally sidestepped in order to make of Valcin's more apolitical novels the standard of the Haitian woman's novel—in order, in other words, to represent the Haitian woman writer as cloyingly sentimental and unaware of the politics around her.[2] Feldman believes that it is time that Desroy's novel be given its due: "in the context of critical revisionism demanded, with good reason, by the second sex, it is of great importance that we reexamine the verdicts—negative or positive—passed on all women authors, for discrimination or male paternalism play a role all the more insidious as it is often unconscious."[3] Feldman not only quite rightly argues that women writers like Desroy have received next to no critical attention; she also points out that what little criticism exists of their texts has been motivated not by an interest in valuing "art for art's sake" but by an interest in *devaluing* women's works. In Desroy's case, the oversight is all the more deceitful because her novel provides some of the missing pieces necessary to reconstructing a historical period during which Haitian points of view were by and large suppressed. Here, I am in agreement with Feldman, who writes that the "uniqueness of *Le joug* emanates from its role as a crossroads for cultural exchanges."[4] By pairing Valcin and Desroy's novels in this chapter, I am thus aiming to create a literary crossroads that will enable readers to better apprehend how Haitian women's early literature served as a tool of ideological revolution, not only by its criticism of the literature that emerged outside of Haiti and demonized our culture, but also by its revelation of the ways in which Haitian culture was rudely altered by the crucial disruption of its independence. That two novels should appear so precipitously in 1934 by two Haitian women writers can be understood only by clarifying here the impact the Occupation had on Haiti as a whole.

Historians who contend that the Occupation had a beneficial effect cite the building of roads and conveniences such as electricity and running water as evidence for their argument; they do not go further to explain that, as has been the rule for subsequent Haitian governments, "modernization" appeared in selective areas of the country in which the ruling class (in this case, the U.S. military and private citizens) resided, nor that the new structures were built through the reinstatement of the "corvée" (Bellegarde-Smith 78), whereby the poor were forced to provide free labor (the practice had last been used by King Christophe to build his (in)famous Sans Souci palace and Citadelle Laferrière). Robert Kaplan, for one, has written that the U.S. mission was "to heal the body politic of a land that lacks the basis of a modern political culture" (qtd. Chomsky, 17). Haiti's history of political, post-independence, instability was the source of the idea that Haiti lacked the basis of a modern political culture. Between 1843 and 1915, Haiti had twenty-two rulers (only one of whom served out his term, and four of whom died in office), suffered through one hundred and two civil wars in seventy-two years of independence, and had its waters navigated by U.S. warships twenty-eight times between 1849 and the first year of Occupation (Heinl and Heinl 404).

Though many factors could be cited for the country's political unrest (hence its reputation amongst Haitians as *tè glissé*), it seems that much of it was due to the imposition of European norms of governing by the first rulers of the country, from Toussaint to Dessalines (Price-Mars 7), who, in their own way, sought to preserve oppressive elements of European imperialism. (Christophe, for example, followed the model of the British aristocracy in declaring himself monarch of Haiti in the early 1800s [Dash 51].) Michel Trouillot observes further that "the Haitian state has always been authoritarian: from Dessalines to the two Duvaliers, Haiti has known nothing but dictators" (164). The *cacos*—descendants of Taino and African maroons who lived hidden away in the mountains and resisted French colonialists during the seventeenth century—had begun their war of resistance in 1869 (Heinl and Heinl 342) and represented an active force of resistance against the looming U.S. invasion. Nonetheless, the last president before the Occupation, Guillaume Sam—a former *caco* dissident—was killed by a Haitian mob for his misdeeds while in the seat of power. The country was thus experiencing the growth pains, so to speak, of a movement toward a syncretic form of government that could more successfully combine the interests of a fiercely Afrocentric populace and a Eurocentric elite.[5]

The "modern political culture" the United States sought to impose was supposed to rid Haiti of its dualistic "unrest"; what happened instead, however, was that the Occupation, the purpose of which was to protect U.S. interests, disrupted the natural course of Haiti's evolution after relatively few years of autonomous politics. These interests included establishing distance between the Caribbean nation and the European powers that dominated the area, such as Germany (this is important to note given that the First World War had begun in 1914) and protecting loans made to Haiti by U.S. firms between 1900 and 1911, as well as private investments such as export-oriented plantation systems that had been operated by U.S. citizens since 1910 (Trouillot 100). By the time of its invasion of Haiti, the United States had garnered a history of military "intervention," intervention that it justified by way of an appeal to "manifest destiny"—the idea that the expansion of its borders was warranted by its divine right to rule neighboring, smaller nations in the Caribbean basin and Latin America.[6] Haiti was ruled by martial law starting in 1915 (Trouillot 105), and over 5,000 Haitians died during the thirty-year period of its imposition (estimates range between the conservative figure of 3,000 by U.S. accounts and 50,000 by Haitian accounts). The result of what the United States called an "intervention" was a country worse off than it had been before that interference. Fully conscious of its misdeeds, the U.S. military imposed broad censorship in the country (Pamphile 97), preventing Haitian journalists from writing, printing, and disseminating information on various infringements of civil rights taking place in the vast countryside.

Woodrow Wilson, the president of the United States at the time of invasion, is said to have declared before it took place that "Only an honest and efficient government deserves support. The Government of the U.S. could not justify the expenditure of money or the sacrifice of American lives in support of any other kind of government" (Heinl and Heinl 391). The government the United States put in place was formed in such a way as to enforce complete dependence upon Haiti's northern neighbor: in 1915, the United States signed a convention with Haiti that gave it the power to impose the right to police the country and control it economically for ten years; in 1916, the Haitian Senate was dissolved; in 1917, the convention of 1915 was extended to give the United States economic control over Haiti for a total of twenty years. As *caco* revolts were squelched, a new Haitian army trained by the Marines was formed, and, by the end of the Occupation, the United States was the chief source of Haitian imports and Haiti was sixth among its buyers of exports (Trouillot 101–103). Largely exploited for its coffee and other natural resources, Haiti lost much of its revenue through inflated custom duties that benefited plants owned and operated by U.S. corporations. According to Patrick Bellegarde-Smith, the real economic goal of the United States was "to dispossess the Haitian peasantry and reinstitute the plantation economy" (78). Lastly, every ruler that presided over Haiti during the Occupation was put in place by the United States rather than elected through free and democratic processes. Wilson's "honest and efficient" government was, in the end, nothing more than a smoke screen for possessing and thus exploiting the island, the former pearl of the West Indies.

The Plundered Island

Not only was Haiti dispossessed of its economic and political wherewithal (a formula for disaster—one, albeit, that could not have been anticipated—in that this dispossesion certainly made more possible the thirty-year Duvalier regime that soon followed), but it was also irrevocably mired in a racist ideology perpetuated by the U.S. military. Although color prejudice had always been a looming issue in Haiti, it had never been the white on black issue that remains anchored in the American psyche. Haitian historian Michel Trouillot writes that "in spite of color prejudice, Haitian national identity implied a positive identification with the black race"; the presence of the Marines (whom many say were sent from the American South *because* of their supposed overtly racist attitudes) "aggravated color prejudice" (130), which was reinforced through the installation of light-skinned political officials and the systematic ill-treatment of darker-skinned Haitians. As U.S. historian Brenda Plummer writes, "Americans insisted on segregation and introduced jim crow hotels, restaurants, and clubs in the cities" (129). Anthropologist Robert Lawless, in his recent book *Haiti's Bad Press,* contends that racial discrimination under the Occupation "forced the largely mulatto-dominated elite to rethink their identity and to question whether they were imitation Frenchmen or transplanted Africans" (109). By all accounts, the racial tensions exacerbated by the U.S. military gave rise to the academic and literary movement led by Jean Price-Mars called *indigénisme,* which provided the underlying tenets of the ideology that later became known throughout the African diaspora as *négritude* (Lawless 109; Bellegarde-Smith 334). The movement called for the reclamation of a denigrated African heritage, no small feat considering the overt demonization of Haitian culture during the height of the Occupation.

Joan Dayan writes in her article "Vodoun, or the Voice of the Gods" that "during the American occupation . . . tales of cannibalism, torture, and zombis were published in [the United States]. What better way to justify the 'civilizing' presence of marines in Haiti than to project the phantasm of barbarism?" (33). Until the mid-1930s, literature on Haiti had been penned mostly by visiting Americans—both black and white—whose visions of Haiti were quite unlike those of Haitians themselves and were fueled by racist and/or jingoistic ideological sentiments that dated back to former years of enslavement. One of the most popular of these writers was William Seabrook, author of *The Magic Island,* whose depiction of Haitian *vodou* as alternately demonic and unfathomably beautiful resulted from his focusing his attention on what he viewed as the ultimate representative of the culture—the Haitian *vodou* priestess. Desroy's and Valcin's novels are, in large part, devoted to redressing the myths promulgated by Seabrook's account of the *mambo* priestess at the same time that they advance a different, less demonized (albeit at times overromanticized) vision of women within Haitian society.

The Magic Island, a tome replete with black and white lithographs depicting ghoulish, bloodthirsty caricatures meant to be representations of Haitians involved in mysterious acts of *vodou* worship, has only recently been reclaimed as a significant ethnographic text.[7] Anthropologist Steven Gregory describes the text as "both unscientific and potentially subversive." He further claims that Seabrook's inability to neither condemn nor laud the culture he describes leads him to produce a double-voiced text through which he is forced to become his own Other (173, 180). Seabrook is enchanted, as the title of his book reflects, with the secrets of Haitian *vodou*. This enchantment is confirmed in his description of Madame Célie, the *mambo* priestess of whom Seabrook writes: "It was as if we had known each other always, had been at some past time united by the mystical equivalent of an umbilical cord; as if I had suckled in infancy her dark breasts, had wandered far, and was now returning home" (28). Gregory interprets such descriptions of Madame Célie to be "unmystified and unsexualized . . . a maternal figure in a concrete sense" (189). The attribution to Seabrook of such pure intentions, of a desire to transcend the very raciosocial literary discourse that he himself had a tremendous part in shaping, is to neglect the historical context in which his words were penned.

Seabrook's words themselves contradict such an interpretation. Take for example his description of his experience of a *vodou* ceremony: "It was a terror of something blacker and more implacable than they—*a terror of the dark, all-engulfing womb*" (my emphasis, 37). Seabrook's language is intentionally feminized, just as it is intentionally double-voiced, in order to give the *deceptive* appearance of racial and cultural openness. After having described Haitians and *vodou* in the most racist and fantastic of terms, coupling his descriptions with the perfunctory caricatured illustrations, Seabrook writes:

> I notice I have been continually writing "they," using the time-honored pronoun employed by so many otherwise veracious and candid traveler-authors when describing wild happenings which they feel may be regarded dubiously by *sisters and aunts* back home. Very well: the truth. I drank like the rest, when the bottles were passed my way. I did *willingly all else that Maman Célie told me,* and now with good appetite stuffed myself with goat flesh and washed down the meats with more white rum, and dozed, replete and vastly contented, in the bright sunshine. It was for this I had come to Haiti. It concerned me personally. It justified something in my soul. I cared not if I never wrote a book. *I merely wondered,* without worrying— since it is impossible ever to be utterly content—*how soon Maman Célie would take me inside her houmfort.* (my emphasis, 45–44)

The author here uses an appeal to an emotional, sentimental readership defined as female to assure his credibility as an authentic ethnographer if not as an anthropologist. He adopts the stance of an apologist to mystify readers who may mistrust his white male, American identity, which is what permits his presence in the occupied country in the first place; as noted, these readers are encoded within the text as female and Seabrook claims to be controlled as well by Madame Célie, his pseudo-mother. Seabrook's access—his possession of Haitian culture through the written word—results from the Occupation. He sees Haitian culture from the clouded perspective of an occupier, a possessor, which permits him to sexualize all his encounters with Haitians and accounts for his wish to literally *penetrate* the culture he has the license to define. Thus he can facilely describe the rituals as speaking to "something that was elemental male" in him (37), as "savage and abandoned," yet at the same time as "not devoid of a certain beauty" (43). Haitians themselves are described in the act of devotion as "writhing black bodies, blood-maddened, god-maddened, drunken, whirl[ing] and danc[ing] their dark saturnalia, heads thrown weirdly back as if their necks were broken" (43)—indeed a pretty picture.

What revisionists of neocolonial texts written by Americans in this period ignore is that throughout the nineteenth century, the sexuality of women of African descent was overdetermined in the service of imperialistic aims. As Sander Gilman has conclusively demonstrated in his essay "Black Bodies, White Bodies," African women were perceived as useful only for their labor and reproductive capacities; their bodies served as the basis for the articulation of a sexual discourse that placed the African woman at the bottom of the "evolutionary" scale in order to substantiate the claims of European women's chaste superiority and justify the enslavement and exploitation of African women. This sexualization gave rise to the creation and institutionalization during the slave era of such gendered racial stereotypes as the matriarch, the sapphire, and the mammy—all of which served to further circumscribe the woman of African descent and deny her the power of self-definition. Seabrook's depiction of Madame Célie recalls the image of the prototypical mammy figure who silently and benevolently nurtures her white charges.[8] But Seabrook is not a child, and the image he invokes of himself suckling at the breast of a Black woman at a time when, in the American South, accounts of lynchings were widespread and cross-racial affairs were declared illegal, implies a pseudo-sexual bond. As is the case with all narrative, the story is a product of its author whose own subjectivity is interpolated with the representation of the characters brought to life within it. This is but the more true when we take seriously the historical context in which any given text is produced, a task that Gregory refuses to engage, even as he espouses it (204). Whether Seabrook succeeds in placing himself in the skin of the "Other" can be debated, but it is another matter altogether—especially in the absence of a full evaluation of texts written by Haitians during the Occupation in response to their depictions in American literature—to defend the resulting colonizing text his adventuring spirit engendered.

Pointedly, Desroy anticipated in 1934 sympathetic readings of Seabrook's text and made use of an unusual protagonist, the American officer Harry Murray, to tackle the insidious rhetoric of the American occupants. Murray is atypical of representations of Americans in Haitian literature produced during this period, who are usually painted as immoral exploiters (Dash 53; Feldman 37). Murray, whom Desroy describes as a pacifist (25) and as as an "indigénophile," is kind, considerate, and a supporter of Haitian nationalism. In the novel, Murray thus serves as foil to the openly racist American officer who is making more difficult already strained relations between occupied and occupants as the nineteen-year Occupation draws to a close. Though Murray, like Seabrook, is deeply curious about Haitian *vodou,* he distinguishes himself from the latter by condemning those who exoticize and exploit the mysteries of Haitian culture for their own gain. Murray, however, is soon revealed to be as misguided as is Seabrook; his liberalism is simply a veneer beneath which are buried deeply-rooted views of racial and cultural supremacy.

Michael Dash contends that "Desroy, through her character [Murray], sees the true villain of the Haitian situation not as the American officer but as the Haitian elite" (53), and further, that Murray "rejects Seabrook's *Magic Island* as an indignity to Haitians" (53). This interpretation leads Dash into a fatal misreading of the text. The Haitian elite, represented by Murray's secretary Frédéric and his wife Fernande, are the *demystifiers* of Seabrook's text and it is they who enlighten a gullible Murray. When Murray reminds his secretary Frédéric of his promise to take him to a *vodou* gathering, Frédéric explains to Fernande the reason why Murray wants to witness a *vodou* ceremony. He says: "You do know that a certain Seabrook has written, probably under contract, a book entitled *The Magic Island* in which we are, as usual, the fodder for these writing buffoons, thirsty for a quick success."[9] The discussion that unfolds is strictly between husband and wife; Murray has long departed. The passages Dash would want to attribute to Murray are all spoken by Frédéric:

> We suffer the yoke of our ignorance, of our passions, of our super-stitions, of our prejudices. It is those barriers which paralyze our evo-lution and deliver us with bound feet and hands into the hands of foreigners who benefit from our stupid disunity.[10]

When Frédéric finally takes Murray to a *vodou* ceremony, the latter discovers that the rituals Seabrook had described as barbaric are at once mystical and fantastic. The *vodou* practicioners enact religious rituals of devotion that even Murray would like to emulate, as they dance and sing to Damballah (the serpent god): "Murray was no longer the being for whom Civilization had forged a refined and snobbish soul. He had the uncontrollable desire to throw himself in the midst of the frenzy."[11] Murray's desire turns to horror as he thinks he is about to see a child sacrifice; in fact, the "sacrifice" is a simulacrum devised with a doll and the blood of a goat. Frédéric explains that the performance is tacked on to the ceremony to please curious outsiders. Murray is satisfied, but his transformation from elitist bystander to participant is short-lived. He learns nothing from his experience.

Desroy's sympathetic protagonist serves as a vehicle through which the author unveils the true tragedy of the Occupation: cultural invasion at all levels—in other words, neocolonialism. Murray is not, in fact, espousing Haitian nationalist ideals; rather, he adopts a pseudo-liberal approach to his position of authority in Haiti that simply masks a deep-rooted condescension toward Haitian culture. Dash claims that Murray "argues for a revaluation of Haitian culture around its African base" (53) in keeping with the *indigéniste* movement. But even a cursory textual literary analysis of Murray's views on this topic demonstrate his inability to grasp the basic principles of *indigénisme*. In conversation with his secretary, Murray misconstrues Price-Mars' pivotal writings in *Ainsi parla L'Oncle* and declares that "In order to evolve, you would have to affirm your identity, that is, never to abandon the fact that you are all negroes without any perceptible differences."[12] Had Murray read further than the preface from which he quotes, he would have discovered Price-Mars' detailed ethnography of the various West African origins of Haitians and the cultural aspects taken from each and syncretized on Haitian soil. Price-Mars was aware of and confronted skeptics such as Murray when he wrote in *Formation ethnique* that "For some time, a serious debate has been raised in our intellectual circles regarding Haitian culture." Pointing out that "Some deny or doubt its existence," he countered this misconception by locating Haiti's claim to its own unique culture in the "sum of its beliefs, superstitions, legends, stories, songs, riddles, [and] customs"[13] as reflected in its oral foundation. On this point, Price-Mars boldly asserted that "there was not one country which possessed a richer well of oral traditions than our Haiti" (43). In fact, his well-known tomes directly contradict outlooks like Murray's; they *affirm* that Haitians have not only one tradition, but many, which taken together have resulted in the creation of a distinct culture.

In contrast to Murray, his secretary Frédéric (labeled by critics of the text as an "elite") is described by Feldman, for one, as "indifferent" and "antagonistic" in his discussions about Haiti with Murray (41–42). Both Feldman and Dash ignore the racial dynamics at work in the novel between the two men: Frédéric is Murray's employee, his "subaltern," not an equal. He and his wife cannot even be considered truly of the "mulatto elite" since they *aspire* to that status and dream of owning a summer home in posh Kenscoff. Understandably, Frédéric is not overt in presenting his views, however conservative they might be; he does, however, upbraid Murray for his views—for instance, he criticizes Murray's inability to endorse the practice of *vodou,* even in light of his new-found appreciation for the religion, and his unwillingness to acknowledge the failure of the American Occupation to improve educational standards among the less privileged classes of Haitians. More importantly, Murray and Frédéric mirror each other despite the racial divide between them: the two men are unable to articulate broader ideological positions because they are invested in their own discrete sets of privilege; that is, they wish to protect their own interests at the same time that they play at finding solutions to Haitians' ails between themselves. Through their impotent dialogue, Desroy demonstrates that as long as those who occupy relative positions of power with respect to the impoverished Haitian underclass refuse to give up their sense of authoritarianism (Murray) or their apathy (Frédéric), redress can never occur.

Like Desroy, Valcin uses her novel to counter American portrayals of Haitian culture as a bastion of demonized African animist rituals. Her chief target is also Seabrook, who appears in the text in the incarnation of his alter-ego, the thinly-disguised Leabrook. Leabrook appears in the novel only to affirm the shallowness of the typical American in Haiti. Readers are introduced to Leabrook in a chapter that begins with a harsh and lengthy description of the occupants as seen through the eyes of the occupied:

> To be American in Haiti, since 1915, is to dispossess the peasants
> by re-establishing serfdom, to declare oneself an expert for the price
> of four to five hundred dollars per month; to be an American is to
> speed dangerously in a fancy car, emprison the journalist, to get
> drunk, to kill the most peaceful of Haitians and find someone to de-
> clare you an idiot; it is to walk about in an atmosphere of peace with

machine guns pointed on defenseless students on strike; to be American, finally, is to live extravagantly, to die of indigestion beside the Haitian whose intestines have shrunk from deprivation.[14]

Valcin's Leabrook is all of the above and more: he fancies himself a poet and is admitted to the intellectual circles of the Haitian elite. His themes, in keeping with Valcin's depiction of Americans, are limited to those through which he can justify his debauchery. Not surprisingly, in Leabrook's mind, *vodou* is inextricably linked to his loose-living and he proceeds to turn his thoughts to extolling these "virtues" of the island in his writing: "Why should he resist the desire to sing of the rum and moonshine of this little black island? to write a book about her?"[15] Valcin clearly intends to bring into question Seabrook's credentials as a writer by recreating his persona in the form of an opportunistic caricature; Leabrook is without literary talent. Furthermore, Leabrook's interest in Haitian culture is colored by his racist and imperialist attitudes. For instance, Leabrook, whose joy-ride is made possible by his position as occupant, declares the impossibility of Haitian revolt, even in the face of the *caco* revolutions, for he sees Haitians only as a "horde de sauvages [savage horde]" (63).

Nonetheless, Leabrook condescends to come face to face with this "savagery," as he asks to be led to a *vodou* ceremony. It is in this scene that Valcin exposes Leabrook's own hypocrisy as he searches for the *zombies* that would confirm for him the "otherness" of the culture he exploits for his own pleasures. Like a tourist, Leabrook takes pictures as the *vodou* celebrants dance, drink, and give homage to their *pétro loas*. He sees a small boy afflicted with tuberculosis and becomes excited at the thought that he has finally encountered a *zombie*. His guides laugh at him and tell him: "We worship the spirits with the Great Master's permission. Those who have zombies are evil persons who use them to guard their holy places, or to work their gardens. We are not into that at all."[16] Leabrook feverishly takes notes to write a book for the "gogos américains [gullable Americans]" whose heads he will fill with visions of zombies he has never seen. Only pages later, readers will find that Leabrook, like his real-life counterpart Seabrook, has made a small fortune writing on the supernatural mythology of Haiti.

Valcin's painstaking depiction of Leabrook as an anthropological parasite may seem harsh and perhaps hypocritical but it demonstrates the destructive effect Seabrook's text had on the Haitian psyche. Valcin buttressed her criticism of Seabrook by decrying the continued existence of *vodou* worship in Haiti in the face of the implementation of laws that Valcin contends made such religious practices illegal (154–155).[17] Valcin could not, in the context in which she was writing, both laud *vodou* and demystify it. She chooses the course of demystification because it achieves her primary aim: to unmask the more harmful hypocrisy of non-Haitian writers who claimed to "know" Haiti when they in fact were only putting into words projections of their own fantasies upon an alien landscape. For her, Seabrook's *Magic Island* is the product of a cultural invasion and as such cannot be read as an ethnological experiment, which, by turning him into the Other (that is the "savage") he despises, as Gregory suggests, ex-onerates him of his blind plundering. The unfortunate side effect of this literary defense is that it leads Haiti's first woman writer to deny the very features of the culture that provide it with its own unique form of resistance. Nonetheless, both she and Desroy attacked Seabrook as women writers in order to free Haitian women from the neocolonial yoke with which his text burdened them. They were less equipped, however, to construct a realistic image of the Haitian woman, one that could replace Seabrook's image of the nurturing *mambo*/mammy (and those of the lascivious figures in the accompanying illustrations) and solidify a sense of the Haitian woman's complex identity.

Conflicts of Identity: Where and Who Is the Haitian Woman?

In *La blanche négresse,* Valcin's characters confront the important dilemma that arose during the Occupation, that of interracial unions—not simply between "black" and "white," but between occupant and occupied. Set in the historical context she herself brings to life within the pages of her novel, the tale is not a simple one of "miscegenation" that became normative in African-American literature up to and during the Harlem Renaissance of the twenties and thirties in the United States; the novel distinguishes itself at the level of plot from novels written in the United States (such as Frances Harper's *Iola Leroy* or Nella Larsen's *Passing*) in that the "tragic mulatta" is not a vehicle for the affirmation and legitimization of the Black race but a vehicle for the denunciation of American hypocrisy.[18] Haitianness is shown to be racially complex, and a sense of identity is revisited rather than defined through a number of scenes in which real-life *indigéniste* poets and writers mingle with the novel's fictional characters. At the forefront of the project of cultural redefinition is the imaging of the Haitian woman. In the end, the novel seems to be asking a greater question:

Who is the Haitian woman? The answer is ultimately provided through an allegorical reading of the text that suggests that the protagonist, Laurence, embodies the racial dualism imposed by the Occupation and is, as such, representative of a neglected or denied cultural hybridity. With Laurence, Valcin produces an arch-play on Durand's *choucoune:* the French suitor is replaced by a white American and Laurence (in the role of the *marabout*) ultimately rejects him in order to embrace her female, Haitian autonomy.

Laurence initially refuses to marry her American suitor, Robert Watson, because she has promised herself to a Haitian, Guy Vanel, a brilliant young lawyer. Laurence is eventually forced to marry Robert to save her father's failing business affairs. Watson is not only rich, but also shallow. To him, "the heart of a woman was a trinket."[19] Although readers are never provided with a full explanation of Robert's interest in Laurence, by the first night of their marriage he professes his "love" for her in no uncertain terms:

> Laurence, think of the happiness of a miserable man who prefers giving up his power as master for the docility of the slave. I am your slave, no, less than that . . . your thing. I throw myself at your feet. Dear Laurence![20]

His words have the desired effect of eliciting pity and sympathy from his wife. She is effectively seduced by the power Robert bestows upon her—ironically, the power of subjugation. The language of the passage is couched in the discourse of enslavement: Robert unwittingly declares his spousal adoration in racial terms. He does so not because he believes that their roles as "occupant" and "occupied" have truly been inverted but because he retains the power of his privileges as a white male American and *perceives* the woman before him as being white (even if she had been white, she still would have had no legal rights in American society at this time in history). What is crucial, then, in this scene is that Robert has placed himself *in a false position of object to Laurence's subjectivity.* It is a deceptive reversal, the playing out of which remains Robert's prerogative. Laurence thus blindly continues in the marriage in the belief that she has more than passing value; she eventually concedes to consummate the marriage and has a daughter whom she ironically names after her husband's mother rather than her own—Anne, a woman who, years before Laurence's own birth, had also been mistaken for white and taken by friends to witness a public lynching in the United States. In the opening pages of the novel,

Anne describes the lynching in the following disturbingly prophetic image: "Full of rage, the American . . . pulled out his knife and cut out [the Black man's] tongue. He stopped speaking, since he no longer had a tongue, but he began to laugh."[21] The passage invokes the American's absolute power and control at the same time that it images that power in terms of the tongue, tool of communication. Robert, in his adoration of his wife, controls the very linguistic terms on which their relationship rests. Laurence's tragic flaw lies in her failure to see that she is a pawn in Robert's power games; she is never fully conscious of the impact her heritage could have on herself and her daughter in a marriage in which she has no leverage, legally or socially.

To complete matters, at the same time that Laurence is rejected and abandoned by her husband when the two discover that she has "African blood" after her Black great-uncle wills her a small fortune, she also risks rejection from the Haitian community, which, however elitist, has begun to question the European prototypes of beauty and acceptability she embodies. Paradoxically, it is Robert's rejection that finally jolts Laurence into some measure of consciousness about the complex world in which she lives. When her husband leaves her a first time, she realizes that she has no autonomy in her marriage. She calls herself a martyr and concedes that she is worse off than a slave (125). She acknowledges that she is trapped, in her role as woman and wife, in the web that was marriage for Haitian women during the historical period in which the novel is set. Here we should remember that the Haitian woman—whatever her racial background—had no protection under the law, no voting rights at the time of the Occupation; the only rights she did have were those extended to her as a dependent of her husband, her "protector" under the law. Thus, Laurence remarks: "The law of marriage? But it is barbaric. It is obvious that it was made for men to terrorize women, to make of them eternal children. Don't speak of it to me. Oh, no!"[22] She continues: "It is time that marriage no longer makes of a free woman, an oppressed woman. . . . Look at me—because of this marriage I am a slave that only a divorce will free."[23]

Laurence's step-mother accuses her step-daughter of being a feminist, as pejorative a label then as now in the Haitian context, to which Laurence can only reply: "Les malheurs m'ont émancipée [My misfortunes have emancipated me]" (126). Ironically, however, Laurence yearns for protection; she does not believe in her own strength and turns to the Catholic religion for comfort:

She would like to have someone to protect her, someone devoted to her. . . . She turns once more to the large silver Christ that she had implored long ago in her first days of anguish, and whispers: "My God, protect Eveline. If I am guilty of hurting Guy, punish only me."[24]

Valcin's protagonist thus fails in her bid for complete self-empowerment, which implies that she is but simply a pale imitation of the average Haitian woman.

Laurence is not in fact presented as a prototype of the Haitian woman. She is enigmatic, a *mystère,* as the following passage suggests:

She sleeps. One could mistake her for a goddess, to see her in this way, her head thrown back, decorated with a cluster of wild jasmine. . . . Her two blond braids fall neglectfully like two pale yellow ribbons against her bare shoulders. She sleeps deeply in an unconsciously lascivious and naturally seductive posture. A smile flickers on her pink lips.

Everything is quiet, it is night, a night cushioned in mystery.[25]

Disturbingly, the characteristics of "lasciviousness" and "seduction" are meant to hint at Laurence's African ancestry. More ironic is the fact that Laurence does not fit the image of the new Haitian woman put forth by the poets of the day represented in the novel by the fictional Lucien Boyer in his poem "Ignorance":

We do not tell you that you are exquisite,
In all our songs and all our sonnets,
We always celebrate some pale marquess,
You are exciting, we never speak of it.[26]

Laurence, "au naturel," is sexually "exciting" when she is unconscious of her racial identity but she remains, in her conscious state, a member of the privileged landowning class, a "pâle marquise," the honored white woman. She does not have to emulate white society because she is already ensconced in it. She need not ask whether she resembles the Greek Venus as does Boyer's effaced Haitian heroine:

Do I look like Venus with this pale complexion?
You think yourself already blond like Cybil,
But the mirror is quiet out of politeness.[27]

Laurence's mirror image *is* that of Venus rising from the sea in all her blond splendor. She can never fully be sung as a part of the new order that was at the time seeking to break from its Franco-European legacy to laud the Africanness of Haitian culture. She is not and cannot become the beauty eulogized in the final lines of Boyer's poem:

> As for me, I have too often sung the white woman,
> . . . .
> I am going to erect—to seek revenge—
> A statue with the bronze of your skin.[28]

The poem is significant not only because it underscores Laurence's inadequacies as either a French or an African goddess, but also because its title highlights one of the major themes of the novel, that is, ignorance. Textually, it exposes Laurence's ignorance of her own heritage, an ignorance compounded by the social context in which she has been brought up and lives. But Boyer's poem is also an attempt to point out and condemn the ignorance of African beauty on the part of Haitian writers and poets; that Valcin foregrounds it in the novel suggests that she agrees with the *indigénistes'* exultation of Africanness in the Haitian context. The remainder of the novel reveals, however, that Valcin yields to this ideology only up to a point. As the travails of her protagonist reveal, she firmly believes that, taken too far, that ideology will result in the denial of a hybrid or syncretic racial identity for Haitians.

It is through the protagonist's interaction with Myrtana, the only self-identified Haitian female nationalist in the novel, that a realistic portrait of the Haitian woman emerges. The ultimate image of the Haitian woman proferred by the text is suggested in the fusion of the two characters. As they sit together in the final pages of the novel, Laurence says, "I love these sacred silences when one speaks to the soul of her soul."[29] Laurence and Myrtana share a soul that has become unified through the one's individual struggles within the institution of marriage and the other's political consciousness of occupation. Laurence, as she emerges from her own personal misery at the novel's end, is only beginning to understand the impact of the Occupation. She happily declares, upon hearing that the Occupation is over, that Haiti's revolutionary ancestors must be pleased with what she calls the "second independence" (213), but Myrtana swiftly corrects her:

> Let us not compare 1934 to 1804. Two historic dates, yes, but how different one from the other. 1804: glorious proclamation of Haitian

Independence after continuous battles fought by black and yellow
citizens of the little island oppressed by the French! Alas, 1934!; liberation . . . the non-violent evacuation of Haiti . . . due only to the *political needs* of the President of the United States . . . and, irony! . . .
second Independence.[30]

These words realistically convey how bitterly Haitians reacted to the departure of the Americans, a departure orchestrated to benefit the United States
rather than Haiti, whose economy and natural resources had been utterly
depleted. On another level, the words provide readers with a guide to an allegorical understanding of the text.

Laurence, in effect, represents Haiti in her state of political and cultural flux. Her marital trials, her relationship to Robert, mirrors Haiti's dependent relationship with the American occupants whom she resists but
cannot free herself of alone. Haiti is no more freed by her own actions than
are the intellectuals debating Haitian identity in the midst of the Occupation in Valcin's novel. The latter's failure to support the kind of revolutionary acts that only Myrtana, of all the characters in the novel, evokes on the
last page of the text when she utters the name of Charlemagne Péralte and
other slain *caco* leaders, reveals Valcin's own misgivings about the potential of the *indigéniste* movement to free Haiti from U.S. hegemony. Like
Laurence's inertia, the movement is depicted as stagnant, played out in the
comfort of establishment sitting rooms. The racial consciousness Laurence
is forced to realize is debated through academic speeches entitled, for instance, "Does Color Prejudice Still Exist in Haiti amongst Those Native
Born?"[31] that treat the theme of the "négrophobie nègre [Black negro-
phobia]" (72). Such presentations end in the affirmation of Africa as Haiti's
foremother and the caution that "the greatness of a nation is measured by
the persistence of its memories."[32] Those remembrances, however, appear
to refuse or substitute the French-European legacy for an Afrocentricity
which is not embraced in everyday life in the most elitist of social circles.

The meeting Valcin recounts, at which "real life" historian Pradel and
writers Aléxis and Price-Mars are present along with Laurence's thwarted
love, Guy Vanel, ends in the impotent appreciation of a Haitian night, "a
pink night, hesitant, fearful, bewildered, a night which advanced and re-
ceded, conquered yet triumphed."[33] As they all look upon the sunset, Guy is
reminded of nights spent with Laurence. This scene, juxtaposed with the
earlier presentation of a slumbering Laurence, points to the inability of the
intellectuals to pierce the mystery of the Haitian night—that is, to see the

truth of cultural syncretism that Price-Mars himself advanced in the theory of *indigénisme,* which fell away with the rise of *noirisme* (as articulated by Duvalier and Denis) and *négritude* (Césaire and Senghor). The fusion of two or more disparate cultures is affirmed in the deceptive body of Laurence but more so in the potential of her ideological amalgamation with Myrtana—a fusion the implications of which are, interestingly, left unexamined at the novel's end.

Desroy, on the other hand, is not content simply to explore the racial tensions exposed by the Occupation; she also demonstrates that claims to racial or class privilege exist alongside a pervasive sexist ideology whereby Haitian women are viewed as erotic creatures deserving not only of disdain but also of overt violent treatment.[34] In fact, the only fully described violent scene of the novel occurs when a woman is arrested after her husband is tortured and confesses that she has stolen goods. The police chief, an American, hits the woman so violently that she falls to the ground "holding her stomach with both hands, while blood flowed from her, falling in pools."[35] Mac, the police chief, reacts without sympathy, saying "Take her away . . . if she drops dead it will just be one less of these damned negresses."[36] Murray's wife, Arabella, sees no cruelty in Mac's actions for she believes that Haitians are inherent thieves (94). Murray is appalled when he hears of the American soldier's behavior, but Desroy holds him as responsible for the woman's fate. Writes Desroy: "In Murray's account of the entire event, the one thing he had not seen, *what he could not see,* were two little girls in their Sunday best holding hands; their emaciated legs oscillated in oversized shoes" (my emphasis).[37] Desroy reveals, once again, that Murray's humanism is a mask for a more deepy entrenched condescension directed toward Haitians as a whole; although he feels that the actions toward the impoverished woman are beyond the bounds of human decency, he is unable to connect the story he is told of this violence to the impact it has not only on the woman but on her entire family. For Murray, stories such as these circulate as minor and unfortunate incidents during occupation of which he is an important part, not as indicators of the violence, both physical and cultural, implicit in the activity of the Occupation itself. Desroy reveals Murray's limited vision by shifting to the third person omniscient narrative voice to reveal to readers what he refuses to see.

It becomes clear that the family is poor and that the parents have stolen food for their children; the tortured husband scapegoats his wife and she alone is left to pay for the family's low-class standing. Her daughters, both less than seven years of age, are left to console their crying mother, who never resorts to attempting to justify her theft by pointing to the presence of her children. The woman is dragged away and the girls are left to fend for themselves. Desroy laments their fate: "Poor waifs, already tossed about by life; disinherited, who did not yet know what it was to be orphans."[38] We find out later that the woman was not only brutally beaten but thrown, still alive, to Mac's dogs. To alleviate their guilt, after her death, the Americans decide that she was a *caco* spy, even though by 1934 the *caco* army had effectively been disarmed and neutralized. It is significant, of course, that the woman's children are also female, for the novel charts the narrow options life holds for them aside from the likelihood of hunger, poverty, and early death within their own culture.

Lamercie, Arabella's loathed maid, is Desroy's glimpse into the life of a working-class Haitian woman whose only means of escaping misery and poverty is through servitude. Lamercie, whose name reflects her underappreciated virtues, is as objectified as the woman who is fed to the dogs by the American police. Arabella, who has never come into contact with a Black woman, does not want a maid because of her hatred for all individuals of African descent. When she meets Lamercie, she is surprised to greet a beautiful, well-dressed woman. Lamercie is described in sexualized terms evocative of Durand's *choucoune*:[39] "a pretty negress, with an arched back, firm breasts, a dress decked with bright flowers."[40] It soon becomes apparent that Lamercie is the envy of all the wealthy American women. Kitty, Arabella's best friend, implodes her friend's racist definition of beauty when she says to her:

> You have a caucasian ideal of beauty. Wait until you get to know the creoles and then tell me if you don't find any of them very pretty. . . . Look at Lamercie's body. What a figure! Naked, she would tempt the most demanding of artists. And that without having to exert herself, without having to break a sweat. She is "nature."[41]

But the "nature" Kitty exalts is simply a stereotype, a clichéd eroticism attributed to Black women. That eroticism is in turn projected upon Fernande (Frédéric's wife) whom Kitty spies from Arabella's window. Kitty exclaims: "She is magnificent. . . . Oh! Arabella, rarely have I seen a more beautiful woman, what beautiful curves! The husband must enjoy himself."[42] Kitty's "appreciation" of Haitian women is homoerotically charged, as she lays in the sun, yearning to grow as dark as the Black women she finds so beautiful (61). In contrast, the objects of such erotic yearnings— Lamercie and Fernande—are the only characters in the text who do not display feelings of extramarital desire. Through these contrasts among the women in her text, Desroy subverts the *choucoune* typology further by suggesting that the Haitian woman does not and could not betray the Haitian man, and hence, national identity itself.

It is white American culture only, Desroy appears to say, that provides and maintains the wedge distancing the sexes from one another. Her American woman attempts to take on the attributes of the Haitian women she subjugates to serve her own needs, that of accessing and possessing maligned "blackness." In so doing, however, she nonetheless remains in full control (like her male counterparts—Robert in Valcin's novel, Seabrook in his own "magic island"); she accesses the "other" without fear of personal or cultural losses, without ever losing her identity or power as a white woman. In the end, the lascivious eroticism attributed overwhelmingly to Haitian women throughout the years of the Occupation is revealed to be a defining characteristic of the occupant women. This is a point not lost on Lamercie who notes the erotic behavior of both Kitty and Arabella. As revenge for a beating that she suffers at the hands of Arabella, who whips her mercilessly when the latter believes that Lamercie has stolen a jewel from her that is later found, Lamercie reveals to Murray his wife's infidelities with Kitty's husband. This revelation has the force of disrupting the marriage and, finally, of evicting the couple from the island; the loss Arabella is made to endure, then, is that of a removal from a seat of power over the Black women she so disdains. It is a loss which is ushered in by Lamercie, but dispensed by Murray, indicating that Arabella's racial identity remains nonetheles secure (bear in mind here too that her infidelity occurs with a white male) and that the couple's departure is a further attempt on their part to hold on to the privilege of race, class, and nationality that the status of occupant affords them.

Significantly, the plot of Desroy's novel not only revolves around Murray's journey through Haiti but also around the main couples' perceptions of one another as they observe each other from a distance. Arabella's in-bred racism is never overcome, Murray and Frédéric engage each other in adversarial yet friendly intellectual debates, but, between themselves, each couple tries to assess their racial and cultural differences. Fernande, for one, dislikes Arabella and all American women. She tells her husband: "They affect airs:—always a cigarette between their lips pursed with disdain in marbled faces, acting too much like grand ladies to be real ladies."[43] Her dislike is rooted in the racism she feels women like Arabella perpetuate. She says that "It's the American woman who fosters color prejudice."[44] Unlike the Haitian intellectuals brought to life in Valcin's novel who pontificate on race matters among themselves, Desroy communicates a very different outlook—for one, that Haitian society is made up of layers of classes that are not necessarily always at odds with one another. Within the novel's world, each class is to some degree oppressed by other, more privileged classes, the top layer of which is comprised not of the "mulatto elites" but of the white colonizers, temporarily replaced by the American occupants. The result of the overlay of American racial prejudice on Haitian society fosters racial divisions. Fernande and Frédéric absorb that racial hatred, but, refusing to internalize their "worthlessness," they surmise that there must be a "positive" side to the racism they experience, that, since American men despise Haitians so much, they will never form deep attachments with the people of the country they oppress and that the Occupation will not be an enduring one (39). They thus resign themselves to the situation; as Frédéric states: "what we cannot prevent, we must endure."[45]

As I stated above, the novel's dénouement occurs when Arabella's infidelity results in the American couple's departure from the island. Fearful of the economic significance of this departure, Frédéric and Fernande are initially concerned over their loss of financial security but Fernande is understandably relieved: "Despite herself, her Haitian hatred rose against the occupant, whose acts forced the young to practically subaltern themselves in order to be able to live."[46] In contradistinction, Murray and his wife sail back toward the American shores like errant beings, unable to assess clearly what they have lost or gained. Desroy portrays them as typical of the elite Americans of the roaring twenties and thirties depicted in the novels of F. Scott Fitzgerald. In fact, her novel ends with an intertextual reference to the ending of Fitzgerald's *The Great Gatsby*. Whereas the last glimmer of a green light at the far end of a dock in Fitzgerald's novel symbolizes the many lives wasted by the pursuit of the shallow rewards of money and decadent lifestyles, the similar symbolism used by Desroy at the end of her novel is meant to highlight not so much loss through decadence but the inability of Americans to come to terms with their own delusions of grandeur. Desroys writes: "As if to signal a final goodbye, the lighthouse in the distance lit up. Then everything disappeared. Slowly, the boat sunk into a darkness not yet touched by the glow of the night's first stars."[47] For Desroy, the behavior of the Americans in Haiti is rooted in a lack of knowledge of self. Murray and Arabella return to the United States in a literal activation of the final line of Fitzgerald's novel: "So we beat on, boats against the current, born back ceaselessly into the past" (149). The line, of course, resonates with the earlier image in the novel of the orphaned children set adrift into poverty and violence. *Le joug* suggests that the fate of Haiti and Haitians will not improve simply because the Americans have finally departed, for they leave behind the darkness of their delusions, the legacy of their narrow racial convictions.

Valcin and Desroy both struggle to demonstrate how their Haitian female characters define themselves in a society in which women are both voiceless and victimized by reproducing that voicelessness textually at the level of plot and characterization. Valcin, of course, explores the theme of female identity in purely racial terms, suggesting that the Haitian woman cannot be represented as either white or Black and that she cannot define herself without being characterized as one or the other. Valcin's *"blanche négresse"* has little sense of her Haitian identity for she is refused entry into both the world of the *indigénistes* and that of the Americans. For Valcin, then, racial consciousness leads to destructiveness because it disallows the crossing of racial lines and hence of class lines as well. Desroy, on the other hand, champions women of the underclass and seeks to expose the violent treatment Haitians faced during the Occupation. Race is not as much of an issue here as is the meeting of class and gender. Haitian women of the middle class in Desroy's work are revealed to be both unaware of, and apathetic with regard to, the lot of impoverished women, though, in the eyes of the Americans, they are seen as being no different from their poorer counterparts. For Desroy, Haitian women's emancipation rests upon the cessation of American influences and on the disruption of sexist stereotypes that result in the objectification of Haitian women.

As I will show in the chapters to follow, that influence has never ceased. Haitian women writers since 1934 have had to contend both with the legacy of the Occupation and with the anti-women, anti-feminist practices of the Duvalier regime (a regime marked not only by censorship but also by unmatched violence directed against women) in their attempts to create a concrete sense of Haitian women's identity and potentially subversive power. That sense of identity has remained understated at the same time that it has become increasingly revolutionary in scope.

CHAPTER 3

Si-m di ou, oua konn pasé-m

GHISLAINE CHARLIER AND JAN J. DOMINIQUE FRAME
THE UNMASTERABLE, MEMORIED PAST

Whatever is buried in the memory by the collapse of meaning under an inadequate or lying language—this will become, not merely unspoken, but unspeakable.
—Adrienne Rich, *On Lies, Secrets, and Silence*

There is a silence that cannot speak.
There is a silence that will not speak.
—Joy Kogawa, *Obasan*

Je sais que je parle, seule, à voix haute parfois, plus souvent au fond de moi, mais j'ai besoin d'écrire ce texte, tant pis pour la prudence, il y aura toujours quelqu'un pour m'empêcher de commettre les erreurs impardonnables, si j'arrive réellement à perdre mes habitudes d'auto-censure.

[I know that I speak, alone, sometimes aloud, more often deep within myself, but I need to write this text, who cares about caution, there will always be someone to prevent me from committing the unforgivable infractions, if I do succeed, genuinely, to lose my habits of self-censorship.]
—J. J. Dominique, *Mémoire d'une amnésique*

*R*emember Solange. You forgot about her for a few pages but now she returns to nag your conscience; she will not let you forget her. She knows too well that to live is to be recalled, an image in the mind, however you conceive of the being she once was. What is left is so little. A child is born; a girl is born; a girl is born and you worry, if you care enough about such realities, about the years it will take

72

for her to grow to be a woman. You have no future sight: you do not know, as the small fingers grip the tip of your thumb in a tight fist, that this child, this girl, will not have the life you already dread to imagine. You look forward to the pictures she will draw, spelling the letters of her name backwards, the "S" like a snake sliding back to Africa as her hair will by the time she is three. You will plait the tufts of her black hair into little braids and she will smile up at you as if in your hands lie all the answers, the power to hold back the world which has rejected her without knowing that smile. If you are lucky, you can look forward to her first steps, the first sounds emerging from her throat, which delight her like the magic of the sun upon her face. If you are lucky, you can read her stories at bedtime and wish her no nightmares. If you are lucky, you can send her to school and she will come home, out of breath, to tell you all that she has learned. She will become something greater than herself, and this will make you proud.

But Solange is not real. She has lived her life without your help. You have not mothered her or pampered her. You do not have the imprint of her hand in a plaster of Paris cast. You do not have bits of chewed crayons lying in the dusty corners of an old schooldesk you bought her at a garage sale: you have bought her nothing, you have given her nothing.

Solange has dreamed about you too. This is something you do not realize. She has drawn your likeness in her notebook alongside the words that represent your worlds: France, Canada, the United States. . . . Sometimes you have a beard, sometimes you have a string of pearls; sometimes you smile; at other times you are frowning. She wonders if you have children and if you are good to them: she would like to meet them and play games but she does not know what games are played in those faraway places. You are not real.

Luck is not something Solange understands. There is life and there is death. Luck has little to do with it. She does not trust in tomorrows that are littered with corpses she must walk around on her way to school; she knows something very thin separates her from those too-still bodies. A string. A tightrope. Wind. Luck has little to do with anything. If she had the words she would say fate or fortune. Those words she might believe in because they mean that someone is looking over her shoulder, someone greater than herself, akin to a god. It isn't you but it could be you. She does not know.

Solange sits on a stone bench on which letters have been carved, joined together in hearts. There are names too but they have been worn down and cannot be read. She has been taught not to carve into objects that belong to the public, like trees or outhouses. She wishes she were brave enough to do it now. Her history book is on her lap and the pictures no longer speak to her, the words blur in and out of visibility. She takes her pencil and writes her name on the bench, first in script and then in print; she feels like a large weight has been lifted from her spirit. Then there is that sound that she has been taught to ignore; it whistles by her like thunder. There is blood and there is darkness and she knows she has crossed that thin line. In the morning, after her body has been removed, they will wash down the bench, the sidewalk; the blood will fade, the pencil marks will be erased. And it will be years before you learn of her name. Years before you realize how lucky you are.

The Unmasterable Past

Stories are the basis of our knowledge of the world around us. In cultures in which orality remains the main locus of collective consciousness, the power of storytelling and of storytellers (*griots,* as they are commonly called in Africa) is paramount. The stories told and handed down from one generation to the next are most often cautionary tales, transferring wisdom from the elderly to the young in order to preserve the self as well as the community. In communities of the African diaspora, and most especially in the Caribbean, orality equals survival. Language, song, and stories have been the means by which enslaved peoples have maintained a sense of culture as they have been denied access to their very roots. Out of necessity, new codes were created out of converging and conflicting cultural matrices: creole languages are but one aspect of this mechanism of survival. Acts of memory are another. Memory, both personal and collective, provides the basis for cultural cohesion in societies where chaos, as defined by those outside those societies, appears to be the only constant. In Haitian women's literature, the importance of memory is a recurring theme precisely because memory is the mechanism by which the African diasporic experience has been preserved from generation to generation through the oral tradition.

My purpose, then, in foregrounding memory as a crucial element of the politics of representation in the Haitian women's novel is to reveal the extent to which the movement from orality to literacy through the process of colonization resulted in a tragic falsification of memory. Thus, Haitian women authors have had to rely on a faulty collective memory to create their own image and their works intentionally reconfigure that memory in the attempt to reclaim that which has been lost to the vacuum of an interrupted culture. They do so through the written text but in such a way as to distance themselves from the machinations of historicization; they are more interested in retrieving memory for the purposes of foregrounding Haitian women's lives transhistorically than in inserting women's experience into a static reading of history.

It might seem appropriate then to theorize the role of memory in the works of Haitian women in terms of an occupation of that site of memorialization that has more recently been associated with French historian Pierre Nora's concept of *lieux de mémoire.* Through this concept, Nora defines a "postmodern" reading of history in which traditional concepts of the historic have suddenly been destabilized and replaced by conflicting, collective versions of the past recounted through individualized voices. For Nora, "[t]he moment of *lieux de mémoire* occurs at the same time that an immense and intimate fund of memory disappears, *surviving only as a reconstituted object beneath the gaze of critical history*" (288, emphasis mine). Further, these sites comprise three elements: archive-memory, duty-memory, and distance-memory. *Lieux de mémoire,* are, nonetheless, inextricably linked with and re-affirm standard modes of historicizing, and necessitate the creation of texts or events that serve as commemorations of given sites, the involvement of politically active commemorators, and the buffer of time and space. But what occurs when narrative imbricates archive-memory? When the individual is politically committed but socially invisible? When hindsight is simply another construction of time meant to delude social participants into believing that "it"—the *lieux de mémoire*—has been evaded? Ghislaine Charlier and Jan J. Dominique disrupt rather than re-affirm standard modes of historicizing and, in so doing, demonstrate that in colonial and feminist contexts it is not possible to think of history as linear; memory, of course, clearly attests to this fact.

In "Memory and Identity: The History of a Relationship," John R. Gillis describes the link between memory, self, and community as follows:

> The core meaning of any individual or group identity, namely, a sense of sameness over time and space, is sustained by remembering; and what is remembered is defined by the assumed identity. . . . Memories help us make a sense of the world we live in; and "memory work" is, like any other kind of physical or mental labor, embedded in complex class, gender and power relations that determine what is remembered (or forgotten), by whom and for what end. (3)

Memory, then, is in a sense the signifier of identity, outlining the frame in which a singular or plural body believes itself to be contained and through which it comes into lexical being. The frame, which is created out of social perception, is thus not as objective as some might assume: even defined as "history," memory remains at the mercy of those who seek to create meaning out of "what is" by supplying, out of past experience, the contours of "what is not." Memory is thus, as Gillis points out, political, even though, as a term, it often implies empty nostalgia.

Memory is by definition selective: recall is subjective. Memory may frame what has been as well as what will be, but the past can only affect our sense of the future (and even of the present) if we know enough (or are willing to know enough) about the past to remember it. It is this element of choice which forces cultures that have experienced a tragic loss of lives and traditions to insist on reminding a larger public—usually the cultures which have caused their tragedies—that loss has occurred and must not be repeated. Memory, then, can also serve as handmaiden to justice. As Iwona Irwin-Zrecka notes in her book *Frames of Remembrance: The Dynamics of Collective Memory,* collective memory is not infallible: "Attending to an absence-which-ought-not-to-be also rests on a theoretically crucial, albeit often implicit principle: that which is not publicly known and spoken about will be socially forgotten" (115). We cannot presume that collectivity is all-inclusive simply because we speak of oppressed Third World nations as unitary. Gillis writes that "national identities are, like everything historical, constructed and reconstructed; and it is our responsibility to decode them in order to discover the relationships they create and sustain" (4). Although Gillis appears to be certain that this is a Western phenomenon, that is, that the notion of national identity implies what I can best describe as "First World stability," the Caribbean space on which Western ideology has constantly been imposed reveals that national identity is a global phenomenon. Without it, Third World nation-states can be victimized on the basis of a perceived lack of "coherence."

In both Jan J. Dominique's *Mémoire d'une amnésique* (1984) and Ghislaine Charlier's *Mémoire d'une affranchie* (1989), "coherence" is achieved with difficulty; both authors present stories in which characters' frames of reference undergo constant change and are mediated by the authors themselves who appear as actors in their texts; fiction and reality are blurred as the identity between author and narrator blends and becomes inseparable. The narrators each author presents are intent upon revealing their own silences, which are also those of a collective women's experience in Haiti. That collectivity cannot be confused with nationality as it is commercialized globally, and neither can it be reduced to a singular identity: collectivity is here synonymous with plurality. In both novels, the absence of women's presence in national collective memory results in the production of the narrators' texts. There are significant ellipses in the stories they tell that suggest not that some memories cannot be reclaimed but that self-preservation demands cautiousness. Truth is as elusive as trust precisely because, as Gillis writes, "Women and minorities often serve as symbols of a 'lost' past, nostalgically perceived and romantically constructed, but their actual lives are most readily forgotten" (10). Continuing in what for me represents a recognizable facet of a Haitian women's literary tradition, Charlier and Dominique elude this sort of co-optation by demonstrating an awareness that history is repeated exactly because the models that have typically been invoked to define Haitian women's identity revolve around mythical norms and mythical deviants. Located on the margins, rejected from the center, Haitian women writers occupy the unenviable position of having to speak from a position of silence. They render that position productive by inflecting it with the distinctly Haitian sensibility reflected in the proverb *si-m di ou,* if I tell you, *oua konn pasé-m,* you'll know more than I do; they refuse to surrender the power of their voice to a center which has suppressed their stories at the same time that they reveal what they must of their life conditions. The most transgressive aspects of women's lives—their tenacity, their use of violence to attain liberation, their expression of sexual desire, to name but a few—are therefore told at a slant, as if they are secrets to be whispered and preciously preserved. In making use of this sort of doublespeak, then, Haitian women writers embody, as they articulate, what I have termed a *culture-lacune,* or a culture of absence. Silence, in this context, is redefined "as opposition both to what is being said . . . and to whom is saying it" (Quinn 23). Ironically, then, the text is both the liberator of voice and its silencing agent. What is made visible in this dualistic process is the desire of Haitian women to create their own frames of reference. They do so by attacking the novel form itself, by reshaping the parameters of textual representation.

Narratologically, this poses an interesting theoretical problem, that is, the extent to which both Charlier's and Dominique's novels might be construed as postmodern texts. In Dominique's *Mémoire d'une amnésique,* a postmodern effect is produced by the two biographical authors' notes and accompanying portraits on the back cover of the text, which are meant to contribute to our understanding of J. J. Dominique, the author of the novel (labeled a "récit," an account, rather than a "roman," novel), and Paul, its narrator. This representation of J. J. and Paul as pivotal to the creation of the "récit" subverts the kind of closure usually associated with the novel genre. J. J., we are told is 31; Paul, "l'autre [the other]," is 33. Both write, but it is J. J. who holds the power of memory: "as far back as she can re-member, she has always written";[1] Paul, on the other hand, "écrit [writes]," and lives only in the context of an immediate present. J. J.'s black and white photograph shows her in profile; the frame that should hold Paul's picture is empty, a blank, demonstrating that she exists only within the pages of the memoried text. We are told that J. J. will produce other texts besides the one we are now holding; Paul will not. But it is Paul's willingness to write and be written that has resulted in their collaboration, "because she likes to do it, because she needs to do it."[2] And yet Paul, as the title of the novel suggests, has no past and no future of her own: her existence depends ex-plicitly and implicitly on J. J.'s creative abilities.

Likewise, Charlier's narrator is linked to her narrator beyond the pages of the novel itself. The story she recounts in *Mémoire d'une affranchie* of the Revolution, which roughly spans the years 1786–1806, is told through a freewoman's eyes whose image graces the front cover of the text. In the biographical author's note on the cover of the text we are told that this woman, whose eyes look out beyond the viewing frame, is one of Charlier's foremothers: "This portrait adorned the home of her relatives in Haiti and thus she decided that it would adorn the cover of her novel."[3] Her clothes, we are further told, are of our century as well as of past centuries: history, heritage, and tradition are thus invoked at the very site of produc-tion, before we have even had an opportunity to interact with the written text. Moreover, like Charlier herself, who fled the Duvalier regime with the picture of the woman who adorns the front cover, and a copy of the novel-in-progress, the text is a product of flight, of cultural mutation: "the writing began in Haiti, was carried on in Paris and in New York and completed in Montréal."[4] *Mémoire d'une amnésique* and *Mémoire d'une affranchie* are connected in my own mind in that they accurately reflect the condition of exile many Haitian women authors undergo as they attempt to tell an un-told story. Further, they reveal the necessity of creating innovative narrative forms which can contain the untold, but which ultimately alienate the au-thors from the mainstream, Haitian literary scene.[5]

Both novels are fragmented in their delivery; the voices of each nar-rator intermingles with that of her author's. In Charlier's text, footnotes act as missives from author to reader and disrupt the linearity of the text; in

Dominique's novel, the narrator creates a multitude of characters to tell the story of her life, a story which cannot be completely disclosed. Is this seeming confusion of authorial agency postmodern?

Linda Hutcheon writes of postmodernism that it "has called into question the messianic faith of modernism, the faith that technical innovation and purity of form can assure social order, even if that faith disregards the social and aesthetic values of those who must inhabit those modernist buildings" (12). Postmodern texts, on Hutcheon's account, thus interrogate the very means of production, questioning what constitutes genre and period and concluding that there are no fixed categories. On the surface, this would seem to accommodate well the reconstructive project of both Dominique and Charlier. Hutcheon argues that

> postmodern fiction does not . . . disconnect itself from the history of
> the world. It foregrounds and thus contests the conventionality and
> unacknowledged ideology of that assumption of seamlessness and
> asks its readers to question the processes by which we represent our-
> selves and our world to ourselves and to become aware of the means
> by which we *make* sense of and *construct* order out of experience in
> our particular culture. (53–54)

Contestation, however, is not necessarily political. In fact, self-conscious postmodern artists have often proven themselves to be more interested in creating an infinite playground of free associations and border crossings than in creating a new sense of the world in which an equitable social organization might be achieved without exclusivity. In fact, postmodernism as a theory or discourse can function only if one truly believes that metanarratives have existed for everyone, that they have been unified, singular, and heretofore uncontested. The history of the world tells us differently.

Postmodernism, viewed either as a historical moment or as a philosophy, denies that societies which have emerged out of disruption can produce art and artifacts that simultaneously respond to the primal moment of disruption, contest ideologies of subjugation, and deploy their own agendas. In postmodern theory, writers who occupy "colonial" positions of marginality are brought into the center through an ideology that appears to describe the modes of production of their texts but that ultimately denies the authors' political impetus (whether those politics are implicit in the texts or are imparted to them by readers). According to theorists Linda J. Nicholson and Nancy Fraser, "Lyotard [father of postmodern theory] rules out the sort of critical social theory which employs general categories like gender, race, and class. From his perspective, such categories are too reductive of the complexity of social identities to be useful" (Fraser and Nicholson 24). Women of color in particular are thus denied the agency to create their own political, social, and artistic realities, realities that can only be articulated through a mediation or negotiation of the very "reductive" categories postmodernism annihilates. This is to say that, though the categories of gender, race, class, and sexuality may be reductive, they *constitute the complexity of contemporary social interactions.* As Hutcheon notes:

> Feminisms will continue to resist incorporation into postmodernism, largely because of their revolutionary force as political movements working for real social change. They go beyond making ideology explicit and deconstructing it to argue a need to change that ideology, to effect a real transformation of art that can only come with a transformation of patriarchal social practices. Postmodernism has not theorized agency; it has no strategies of resistance that would correspond to the feminist ones. Postmodernism manipulates, but does not transform signification; it disperses but does not (re)construct the structures of subjectivity (Foster 1985: 6). Feminisms must. (168)

Postmodernism is ineffective as a political discourse because it is complicit with the modes of production it interrogates. Hutcheon concludes, therefore, that it cannot form the basis of a feminist politics even though some feminists use, or may appear to use, its tenets to articulate their politics.

In the Haitian context, commitment to the "real" is paramount for survival; the idea of the "real" cannot be rejected simply because power relationships are shifting. Again, one need only to recall here the Haitian phrase: *Haïti çé tè glissé.* Haiti's ground has always been shifting and its women writers have attempted to still that landscape through varied images of the material and social realities of Haitian women's lives. In order for their words to have resonance in contexts which mishear and silence their voices, they must use methods of subversion that appear to embrace literary and social norms but that in fact disembowel them. This is an African (and thus Afro-Caribbean) mode of communication which survives orally in tales of Anancy, the trickster-spider; it is not a postmodern impulse but an Afrocentric one.

What is posited as "unmanageable" and "unmasterable" in postmodern thought is only so for those whom it uncomfortably places at odds with ideologies of insurrection. Postmodern theory therefore simply recapitulates the power dynamics proper to the West that it claims to be contesting. The process of memorializing the slain or the survivors of international wars, of making selective heroes while denying the existence of others, is a Western phenomenon produced for and by a narrow ideological elite. Writes Gillis: "it was the dominant male elites, who imagined themselves at the cutting edge of progress, who, feeling the loss of the past most acutely, were most insistent that it be restored and preserved" (10). It seems to me that postmodernism is the "hysterical" response of those "male elites" whose reality and sense of history has been contested by those they have relegated to the dusty corners of collective consciousness; postmodernism makes theoretically possible the dissolution of the categories of race, gender, class, and sexuality rearticulated by the marginalized for the purposes of self-empowerment. The male elite can thus easily believe, as Fraser and Nicholson note in summarizing Lyotard's thought, that "the social bond is a weave of crisscrossing threads of discursive practices, no single one of which runs continuously throughout the whole" (24). What this logic conveniently ignores, however, is that there is a continuous thread in the history of the world, namely, that of the oppression of women and people of color, even though that oppression has assumed various forms. As Irwin-Zrecka points out, those who occupy relative positions of power often fail to acknowledge their participation in the modes of oppression they institute and/or perpetuate, even unconsciously. She speaks here, specifically, of the Holocaust and the lack of "remorse or even regret . . . among the direct [German] participants": "The 'unmasterable past' is only unmasterable to those morally challenged by it" (50). It is therefore left up to those who have been mastered by that past to make visible their losses, oppressions, and alternative visions.

Nation and Consciousness

The Haitian Revolution which took place over several years in Saint-Domingue, the nation center that was later to become Port-au-Prince, has maintained its status as a prominent event in the history of slave rebellions in the Americas. Toussaint L'Ouverture, Napoleon's "darker brother," emerged as its hero. The independence of Haiti, finally established in 1803–1804, struck a resonant chord thoughout the islands as well as on the continent, where similar battles were being waged but not as successfully. Haiti, as ironic as that might seem now, was a model of hope, as slaves, free Blacks, and some landowners joined together to topple the French empire, which had sunk its roots deep into the rich soil of the land Columbus had once dubbed the "pearl of the Antilles." Hispaniola, as it was initially named, became the first independent Black nation in the Western hemisphere. That triumph, however, was short-lived, and the down-spiralling of a nation newly shaped by the experience of *métissage* has resulted in the production of numerous texts meant to elucidate the character of the Revolution and recapture its significance in a modern context.

In more recent times, such efforts have primarily focused on analyzing Toussaint L'Ouverture's role in the Revolution, and on reclaiming him as hero, for his incarceration and death in a French prison in 1807 had stripped him of his legendary stature. In the foreword to his popular historical narrative of the Revolution, *The Black Jacobins*, C.L.R. James comments that "To this day I am convinced that, apart from Napoleon himself, no military commanders or strategists of 1793–1815 exceed Toussaint L'Ouverture and Dessalines" (vi). He also contends that "it was not so much the slaves but the maroons, those who had run away and made a life for themselves in the mountains or forests, who . . . led the revolutions and created the foundation of the Haitian nation" (vi). James emphasizes the integral part played in the Revolution by maroon communities because he believes that they are representative of revolutionary currents in other Third World nations and those nations (like South Africa) in which the lines between colonizer and colonized have continued to be upheld and managed. So he writes in 1980: "It is obvious to me today, as I saw in 1938, that further study of the revolution in French San Domingo will reveal more and more of its affinity with revolutions in more developed communities" (vii). Although this realization is crucial to the creation of an international coalition, it sidesteps the fact that the Revolution, now almost two hundred years in the past, failed in many respects.

Any assessment of the Revolution must indeed pay close attention to the various factions that supported or contested it, and that, more often than not, opposed one another even as they struggled toward emancipation. The rigid caste system instituted under colonial rule affected the ways in which various groups within Haitian society interacted and visualized their advancement into the future; this system, which has grown many tentacles informed by race, gender, color, class, and nationality, is firmly rooted in Haiti. To deny it is to perpetuate the ideology that makes heroes of a few men and denies the presence of the masses, without whom revolutions cannot take place.

Our desperate need for heroic figures results, I suggest, from living in a world that cannot face its own social stratifications, stratifications which are deeply embedded in matrices of difference that we deny exist in order to pursue a unitary truth, a unified social consciousness. Without denying that revolutionary leaders have, at various times, galvanized the energies of the masses and made the Haitian populace visible on an international scale, I would suggest that Haitian women's political visions depart drastically from the model in which a country is governed by a single leader. In *Mémoire d'une affranchie,* Ghislaine Charlier reconstructs the events leading up to and immediately following the Revolution from a female point of view and from the point of view of a specific class, heretofore neglected in the study of the events that took place in Saint-Domingue at the turn of the century. Her purpose appears two-fold: to distance the collective memory of the Haitian Revolution from its French associations, and to acknowledge those people whose identities are clearly both French and African, in short, Haitian.

Charlier's narrator is "une affranchie [a freed woman]," who occupied a precarious position in Haitian society at that time. According to Dantès Bellegarde in his *Histoire du peuple Haïtien (1492–1952),* the class of the "affranchis" was made up of children of mixed-race couples. Few, if any, slaves were freed before the *Code noir* of 1685; those who were free before this time were most often the offspring of white male plantation owners. For the most part, however, these offspring were condemned to a life of servitude, though it was possible that they might attain privilege, might access the riches of their fathers. Although the ninth article of the *Code noir* stipulated that illegitimate children of cross-racial unions could never be freed, it also stated that through marriage enslaved persons could be freed as could their offspring (Bellegarde 38–39). From this point on, however, the products of such alliances were labeled *de couleur,* a designation that served to uphold the racism of the time and to disenfranchise this growing class of non-whites/non-blacks. Nonetheless, by 1789, 28,000 "coloreds" occupied Saint-Domingue and owned over two thousand plantations (Bellegarde 42); this accessing of class privilege was, of course, due to their white heritage; many passed as white in an attempt to surmount the constraints of their narrowly defined freedoms. Thus, the Haitian Revolution involved a complex struggle for independence that did not involve the discrete categories of "oppressor" and "oppressed" battling each other. The rise of a middle class, dubbed *gens de couleur,* who transgressed the bounds of race and class through their physical makeup, resulted in a series of internal conflicts within the Haitian caste system.

It is this aspect of Haitian history that Charlier seeks to memorialize in her novel. Charlier opts to center her historical focus on distinct figures of the Revolution who rose from the mulatto/mixed-raced/*gens de couleur* class, such as Pétion and Ogé. While Boukman, a "gros Nègre" shaped the slave revolt in the North, using the unifiying spirituality of Haitian *vodou* in order to galvanize those enslaved throughout the plantocracy system (Ott 47), Pétion organized the *affranchis* in the South, most notably in Jacmel. In 1791, Boukman was killed and decapitated by the white *colons* during the insurrection he engineered. Because of his militancy—which compares to that of Malcolm X at the height of his involvement with the Nation of Islam in the United States—the importance of Boukman's role in the Revolution is generally diminished. Toussaint L'Ouverture's rise to power was the direct result of Boukman's unfortunate end. Ironically, Toussaint's hero-status is as much a consequence of his having been an African slave as of his having used Napoleonic military strategies in order to subvert and topple the slave system. He too was ultimately defeated by the French, by Napoleon himself, but more so because of his collusion with the purveyors of that system than because of his adopting a thorough-going politics of opposition. If an African revolutionary such as Toussaint could have succumbed to the trappings of European models of power at this time, one might assume that those of mixed-race, like Pétion and Ogé, who under some circumstances (especially after the institution of the *Code noir*) may have benefited from white parentage/patronage, could have faced greater difficulty in divesting themselves of such a system. Charlier attempts to demonsrate the opposite.

Ogé is presented in the novel as a charismatic leader whom few could resist. The narrator's father notes that he is measure-made for martyrdom. Julie, the protagonist, declares: "if he had asked me to follow him, I may not have said no, which proves that I was not destined to be a victim of oppression."[6] Ogé, studying in Paris in 1790, worked with the powerful Club des Amis des Noirs (which included among its members the philosophers Mirabeau and Robespierre) to pressure the National Assembly to affirm the civil rights and liberties of the *gens de couleur* class (Bellegarde 61). When calls for his death were issued by the *colons,* he, then age thirty-three, returned to Haiti in order to see to it that the decree became reality. Armed, Ogé and a militia of two hundred fifty successfully resisted a force of six hundred whites. Unlike many slave groups, Ogé's troop consistently released its prisoners. Six months later, in 1791, Ogé, having been captured, was dismembered alive along with Chavannes, another *mûlatre* (Chavannes is interestingly remembered as a son of a *négresse* rather than as a mulatto; Heinl and Heinl 40–41; Bellegarde 63).

The accounts of this execution are conflicting: in Haitian reports, Chavannes is said to have screamed for vengeance as his body was torn in half; in the reports by outsiders, Chavannes is said to have remained mute while Ogé "gave an extensive confession, which included details of mulâtre plots for a general uprising, slaves included" (Heinl and Heinl 63). Which-ever account is true (or truer), this historical incident reveals the complex-ity of Haitian politics: Ogé and Chavannes were captured by a coalition that included *affranchis,* whites, and a volunteer slave force. They were thus caught in the center of the revolutionary maelstrom erupting from all corners of the island. Charlier's protagonist concludes that what caused Ogé's defeat was his ideological blindness: "Ogé died, a victim of his own blindness. He did not know, what we have come to learn since, what causes all revolts, that is, that the oppressor understands only one language: that of force."[7] As a result of this setback, Julie begins to believe that her own des-tiny lies in following in Ogé's footsteps. In his downfall, she sees an oppor-tunity to redefine the shape of things to come. The dismembered bodies of Ogé and Chavannes serve as a rallying point of resistance for Julie as well as for Pétion.

At eighteen, Pétion took part in these internal waves of revolution and was distinguished by his "calme bravoure [calm bravery]" and "gran-deur d'âme [generosity of spirit]" (Bellegarde 116). He was characterized by his "bonté [goodness]" (Bellegarde 117); in fact, he was nicknamed "Papa Bon Coeur [Father Goodheart]" by the Haitian masses (Heinl and Heinl 152) even though he showed himself to be an inept political leader when he became president for life in 1806. In *Mémoire,* Charlier fore-grounds Pétion's despotism from the outset, but also qualifies the image of him as a tyrant by underscoring his attempt to redistribute land and wealth (13). Her real emphasis, however, is on the young and unknown Pétion. Charlier paints a flattering portrait of this legendary figure when Julie first encounters him at her father's home. Julie meets Pétion before the Revolu-tion, when he was known as Anne-Alexandre Sabès, the illegitimate son of a white landowner. Julie describes Pétion as follows: "Of cheerful tempera-ment, peaceful, he accepted kindness with good grace and thanked with delicacy. When he provided a service, which he did often, he always made it seem as if he were the one in need."[8] The two have a brief flirtation dur-ing which Julie uses Racine's poetry to convey her admiration for Pétion. He refuses her kind words, her suggestion that he is a "prince," and Julie wonders "what could become of a dark-skinned, impoverished, quarteroon in this society of whites."[9] Pétion, of course, is to become "prince" to Christophe's kingdom when the two ascend to power after Dessaline's death in 1806, each taking over one half of Haiti—Pétion the south, Christophe the north.

Charlier, then, points to a new version of history, one in which Pétion is remembered as humble, generous, and unpretentious. Despite his despotism, Pétion did, in fact, attempt to correct wrongs. Among his better deeds was the founding of a girls' school in Port-au-Prince (Heinl and Heinl, 152). Tellingly, Julie's only explicitly revolutionary act in the novel, other than her returning to Haiti to follow in Ogé's footsteps, is her establishment of a school for girls of the mulatto class. Julie says: "We began again to enjoy life. In our afflicted souls, the pain was beginning to dull and we were rejoicing for having finally obtained equality."[10] But flanked by her mother and her enslaved grandmother, Ninnaine, an African, Julie reveals her own ultimate lack of vision: she fails to see that her mother and grandmother are far less free than she, and that caste creates a transparent barrier between the participants in the movement for emancipation.

The role of caste takes on added importance when one considers that Charlier's protagonist is ironically named after Rousseau's 1761 heroine in his *Julie, ou la nouvelle Héloïse.* Charlier's Julie is the illegitimate daughter of a Jewish-French landowner, Joseph Maurer, and Man Vonne, a "grifonne," that is, a woman born of two mulatto parents. Despite this mixed heritage, the link between Charlier's Julie and Rousseau's Julie cannot be underestimated. By naming her character after Rousseau's, Charlier places her Julie within the framework of the French literary tradition; moreover, Charlier, in fact, rewrites Rousseau from the perspective of Haitian *métissage. Mémoire d'une affranchie* thus subverts *Julie, ou la nouvelle Héloïse,* which, in its time, was an important part of French literary history.

According to Ronald C. Rosbottom, Rousseau's *Julie* was important in that it legitimized the novel as an art form: "The issue of literary genre was gender-specific . . . for one of the most persistent myths of the 18th century—and since—was that the novel was written primarily for and . . . by women, not for and by men. Although novel-writing did offer women a rare entrée into the literary world, allowing them to attain increasing prominence as writers, it was regularly criticized as an activity unworthy of serious *men* of letters" (483). Consequently, the fact that Rousseau's text centered on a "modern" woman's desires made him a target for ridicule, in keeping with the devaluation of women's stories and women's sexuality, and an agent for the legitimation of the same because of his gender. Writes Rosbottom: "Rousseau's novel describes how difficult it is for a desiring *woman* to influence the social codes of a society defined by male values." Although Charlier's novel bears only surface likeness to Rousseau's tale in terms of its plot—we learn quite late that Julie is in love with an African male whom she considers below her own station—Charlier painstakingly documents every facet of her characters' lives within a chronological, historical, geographical and social framework in the same way that Rousseau uses chronology, detailed descriptions of daily life, and geographical and social references to provide a *realistic* yet fictional account of impossible love across the races (Rosbottom 481). Furthermore, Charlier duplicates an eighteenth-century approach to female desire, relegating Julie's own yearnings to the margins of the story. The new Héloïse is not so much a liberated woman as she is the prototype for a new Haiti; she speaks for the forgotten, male and female, and consequently effaces herself.[11]

Charlier's heroine tells her story to her son, André, and she does so to counter the very education provided him through the independence movement, which spanned the years 1789–1806. She seeks to erase from his imagination the figure of Helen of Troy and her Persian heros. "The men of whom I am speaking" says Julie, "were greater than the heroes of antiquity. They had to reconquer a possession much more precious than the most beautiful of mortals . . . liberty."[12] As the incarnation of the Haitian Helen, Julie cannot be at the center of political discourse: she is merely a vehicle for the *voicing* of the pursuit of liberty, not its agent herself. Julie's voice is released through Charlier's historiographic narrative and acquires a doubleness.

Julie's "memories"—some adapted from Charlier's own readings of Haitian historical texts—are the author's and vice versa. Through numerous "cultural" footnotes, Charlier's own voice glides through the text in a seemingly seamless fashion to join Julie's across time and space, and underscores the fact that storytelling is a decentralized act. In this montage of fact and fiction, history and story, the novel disassembles as it reassembles the forgotten past. In one instance, Julie conveys to her son/readers the political thought of her father who believed (unlike most of the land-owning class) that the enslaved ought to be immediately released. Her father makes her read "a memoir written by a colonizer of Jérémie in which he proposes to free the slaves to become farmers by distributing to them the vacant lands."[13] This "distribution" was begun under Toussaint, Dessalines, and

Pétion, though it did not go far enough to dismantle the caste system. The novel refers us to a footnote wherein the author authenticates her heroine's memoir/memory by stating that the text in question was found "in an old trunk which belonged to Mrs. Théophile Noël, born Zulma Laraque, by her relative Octave Petit."[14] The chest thus serves as a "lieu de mémoire" in that it contains a text that commemorates a historical turn of events and articulates a vision for class/social equity. That it has been lost or forgotten in the chest underscores the fact that despite the presence of a "text" there can be no firm hold on the past without the active involvement of generations of real people: the "memoir(e)" of one man survives only through the transmission of the textual evidence of his thought from one parent to his child, who keeps it until it is rediscovered. The chest is representative of *culture-lacune* in that it symbolizes the painstaking process of simultaneous uncovering and dissimulation. Julie mirrors the extra-textual transference of text by telling her son about the memoir, planting her memory in her son's imagination.

Lieux de mémoire are thus displaced by the explicit refusal to believe that texts can efface an oral legacy; despite textual codification, orality remains a constant and determining feature of African diasporic literature. Other footnotes underscore the incompleteness of textualized oral narratives: the memoried text remains selective, limited, filled with gaps, holes, fissures, stops and starts. As readers are led through Julie's historical memoir and repeatedly made to pause during her narrative in order to read the explanatory notes, they cannot remain unaware of the exacting process of reclaiming a dormant history. For instance, when Julie tells of her mother and grandmother's survival of the burning down of their home by white settlers, and the imprisoning of their slaves, she wonders about the fate of a member of the household, Georges: "Maybe he had his head cut off? Or, having fallen into the hands of the royalists, he had expired in the hell of NEW LOVE."[15] The footnote pointedly answers the question raised in the body of text by explaining the hidden meaning of "NEW LOVE," which is code for a prison in Jérémie where both the freed slaves and those remaining enslaved were "torturés, tués ou jetés vivants à la mer [tortured, killed, or thrown alive into the sea]" (161). In this note, the *affranchis* and the African slaves are connected in a way not revealed by the narrator. Julie is ignorant of the world inhabited by her own family and close others. Torture, death, and, ultimately, the Caribbean sea bind the struggling, invisible heroes and heroines of the Revolution to each other. Their experience of dispossession ties them to the landscape of Haiti.

Charlier's heroine, then, is hardly aware of her potential as a revolutionary. She sees teaching as being diametrically opposed to fighting in the
streets and she lovingly but condescendingly reflects on her relationships
with her family's slaves. She eventually repeats her mother's past by becoming a concubine to a Frenchman, Monsieur Pierre Desmar, who himself believes that "it was good politics to have an ally in the rising class of
Saint-Domingue."[16] She and Pierre use each other in order to maintain and/
or access class privilege in the newly freed colony. In pursuing a union
with a *colon* to maintain class status, Julie consequently undervalues herself. Moreover, the way she reacts to the few stories she tells of women's
acts of rebellion—a subject I will come back to below—suggests that she
undervalues other women as well.

Although many contemporary historical texts depict the slaves of
Saint-Domingue as a hateful and vengeful, bloodthirsty mass who committed unspeakable acts against the white upper classes, Charlier disregards
those representations and focuses on the atrocities committed against
women and children in all classes. Julie tells us that the "whites entered the
city carrying the heads of mulattoes triumphantly on the ends of their
bayonettes" and "had themselves preceded with a pick on which they had
stuck a child of color alive."[17] In the novel, there are numerous accounts of
battles in the main cities of southern Haiti in which women are killed, violated, raped, and their children killed (146–147). After the insurrection of
the *gens de couleur*, the male *affranchi* is targeted for persecution and,
notes Julie, his wife and daughters "if he has any, undergo the ultimate des-
ecrations."[18] Still, characters like Tante Yaya, a vodou priestess, or *mambo*,
and Mme. Martin, a white woman accused of concealing an African ancestry, take an active stand against the oppression of women in particular and
Haitians generally by militantly opposing class stratification and the devaluation of Haitian folklore.

Mme. Martin has enough power to "excite" a crowd. She is described
as "a tall and strong woman from Provence, always armed with a saber and
pistols, her head festooned with red feathers, her long dark hair covering
her naked shoulders."[19] Although white, Martin assumes the identity of a
military commander and has (despite color) the markings of the *marabout*
with her long dark hair and striking appearance, and so is able to access the
ranks of Haitian women who are of color or African. Under her leadership,
a crowd of women encircle M. de Mauduit, a commander in the French
army, and execute him. The scene is vividly recounted and belies the idea
that women did not take part in armed resistance:

The women accompanying Mme. Martin take hold of him and a
sapper cuts off his head. With his limbs cut, thrown here and there,
his head was carried through the city on the point of a pick while
Mme. Martin, having sliced his genitalia with a knife, took them
away with her in triumph.[20]

Julie is presumably disgusted by the tale of Mme. Martin because of its
violence and because of the sexual, erotic overtones that mark that violence. In that disgust, Julie reveals that she has not taken to heart the lesson
she extracted earlier from Ogé's downfall, that the oppressor can only be
answered in his own language, force. Having accessed certain class privileges, Julie does not want to see the symbol of the system that has made
the maintenance of that access possible so utterly desecrated.

It is unclear the extent to which Charlier herself would like readers to
understand or come to terms with Julie's stasis throughout the novel. What
is clear, however, is that even though a woman tells the tale of the Revolution, her lack of political motivation makes it impossible for her to move
out of *lacune* consciousness completely or transform it productively.
Memory, then, is posited as a social *lacune,* an absence that is palpable but
not completely describable, felt but impossible to fill.

Memory and *Auto-Censure*

The title of Jan J. Dominique's first novel, *Mémoire d'une amné-*
sique, reveals a similar bind: the narrator here is struggling to articulate the
past in the face of a loss of memory that is imposed from both within and
without. Yet, her strongest desire is to write the text of her life. As we shall
see with Nadine Magloire's narrator in *Le mal de vivre,* she cannot find the
right words, the right form. She writes: "I want to destroy the pages already
written; they aren't right; they don't reveal what I feel, think, live."[21] The
inadequacy of her written work stems from her feeling that she is being silenced: "I am gagged. I gag myself; I would like, I want to remove this gag
but it holds tight, I feel it imprisoning my fingers like it often closes my
mouth."[22] She fears the consequences of releasing her voice. She thus de-
cides to adopt a variety of masks so that she can tell the story that needs to
be told—the story of the effects of living under the Duvalier regime, of living in a society where sex roles are strictly defined, of being denied vital
connections to other women like herself, and of living without a voice.
Writing "I," she says, is not a strategy that will reveal all aspects of her

story; in fact, it would lead her to fabricate more lies. To tell her truths, then, she finds it necessary to write in the third person—a strategy she adopts "pour me cacher [to hide myself]" (11). As the story unfolds, it becomes clear that secrecy and silence are imperative in a society where "you never know who you're dealing with."[23] Nonetheless, the narrator is clearly intent on denying the society that has thwarted her attempts to shed that skin of fear.

The narrator's fear and intense desire to tell her story is reflected in the syntax of the text. Sentence fragments and run-on sentences abound as if to signify or mirror the machinations of a memory in the process of self-retrieval. Nothing can be told in succession since memory is by nature achronological, moving back and forth across the boundaries of time and space. Dominique's narrator thus writes:

> I can no longer be afraid but I need to find a way to no longer wear the masks. Always the masks. It is not a matter of being careful, of not saying enough, on the contrary, I need to say too much, find a way to transmit this order to my fingers, it's a question of survival, I can no longer be quiet. I know that I speak, alone, sometimes aloud, more often deep within myself, but I need to write this text, who cares about caution, there will always be someone to prevent me from committing the unforgivable infractions, if I do succeed, genuinely, to lose my habits of self-censorship.[24]

The intensity of the text is owed to the vital connection posited between remembrance and survival; one cannot be without the other. But the narrator is telling her "récit" not only for herself but for other women. She says: "I must write so that there will be no lack of sources."[25] She is thus filling the *lacune* that her own experience informs her is that of other women as well.

The narrator's void begins in a childhood filled with seemingly unimaginable horrors. The horrors are those perpetrated by the Duvaliers and their *macoutes* between 1957 and 1986 during a reign whose effects are still in the process of being deracinated, a reign that marked the spirits of all Haitian women and men in Haiti or in exile who lived through it. The narrator, who is named Paul after her father and nicknamed Lili as a child (she will use her formal name only when she has departed Haiti in adulthood), begins her account with the fragmented remembrances of her childhood. Her story begins in 1957, at age six, with the downfall of Haitian president Paul Magloire and the rise to power of François Duvalier. As these events are occurring, Lili's father, from whom she has been separated for several years (she lives with an aunt and uncle) returns from exile to Haiti. Lili is forced to change cities, homes, and parents. In her new house, she throws her toys over a balcony into the street in an attempt to renounce class privilege. With this gesture, Lili abandons her childhood, and it remains in her memory as evidence of her first rebellion: "The first gesture of discomfort. The first manifestation of this difference that will never cease to scream in her head."[26] The difference Lili is beginning to understand resides in her own identity. She is named after a father, who, at six years of age, in the midst of the U.S. Occupation, stood on the same balcony paralyzed by the sight of the soldiers taking over the streets, his streets. Paul, her father, is not a rebel; the heritage he passes on to Lili is one of fear and flight.

Heritage looms large in Lili's story. Dominique uses Lili's family life as a symbol of the effects of a history of domination on Haitians. As a social institution, the family thus reflects the power dynamics inherent in the stratification of human beings by race, class, and gender. As Honor Ford-Smith writes in her introduction to *Lion-heart Gal,* a collection of autobiographical stories by members of the Jamaican theatre collective Sistren, "For most [women] the institution from which their first consciousness of oppression emanated was the family—either in the form of the exploitation of child labour, through the violence of fathers or brothers, or in the case of the middle-class women, through the hypocrisy surrounding race and class relations in the family" (6). Lili's consciousness is formed through the family, where her identity as a girl-child is denied at the same time that it is exploited. Lili alludes to a crucial event in her childhood early on in the novel, which revolves around the image of her father's open hand striking her for daring to gaze defiantly at the *macoutes* (and here the link between the *macoutes* and the American soldiers of the invasion of the early 1900s should not be overlooked).[27] She remembers "revolting before this man speaking to her of heritage. This man telling her that she was his son."[28] Her female identity thus becomes mystified. Amidst this gender confusion, Lili "recherche la précision [seeks precision]" but she does not know which way to turn or whether to recall historical events or her own personal history (54); neither seem real. She thus arrives at a state of self-denial: "she thinks of herself as nameless, she no longer has a name."[29] Her sense of identity becomes bound up with her *auto-censure,* but her memory will not be so easily erased, even if it is silenced: "If she laughs at everything, even if she sometimes scoffs at her memories, she will never speak of that school bench where she huddled, trembling, with the endless sound of the bullets, which did not ricochet, in her ears."[30] Lili's self-censorship cannot imprison her voice, which has begun to break through the wall of fear imposed on her by her father/land. Her personal memories demand her loyalty and she is faithful to their calls. As Dominique writes, "I scream my silence to learn to speak."[31] That scream reverberates from fragment to fragment as Paul/Lili refuses the heritage her father seeks to impose upon her in favor of "l'héritage du non [the heritage of revolt]" (23). She replaces one "nom," name, for its double, "non," no: her name becomes the cry of revolution as she confronts the hypocrisies of her childhood under the Duvalier regime.

In 1957, François Duvalier was "elected" to power in Haiti. By 1960 he had declared himself president for life and proclaimed: "Je suis le Drapeau Haïtien [I am the Haitian Flag]" (Heinl and Heinl 585). At the time, this phrase might have seemed revolutionary in the sense of creating a visceral image evocative of a Haiti moving towards complete self-rule and away from French/European and U.S. influences. Duvalier, in his early years, was associated with the *indigénisme* movement I spoke of in earlier chapters. As Robert Heinl and Nancy Heinl recount in their book, *Written in Blood,* "Duvalier was . . . steeped in the history and folk culture of Haiti and was committed to the proposition that Haiti should wipe away its French veneer and proudly acknowledge its African origins. . . . Rejecting any goal of assimilation into Euro-American cultures, Duvalier was determined that his government would become the political expression of that Africanist mystique, *négritude*" (586). In his inaugural speech, Duvalier declared that "My government will guarantee the exercise of liberty to all Haitians and will always give them the necessary protection in that exercise"; he later declared: "I have no enemies except the enemies of the Nation" (qtd. Heinl and Heinl, 589). The phrase "enemies of the nation" took on an ominous quality as Duvalier rather quickly turned his back on the underlying principles of *indigénisme/négritude* and emulated the very oppressive strategies of his predecessors, white and black. In her novel, Dominique clearly equates Duvalier's regime with that of the U.S. Occupation by suggesting that Duvalier's creation of his own "secret" police, the *Tontons macoutes,* was merely the extension of military might into the private sector.

According to Elizabeth Abbott in her book *Haiti,* the notorious *Tontons macoutes* came into being as a result of a foiled Haitian-American coup attempt against Duvalier père in 1958. Headed by an exiled Haitian military man, Alix Pasquet, the would-be invaders descended on Port-au-Prince and took over the main military barracks with a force of only a few men. Gaining control of the main arsenal should have immobilized Duvalier, but Pasquet made the error of failing to secure the supplies kept at the Palace itself, and of revealing that his force was miniscule. "Nonetheless," writes Abbott, "the invasion tested Haiti's popular political waters, rallied support for the President, and gave him justification for ever-widening and deadlier repression" (83). Since the anti-U.S. sentiment generated by the invasion of 1915 remained ingrained in popular consciousness, Duvalier was able to use the incident to his advantage. He accused "the U.S. of encouraging the invasion . . . then accepted increased aid and, as a Christmastime offering, allowed a Marine mission to train Haiti's army, now equipped with Italian weapons" (Abbott 86). Through international collusion, then, Duvalier secured the arsenal that enabled him to establish his secret police force, which was originally dubbed the Volunteers of National Security and included both men and women.

The *macoutes,* writes Abbott, "were bogeymen of Haitian folk belief who prowled at night in search of bad little boys and girls whom they thrust into their *macoutes,* the straw satchels peasants carry." Duvalier's *Tontons macoutes,* she continues, "carried guns instead of satchels but they also prowled at night, and their victims were seldom seen again" (86). Drawing, then, on a folk image, Duvalier was able to turn the military might associated primarily with the United States into a power sprung from the masses themselves. Thus, in *Mémoire d'une amnésique,* Paul/Lili lives in a world in which *everyone* can assume a masked identity. She cannot tell who can be trusted and comes to understand that in Haiti "there is no such thing as all good or all bad people."[32] The men in black (as the *macoutes* are called in the novel) are in the streets as well as in the home.

There are two developments in the plot of *Mémoire d'une amnésique* that serve to bring together the historical context of Paul/Lili's life and her private childhood experiences. In one, she remembers herself running barefoot to get to school on time for the national anthem and the salutation of the flag. In the other, she finds herself on the roof of the school during a raid staring into the eyes of a military man. The two events are inextricably linked because they are the key to her understanding her own oppression as a Haitian woman. When she and her best friend, Martin, arrive in the schoolyard, breathless, they are accused of being monsters for disrespecting their flag: "You dare to insult your flag. You present yourselves half-naked, barefoot, to show your hostility."[33] Given Duvalier's words—"I have no enemies but the enemies of the nation" and "I am the Haitian flag"— Lili's infraction has dire consequences. Still a child, she is being taught to censor her sense of self in order to honor a flag that no longer represents the nation but the maniacal despotism of one man, one name: Duvalier. Writes Dominique: "The majority of our country's people go barefoot for lack of shoes. Is that an insult to the flag?"[34] The real economic exploitation of Haiti's citizens is overlooked in the demand for a superficial honoring of the flag.

Entwined with this event is the raid on a house neighboring the school; such raids are not unusual, but they always come unexpectedly: "As usual, everything started with a familiar sound that the memory refused to identify."[35] That sound is the whistle of bullets. Lili leaves her classroom and climbs onto the roof of the school in order to get as far away as possible from the disturbance; once on the roof, however, she finds herself face to face with the perpetrators of the crime:

> But in the second crossing, there is the gaze of the other. She smiles and the other looks at this child-student hidden in the shadows of the riflemen. The other looks, horrified, and fear grips her. The other who, in a fraction of a second, was able to guide the glance of the men ambushed on the balcony of the house. She flattens herself even more and listens to the sudden silence of the guns.[36]

Lili is a child who becomes a student of Haitian politics in the moment that the gaze of the gunman falls upon her. He is shocked by the presence of a child in the chaos of the gunfire and it is her presence that ultimately silences the guns. As a result of this experience, Lili is unable to trust such men. As she walks down a sidewalk one day, she refuses to return the smile of a *macoute*. Her father is horrified by the hatred he sees in his daughter's eyes and she is punished for her insolence. Her father slaps her in an attempt to squelch her audacity, "ce regard méprisant la peur [that gaze scornful of fear]" (37). Lili knows that she has understood too much; instead of giving into fear, she retreats within herself and emulates both the good girl she is supposed to be, and the good son who believes so much in Haitian nationhood that he is willing to sell his soul for day-to-day survival.

The difficulty of exposing the hypocrisies of Haitian life is compounded by those on the outside, namely Americans (both in the United States and Canada), who, seeing them, nonetheless pretend they do not exist, and by so doing, enable hypocrisies to be perpetuated. The narrator pointedly addresses the reader as she gives us a tour of Port-au-Prince that leads the unwitting tourist to the site of a firing squad:

> Your guide attempts at times to speak with you, you do the same. Through words, gestures, you show him your pleasure. He guides you then to the big square: leafy trees, fountain, benches in the shade, you discover another city. . . . you . . . forget the anomaly of your tourism in front of these gardens perfumed by camelia and jasmine.[37]

The tourist (you) is led to a public slaying; everyone, including schoolchildren, have been ordered to attend. The tourist watches in horror, but is able to escape the terror that the public slaying induces in her/him by simply leaving the island behind; this is a story s/he will not tell, that s/he will mask with tales of the hot sun and a sun stroke devised to explain the illness s/he will take back to the continent. The story of the tourist is a strategy that enables Paul/Lili to tell another scarring event of her childhood. For the story is one of her nightmares (67), and the effect of her telling it in the formal second person voice is that she distances herself from the event at the same time that she draws the reader, a tourist to her life, into the Haitian landscape of the Duvalier years. In doing so, Dominique implies that memory can take on disparate collective configurations and distort reality. Even though the tourist has departed s/he should not be able to plead ignorance; likewise, the reader should not be able to stuff the words on the page back into the abyss from which they have risen. In short, the outsiders are placed at the center of Haiti's political vortex even though they refuse to acknowledge that this is a position they continuously occupy. The imagination, then, provides a bridge between two very different political realities: the powerful can no longer assert a gap in awareness that makes the "other" unreclaimable. Lili's gaze is ours.

At the same time that the narrator draws us into the vortex of Haitian politics, she distances herself from that center. She flees the sites of her childhood for Canada and Europe and embodies the *culture-lacune* even as she attempts to evade it. Ultimately, her flight will bring her back to her point of beginning; this she knows: "I attempt to flee in order to return home."[38] Flight, then, is an express feature of exile: through it, Paul, as she is known in adulthood, will attempt to reformulate her self. She does this by exploring her redefinition as a woman fighting against the norms established for her in childhood; she wants to reconnect to her heart, which has been desensitized by the scar tissue of her early experiences. In Montreal, circa 1970, her struggle is misunderstood when she rallies in the streets with other students fighting for their rights: "They thought I was indifferent when I did not manifest any horrified surprise or disgust at the tales of police beatings, the interrogations-phone-book-thick-on-the-head-to-avoid-the-recourse-in-justice-of-victims-because-of-the-evidence-of-blows, the illegal activities of the police."[39] Through her halting diction, Lili conveys just how completely the experience of having lived through the Duvalier dictatorship has affected her perspective: she has seen worse. She has lived in a country where laws are easily evaded. To her eyes, Canada is a lucky country, for in it laws must be respected, and if they are not, there is the possibility of dissent, of rebellion. In contrast to what she has learned in Haiti—namely, that "violence . . . is always exercised against the weaker"—what she learns in Canada is "incivility, assurance, the easy retort, the head upheld, what the police deserved who have to respect my rights, respect a law."[40]

As Paul shifts geographies she finally confronts the legacy of her name: as she unlearns her lessons in silencing, she casts off the legacy of her father, and refuses her assigned role as a surrogate son. In so doing, she becomes a woman; she does not yet, however, have the tools to be independent. The lessons of her childhood, which ironically taught her to see herself as a "male" heir, also taught her how to be the prototypical good daughter and/or good wife. To gain her indepedence, Paul must reject the overdetermination of her gendered identity. Thus, when she has her first love affair, with Steve, she states: "He was not my first lover, I did not have a first lover; Steve was my reply."[41] In refusing to categorize her sexuality within the social constraints of "marriageability," Paul's affair defies the rigidly defined sex roles instilled in her during her childhood. As she writes to her best friend, Liza: "Why do women always have to be the ones to give without receiving anything in return? Only tradition forces them to do so and I refuse this kind of tradition."[42]

In exile, Paul finds a space in which to begin to come to terms with the politics of Haiti. She discusses her feelings of alienation with exiled Haitian men only to find that her presence as a woman continues to be denied. Together they dream of a triumphant return, but that dream does not include equity for women, which is seen as a side issue at best, a non-issue at worst. Paul writes: "I gave them my trust rapidly: they were pronouncing the words corresponding to my quest. . . . I promised myself that I would seek out the men of great courage. And I met them . . . feeling the distance with those who spoke in my name while refusing me the power to speak."[43]

Eli, Paul knows, is one of these men, and she forgives him his weakness in the face of her need to revolt against her lot in life. Paul makes preparations with Eli to return to Haiti, but her adoptive mother Marie insists that she marry Eli before doing so, so as to become a respectable woman. In an aside, Paul tells us in her first person voice that "Eli n'a jamais rencontré Marie [Eli never met Marie]" (123). The lack of contact between these two characters reveals that Marie has little concern for the actual person Paul will marry, as she is more interested in propriety; this is the kind of worldview that Paul is fleeing. More revealing, however, is that Paul *prefers* to keep Eli to herself; this is emblematic of Paul's predisposition to secrecy: she refuses to offer up her personal life a stage for the perpetuation of patriarchally-oriented Haitian politics and pursues instead her heart and its choices. This subterfuge frees her, making it possible for her to broaden her associations with other women who are in full control of their identities if not of their social surroundings. By fully occupying the space of *lacune,* Paul is able begin the process of re-identification.

Paul's most significant relationship is with Liza. The importance of Liza is underscored by the letters Paul writes to her throughout her time of exile from Haiti. Letters to no one else are included in the text, though Paul alludes to letters to Romain, a student with whom she falls in love and has an affair even though, at the time, she is with Eli. Speaking of these letters, Paul writes: "Ma mémoire, c'était ces lettres [those letters were my memory]" (115). Romain is but a memory of which the letters are textual evidence. Liza, on the other hand, is very much alive; Paul's letters to her constitute a vital connection between them. Her relationship to Liza, however, is in jeopardy from its very beginnings. Paul tells the story of their train ride through France during which they encounter an Italian couple with whom they try to communicate. In the narrative, she insists that she is captivated by the man of the couple and that she resists his sexual overtures. Disrupting this version of the story, however, is Paul's awareness of Liza, whom she herself tries to hold captive through a camera: "I continued to take pictures of Liza as if somewhere within me I feared that I would never, for a second time, take off with her to the ends of the earth. Somewhere in me I knew already, because the marriage, which had offered me these days of holidays, was the prelude to the Return."[44] Paul cannot bring herself to tell the story of her relationship with Liza. It is too precious and too forbidden. Her passion for Liza remains a dormant facet of the train trip, even though she then introduces us to Liza as one of her great loves.

When Paul first meets Liza it is "le coup de foudre [love at first sight]" (139). Liza, as it turns out, predates Eli. With her, Paul is completely ungagged; words flow between them without the awkward translations needed between themselves and the Italian couple, and between Paul and her male compatriots. Liza enters her life and a new way of being opens for Paul, one filled with the images and words of women: "women's books, women's talk on the mattresses placed on the floor, women's plans."[45] Not surprisingly, Dominique invokes the image of the *marassa* to describe the relationship between Paul and Liza. Paul says: "eyes wide open I saw my siamese twin."[46] Liza provides Paul with a living model of what it is to be a fully independent woman in a world that does not love women. Their love threatens the social order; for this reason, Paul quickly reverts back to the third person to tell the story of this new and transcendent love.

Strikingly, not only does she tell the story in the third person; she also tells it through Eli's voice. She does so in part to legitimate the story's erotic nature, and in part because she is afraid that if she tells it in her own voice she will be cast out from the "family" that attempted to shape her identity as a little boy and that simultaneously, even as it denied her identity as a little girl, insisted that she grow up to be a self-effacing wife and mother. The effect of her upbringing is that she is afraid to construct a world in which women are the focal point rather than the marginal hearth keepers. Paul, in being denied access to other women by her family, has been isolated from her sex; this isolation serves the dual purpose of keeping her servile and disempowered. Women, then, are forced to participate in their subordination in order to maintain positions of relative power within the family, and, hence, in society. Their subordinate position in both the family and society is sustained by the marital contract, that is, by compulsory heterosexuality. Thus, as Trinidadian-Canadian poet and filmmaker Dionne Brand writes: "If men brag when they're together, women deny. They make sure there is no sign of themselves, they assure each other of their love for men, they lie to each other, they tell stories about their erasure, they compete to erase themselves, they rap each other in weary repetitions, they stop each other from talking" ("Just Rain," 16). In this way, women, as Adrienne Rich writes in her essay "Compulsory Heterosexuality and Lesbian Existence" (1980), fail to take account of "heterosexuality as a political institution which disempowers [them]" (23).

In her essay, Rich challenges women (U.S. women, to be sure, but her comments are applicable to Haitian women as well) to take responsibility for their collusion in a systemic erasure of the history and practice of women-bonding. She suggests: "If we consider the possibility that all women . . . exist on a lesbian continuum, we can see ourselves as moving in and out of this continuum, whether we identify ourselves as lesbian or not" (54). The lesbian continuum, as defined by Rich, is one meant to "embrace many more forms of primary intensity between and among women, including the sharing of a rich inner life, the bonding against male tyranny, the giving and receiving of practical and political support" (51). Paul is clearly a woman who can place herself on such a continuum, but she initially resists this identity because of her status as a Haitian woman exiled from a homeland wherein women lead a precarious existence simply on the basis of their sex. That precariousness is compounded for Paul by the fact of her exile. Therefore, she reveals her love affair with Liza at a slant, through the legitimization of a male voice.

Paul/Eli watches Liza dance with another friend of theirs, Martine (whom Paul once thought her double until Martine denounced Paul's feminist leanings as "not serious"). The scene is erotic, as Eli's account makes clear: "I could not bring myself to feel shocked at seeing these two girls, dancing slowly, cheek to cheek. Martine seemed moved, I could feel her body telling us all 'she wanted to dance with me, too bad if you refuse to understand.'"[47] Paul/Eli describes Liza as camouflaged in long skirts that for her/him bespeak a "common and banal heterosexuality" (142) Liza's own gestures deny. Liza ultimately reveals herself to Paul/Eli when she begins to speak of her family and shares that she is the daughter of a man who refuses to take responsibility for his family. Paul/Eli wants her to continue to speak but grows afraid as s/he hears words that recount a woman's life so much like her own: "I did not want to understand when she told me her woman's life and, sensing my fear, she guessed that I was trying to refuse her proffered phrases."[48] Despite Paul/Eli's fear, however, Liza becomes a part of her life, sleeping at her apartment, and, finally, sharing her bed.

One night, Liza seduces Paul/Eli and s/he, in turn, can no longer refuse Liza's words, or her body:

> I said "Why?," she responded with a gale of laughter "why not?!" I didn't want to know anymore. I was back in my fear and, despite it, I heard myself laughing. Of her unexpected tenderness, of the heat of her skin, of feeling her attempts to hold back when desire made her too vulnerable. . . . I closed my eyes and she was holding out her hand.[49]

With Liza, Paul confronts her fear, the very fear that has created her frac-
tured sense of self. Through their relationship, Paul reclaims her childhood
identity by refusing to accept that her gender circumscribes her desire. Her
true desire, finally, is to be free: free of the *macoutes,* free of her father's
iron-hand, free of Eli's political naivete, free of the "prisoned gaze of men"
(Brand, *No Language,* 48). In the arms of another woman, her silence is
broken; her laughter is her voice bubbling to the surface of the narrative,
even though it is masked under another male name, not her own, but her
husband's.

Paul's story does not end with Liza, who exits the text as freely as she
is brought into it; the narrator persists in her subterfuges and disloyalties.
She has an affair with a married man, Patrick, and realizes while she is
with him that she has betrayed herself. She is still attempting to flee her
self, her home and her ultimate defeat is her reversion to patriarchal models
of womanhood. She seeks fulfillment with a man out of desperation as her
loss of "homeplace" becomes all the more apparent; she does so to her own
demise. Her relationship with Patrick culminates in psychological if not
bodily rape: "he used my dreams, spoke of our rage, he took the right to
want my body because of our common folly" (161); he was, the third person voice tells us, "blind to her screams, understood nothing of her silent
suffering, because he was looking at nothing else but her breasts."[50] She refuses his advances, says no; he possesses her body nonetheless. This is the
beginning of Paul's unraveling; she departs to find Liza whom she can
never reclaim because she is bound to Eli in marriage. Thus she feels that
she must go far "pour retrouver l'équilibre [to reclaim the balance]" denied
in childhood (163). Paul returns to Haiti in order to reclaim her mothers,
her land, her self.

This impulse is clarified as she grows passionate about the women in
her life, including her three mothers:

> I cannot speak to you of the women but rather I tell you of my
> women, those who fill my heart and my life, those who, accomplices,
> respect my strength and sustain my stumbling steps, those who are
> buddies, those who share, those who mother and who want me to
> be good, those crazy ones who protect my peals of laughter, my
> marvel-women whom I wear suspended to my heart.[51]

Paul becomes less secretive about her new-found love of women as she rediscovers herself through the intensity of their bonds. Most notable among
the inventory of Paul's women is Lucie, who apparently takes Liza's place.

She tells Eli: "I cannot yet bring myself to speak Liza to you, I can only promise you another voyage, another continent, to meet Liza. Will I succeed at telling you the story of Lucie?"[52] Paul meets Lucie in a bar, dancing atop tables. The image that binds them together is the same as that which bound Paul to Liza; says Paul: "I went towards her, put out my hand which she grasped with a mocking air and I made her come down slowly."[53] Paul's outstretched hand accurately reflects her embrace of a life among and for women and her acceptance of the power of the erotic as the source of her empowerment.

Audre Lorde has described the power of the erotic as "born of Chaos, and personifying creative power and harmony . . . an assertion of the lifeforce of women" (55). Through all of the women in her life Paul rediscovers just such a powerful source of identity: "I discovered all of a sudden the presence of women in my life. Not simply one woman with whom the bonds became very strong, not simply Julia or Liza, but women for everything."[54] Paul's elation is short-lived, however; she must turn away from these women in order to remain in her marriage because it is her only viable passport back to Haiti where the independent life of women is by and large denied. In the end, she writes: "Paul exists, Lili still escapes me."[55] Her ultimate task remains that of finding the source of her personal power in the memories of her childhood horrors. Through the process of recognizing that she has triumphed over those moments, she may yet reclaim her inner and female self, Lili, and refuse her effacement.

In fact, the fissures in Dominique's fragmented narrative reveal that Lili has not been lost: she exists within those textual gaps. Given that names and naming are paramount to the narrator's sense of self, it is telling that her childhood name is Lili and that her primary female relationships in adulthood are with women whose names, Liza and Lucie, echo her own. Paul is the connection between all three of these women, who are like the sides of an isosceles triangle, three equidistant points on a map. They are exiled from one another simply because their love is silenced in the struggle for nationhood in various contexts. Their exile, as Paul knows too well, is a product of their sex and the social constructions that cocoon them, rendering their creative powers, and the vision of change that attends those powers, invisible.

Resisting silencing, then, resisting burial under what Adrienne Rich has called "an inadequate or lying language" (199)—a language through which a deceptive account of social relations at both micro and macro levels is promoted—becomes the task of the victimized collective. Ghislaine

Charlier and Jan J. Dominique play off of the connotations of the French word for history and story, *histoire,* in order to excavate the socio-political implications of *mémoire.* Their purpose, then, is not simply "to stop time" or "block the work of forgetting" as Nora suggests (295), but is, more radically, to demonstrate that whatever the framework, the histories of silenced and oppressed people have already been swept away and cannot be readily reclaimed. Memory serves as a tool for reclaiming these histories, but is not a vehicle meant for restoring fragments to, or destabilizing, History. *Mémoire* is the thread that links generations of peoples whose various histories have been ignored, displaced, silenced: its invocation continues to place the absence of women's collectivity at the center of feminist historiographic discourse. Remembrance is thus at the crux of the reconstructive moment, and the "text" becomes the intermediary between private and collective consciousness. It is the basis for political renaissance: memory, rebirth, as a revolutionary act.

CHAPTER 4

Léspoua fè viv

FEMALE IDENTITY AND THE POLITICS OF TEXTUAL SEXUALITY IN NADINE MAGLOIRE'S *LE MAL DE VIVRE* AND EDWIDGE DANTICAT'S *BREATH, EYES, MEMORY*

Moon marked and touched by sun
my magic is unwritten
but when the sea turns back
it will leave my shape behind.
　　　　—Audre Lorde, "A Woman Speaks"

Je viendrais à ce pays mien et je lui dirais: "Embrassez-moi
sans crainte. . . . Et si je ne sais que parler, c'est pour vous que
je parlerai."

[I would come back to this land of mine and say to it: "Embrace
me without fear. . . . If all I can do is speak, at least I shall speak
for you."]
　　　　—Aimé Césaire, *Cahier d'un retour au pays natal*

Je n'ai plus le goût de vivre.

[I no longer have any desire to live.]
　　　　—Nadine Magloire, *Le mal de vivre*

*T*he way to the square is fraught with danger. The dirt roads are rutted not from rain but from the weight of army trucks passing day in and day out. The roads are made of compacted dirt; they wind through the impossible brush, unpaved and unlit. In places, trees laden with leaves hover over the roads like the wild tentacles of many-fingered ogres. On a night like this one, dark like the inner chamber of an unexplored cave, nothing is as it seems in the day. Or so Solange thinks as she walks bravely down the middle of one such road trying to avoid the borders: the invisible line between her path towards the lit square and the dark abyss seems no different now from the border between Haiti and the Dominican Republic where two of her cousins disappeared a month ago. Her mother told her they had been stolen to cut the sugar cane. Solange shivers as she feels the cool night air against her skin and imagines the cane leaves cutting through the youthful flesh, blood spilling against the whiteness of the sap oozing from freshly cut sugar stalks. Every noise about her, every whistle of wind, carries with it the sound of fear silenced by the burst of sudden light that comes with the so-early daybreak.

Solange walks quickly in the dark, keeping her eyes wide open. She has heard the stories of the girls and women dragged off in the middle of the night to be beaten and left for dead. But such events are not left only for the night. Solange is not blind. She has watched soldiers break down her neighbor's door and has heard the screaming; she does not know what goes on but it is something terrible, something she hopes will never happen to her. When the screaming stops, the soldiers drag the woman out and Solange watches her friend, the woman's daughter, cry over the heaving mass of her mother's body, and try to cover her where her dress has been torn, the tears forming rivers along the crevices of her sunken cheeks.

The walk to the square seems impossibly long. Solange has been warned about stopping, and cautioned to look out for the bogeymen. Bogeymen here are unlike those anywhere else: they don't live in your mind; they are real and breathing and carry guns in leather holsters against their hips. Here, their names begin with an "m" and they wear dark clothing and gold-rimmed aviator glasses. A few of them are women. The men walk through the crowded streets at high noon like they own everything in sight—even your soul.

The bogeymen smile at Solange from across the street when she gets out of school. Sometimes they try to walk her home as if she were a little sister. Sometimes they try to pull her into the bushes, and this is the moment in which Solange realizes that night and day are more alike than different, that she will never be safe. She wishes for the first time in her young life that she were a boy, that the bogeymen would look at her like they do her brothers, as potential candidates for their ranks. In that case, she could stop after school and join them across the way, learn how to polish the barrel of a gun with gleaming sweat.

Solange finally sees the light of the piazza before her. Her heart beats hard. She looks about; the square is filled with meandering people. She sees some of the schoolchildren already seated on the benches beneath the lights. She chooses the bench next to theirs and sighs heavily. She sits down and opens her book at the beginning of a chapter entitled "The Fight for Independence." She is seeking answers, some sign that she might be able to leave in a few hours without fearing the long walk home.

Defying the Erotics of Hegemony

In Haitian creole, the saying "léspoua fè viv" ("Hope makes (us) live") is a timelesss one, reflecting both the tenacious (yet wary) optimism of a populace that has been denied, to this very day, the fruits of hard-won independence. On the heels of that independence followed imperial colonialization in the early 1800s and the concomitant inescapable and harsh realities that continuous neocolonial subjugation bring into being: poverty, hunger, illiteracy. Hope, elusive and ethereal, often seems the only stable source of sustenance in a world where fully accessible and tangible economic and educational opportunity does not exist and where adequate social(ist) programs have not been put into place. "Léspoua fè viv" is a piece of common wisdom, of "mother wit," which has, of late, been appropriated by those in a position to colonize in order to facilely stereotype the Haitian populace as being the prototype for a "generic" Third World stoicism. The politics of "restoring democracy" to Haiti has resulted in the perpetuation of hardships real people suffer by its rationalizing away the economic and cultural oppression of Haitians. The recent embargo, for example, has had the effect of increasing an already high infant mortality rate and decreasing an already horrifically low GNP: Haitians are hardy, goes the stereotype, so a little more pain, a little more death, justifies the end result, the push toward (Americanized) democracy. How, then, do we begin to unravel this *continuously* collapsing rhetoric (that which First World nations use in an attempt to impose their ideology on Haiti) so as to render visible the ways in which various subgroups resist their homogenization from without and articulate their positionality within a *Haitian* ideology? By focusing on the articulation of women's realities in Haitian women's literature we can arrive at an understanding of the ways in which Caribbean identity is not only multiple, along the lines of sex, race, and class, but is also undergoing constant flux in each of these categories.

Both Nadine Magloire's *Le mal de vivre* (1967) and Edwidge Danticat's *Breath, Eyes, Memory* (1994) demonstrate the extent to which Haitian women have been rendered invisible in a society itself typified through their sexualization and denigration. In this sense, the "othering" of women within Haiti is the means by which the privileged classes attempt to legitimate the myth of a Haitian national identity anchored in male martyrdom. Sexuality, in both novels, serves as a pivotal symbol of Haitian women's attempts to formulate empowering identities. Whereas the conventional sexual mores that Magloire's protagonist, Claudine, attempts but in the end fails to elude are imposed from the outside in *Le mal de vivre,* in *Breath, Eyes, Memory,* these mores are self-imposed and are, further, imposed by women on other women from one generation to the next. In this chapter, I will explore the ways in which both Magloire and Danticat use the novel form to demonstrate the extent to which Haitian women are subject to the same outdated Victorian codes of sexual behavior as their female counterparts in the United States and Europe. Although these two texts, separated by twenty-seven years, portray sexuality in different ways, the authors of both emphasize the necessity of creating a language and a frame of reference through which the Haitian woman can come to represent herself and her sexuality directly, without the need for translations.

An exploration of either text can only be understood, however, in the context of the politics of publishing in the Caribbean and the politics of Caribbean/postcolonial literary criticism. Caribbean women writers have, historically, had difficulty publishing their works and what literature they have succeeded in getting published has received little attention from Caribbean and postcolonial literary critics—this state of affairs explains why issues of literacy, economics, and feminist social intervention feature so largely in literature produced by Haitian women.

In the literature of Caribbean male writers, such as Derek Walcott, René Depestre, Wilson Harris, and Aimé Césaire, women appear as elusive figures who represent cultural loss: they function as symbols of the feminized Caribbean landscape that has undergone pillage and violence. The cultural and geographical "rape" of a feminized Caribbean is linguistically and imagistically rendered in a way that has the effect of sublimating and denying the violence perpetrated against women in both "public" and "private" spheres; Caribbean male writers attempt to represent a "whole" culture, a Caribbean culture that struggles to define itself against European norms and, in so doing, replicate the same hegemonies as those present in colonial thought (the bipolarization of race, sex, class, etc.). Colonial hegemony is constructed as gendered to delineate the colonized (passive, hence female) from the colonizing (active, hence male). Thus, Antonio Benitez-Rojo is able to write in *The Repeating Island:*

> Let's be realistic: the Atlantic is the Atlantic . . . because it was once
> engendered by the copulation of Europe . . . with the Caribbean ar-
> chipelago; the Atlantic is today the Atlantic . . . because Europe, in
> its mercantilist laboratory, conceived the project of inseminating the
> Caribbean womb with the blood of Africa; the Atlantic is today the
> Atlantic . . . because it was the painfully delivered child of the Car-
> ibbean, whose vagina was stretched between continental clamps, be-
> tween the *encomienda* of Indians and the slaveholding plantation,
> between the servitute of the coolie and the discrimination toward the
> *criollo,* between commercial monopoly and piracy, between the run-
> away slave settlement and the governor's palace; all Europe pulling
> on the forceps to help at the birth of the Atlantic. . . . After the blood
> and salt water spurts, quickly sew up torn flesh and apply the anti-
> septic tinctures, the gauze and surgical plaster; then the febrile wait
> through the forming of a scar: suppurating, always suppurating. (5)

The cannibalization of Africa results in the erotics of hegemony whereby
all of the Caribbean is feminized and, consequently, abused: Benitez-Rojo's
use of language replicates the historical, colonial moment he describes in
which "woman" is made the "other" and colonized, because she is there,
useful, and the site of self-replication. This, in the midst of advancing a
useful and necessary theory that revolves around the way in which the Caribbean has been annexed to serve the needs of an exploitative global capi-
talist economy. Such uses of the metaphor of woman as landscape has led
to a textual romanticization (even when garishly construed, as in the above)
of Caribbean women, which denies them a sense of identity separate from
that of island-nations. They are, in fact, denied the possibility of articulating identities divorced from but still relevant to the politics of colonialism.

It is no surprise, then, that, though recent scholarship in the area of
Caribbean and postcolonial studies has begun to focus on literature produced by women (Carole Boyce Davies and Elaine Fido's *Out of the
Kumbla* and Selwyn Cudjoe's *Caribbean Women Writers* are salient examples), women writers continue to be underpublished, as well as
underrepresented in the general study of Caribbean literature. In no Caribbean country has this been more true than in Haiti. As I have alluded to
above, in comparison with the publishing patterns of women writers in
Martinique and Trinidad, Haitian women writers find themselves represented only one-fourth as frequently as women writers in either of these islands. The fact that Haitian male writers such as Jacques Roumain have

accrued considerable recognition since the emergence of the *indigénisme* movement in the 1920s—popularized by the publication of Aimé Césaire's *Cahier d'un retour au pays natal* (1947), the "seminal" text of *négritude*— has not resulted in the fostering of female literary talent in Haiti.

The Female Body as Site of Resistance and Literary Contestation

Nadine Magloire's *Le mal de vivre* accurately reflects the muting of the female voice within Haiti and shows how that silencing necessitates the use of the body, of Black female sexuality, as a strategic site and tool of resistance. Françoise Lionnet's analysis of violence in the writings of Myriam Warner-Vieyra, Gail Jones, and Bessie Head in her essay "Geographies of Pain" demonstrates that the body is symbolic of women's responses to colonial discourse in the African diasporic context. Of her own analytical lens she writes that she aims "to focus on the *literarity* of a group of works whose thematic similarities are uncanny" and, like Maryse Condé, she warns "that we should be wary of too literal or sociological an interpretation of these texts that would lead us to infer from them a complete breakdown of communication between the sexes" (135). I read this latter assertion as an effort on Lionnet's part to heal the rifts in scholarship that have been occasioned by critics who regard Black women writers' exposure of their oppression within their own cultures (and here I am thinking of the criticisms leveled against Alice Walker, Joan Riley, and Joyce A. Joyce by Black male critics in the 1980s) as having the effect of weakening Afrocentric, male, nationalist discourses rather than illuminating an Afrocentric and female point of view on those discourses. It is clear to me, however, that the female characters brought to life in the works of women of the African diaspora function as representative figures of real women whose lives would, in the absence of these literary figurations, remain without shape or actualization in our imaginations and ideologies. Writings by Haitian women writers are acts of intervention, metahistories, which render the lives of Haitian women visible. In this sense, then, my own project is one of *socio-literarity*, concentrating on both the ways in which literature mirrors actual social realities and the ways in which it remains a "discursive practice that encodes and transmits as well as creates ideology" (Lionnet, "Geographies" 132).

Magloire's text depicts Haitian women's struggle to assert both raced and gendered identities that relieve them of their exploitation and stereotyping. Magloire engages her readers in an exploration of Caribbean identity along two intertwined axes, the sociological and the narratological. It is through the novel form that she suggests that women's lives can begin to be given shape; her protagonist, Claudine, struggles to become a writer but ultimately fails because the Caribbean novel, in its traditional form, does not encompass women's lives. Thematically, Claudine is presented as a woman who believes that she can only begin to access a sense of self through an exploration of her sexuality since it is her sex which delimits the parameters of her existence within Haiti. It is for this reason that Magloire uses the Black female body as a metaphor for the contest between the sexes. Her heroine is embroiled in a battle for self-autonomy that must begin at that site of self in order to find its ultimate resolution.

The narrative begins with Claudine's poetic musings as she writes the first seemingly uninspired line of her novel: "a light, fine rain parts the air with pale streaks."[1] The image of a peaceful rainshower that hardly stirs the air invokes the despair of Claudine's creative process as a metaphor for her unfulfilled desires. Claudine is a woman without a past, without a future; she struggles to aggrandize her own being by recreating herself through the written word. As Magloire writes of Claudine's claustrophobic vision: "We believe ourselves to be among the chosen ones and then discover one day that we are, in the final analysis, destined to a mediocre life since this is the life fate has in store for us. . . . What does it matter that I felt destined for greatness. I lead an insignificant life."[2] An insignificant life, a life of mediocrity—this seems to be all that is in store for Claudine. Her life is the perfect example of an interrupted narrative through which she enacts a struggle against the symbolic order instead of confronting the social realities that keep her captive.

As a middle-upper class woman, Claudine shows little compassion for those less fortunate and, in fact, has contempt for those in poverty. "Toussaint Louverture was right," she says. "This nation should be forced to work under the whip while it waits to learn human dignity."[3] Ironically, Claudine also despises her own class, and especially the women within it for their shallowness. As she prepares to host a tea party, Claudine relates: "It's absurd to have invited them since they bore me, but the harm has already been done. We will speak of the usual superficialities. Material things, fashion, gossip. It seems that there can be nothing else of interest to Haitian women."[4] Claudine evades reconciling these two positions, occupying a middle ground that allows her to abdicate responsibility toward the poor as well as to avoid confronting her peers with the destructive quality of their extravagances. Only the novel has special significance for Claudine within this universe as it represents for her a sense of continuity between the separate spheres of her child and adult lives.

Her "tentatives de roman" themselves implicitly suggest the importance of the novel to Claudine. But she also explicitly states early on in her pseudo-memoir that she defines her world within the parameters of art and culture: "Books, music, these are my universe. My refuge against the anguish of my nothingness."[5] It is in adolescence, the hybrid ground between childhood and adulthood, girlhood and womanhood, that Magloire's character loses all zest for life. For as she moves into the adult world in which she is expected to marry and take care of a husband and home, she is required to abandon her world of imagination brought alive through games and wooden dolls. Claudine forsakes desire until she rediscovers a world of endless possibilities, of make-believe, through novels. She says: "I discovered the novel and I threw myself within its embrace with passion. In a way, I regained the enchanted world of my childhood, but a world adapted to my new state of mind. The novel was a fantasy world for grown-ups."[6] The novel takes the place of the imaginary world of her childhood at the same time that it recalls its liberty. The resulting disjunction between the freedom she experiences through the fantastical world of the novel and the limitations imposed upon her in the "real" world leads Claudine to search for her own identity by attempting to write her text, her self.

Embedded in Claudine's attempt to re-vision her past is the reality of her childhood, which is not as rosy as she would have us believe. Claudine is obsessed with dreams of her childhood and with the physical spaces that haunt those dreams: the attic filled with forgotten antiques, mysterious, suffocating, dark, "infesté de rats [infested with rats]" (26). As nightmarish as the attic might be, it holds a sort of morbid charm for Claudine, who is attracted to it precisely because of its alienness, its lack of clarity. Juxtaposed with the memories of the cluttered attic are those of a closet in which her mother locks her to punish her whenever she commmits some childish wrong. Claudine remembers crying herself to sleep in the closet, only to awake with wonder to examine her mother's cosmetic creams, dresses, shoes and hats. Through her mother's violence, Claudine is initiated into the world of Haitian women's lives within the upper classes; the closet space holds her captive to the superficial trappings of womanhood that become her only means of connecting to a distant and abusive mother. She remarks: "It's strange. Every time I desire something, I discover it through my dreams in this closet."[7] Both the attic and the closet are representative

of the spheres to which Haitian women's will to transgress fixed gender
identities—to be disobedient, to desire—is confined. Claudine's dreams do
not, as dreams should, deliver her into a realm of new possibilities; rather
they return her to the enclosures of her childhood. In her novel, Magloire
suggests that the past is inescapable, but that her protagonist must nonetheless begin anew. Unfortunately, Claudine has few tools at her disposal with
which to accomplish this transformation.

Sandra Gilbert and Susan Gubar, in their work *The Madwoman in the
Attic,* show that "[d]ramatizations of imprisonment and escape" (85) in
nineteenth-century literature by women in Europe as well as in the U.S.
were enacted through the textual reconfiguration of domestic spaces. Writers such as the Brontës, George Eliot, and George Sand delimited new
spaces within which the female condition could be inscribed and described
rather than simply circumscribed: the domestic space of the home, the
hearth, the kitchen, the mind. As Gilbert and Gubar make clear, the "attic"
metaphor reflects women's imprisonment within strict codes of gendered
conduct, as well as expresses the psychological effects of this confinement.
The "madwoman" in nineteenth century literature represents a response to
the medical discourse of the time, which labeled women "hysterical" whenever they expressed and/or acted upon desires that did not comform with
their defined social functions as wives, mothers, desexualized spinsters,
and omnipresent caretakers.

In her groundbreaking essay, "The Hysterical Woman: Sex Roles and
Role Conflict in Nineteenth-Century America," Carroll Smith-Rosenberg
describes the role of white, middle- to upper-class women in the United
States as follows:

> She was the guardian of religion and spokeswoman for morality. Hers
> was the task of guiding the more wordly and more frequently tempted
> male past the maelstroms of atheism and uncontrolled sexuality. Her
> sphere was the hearth and the nursery; within it she was to bestow
> care and love, peace and joy. The American girl was taught at home,
> at school and in the literature of the period, that aggression, inde-
> pendence, self-assertion and curiosity were male traits, inappropri-
> ate for the weaker sex and her limited sphere. Dependent throughout
> her life, she was to reward her male protectors with affection and
> submission. At no time was she expected to achieve in any area con-
> sidered important by men and thus highly valued by society. (79)

This paragraph could very well summarize the position of women in nineteenth and early-twentieth century Haitian society, which, as I showed earlier, was deeply influenced by U.S. racial and sexual mores as a result of the Occupation. In order to assess properly the vestiges of colonial life in the Caribbean we must be cognizant of the fact that castes or classes were organized through the dominant social strata imposed in the colonies by imperialist nations such as England and France. The United States came into being itself through the exertion of imperialist might: it is therefore not difficult to understand how pan-European nineteenth-century values became entrenched in the "new world" and thus, how the idea of "separate spheres," that is, of strictly defined sex roles, came to figure so largely in the organization of the upper classes in nineteenth century "America." It has been less easy, however, for mainstream U.S. historians and literary critics to understand how these same narrowly defined sex roles came to be imposed on the citizens of already existing countries in the same hemisphere, countries which were labeled "black" or "of color" in contradistinction to the United States. From the creole woman (such as depicted in Jean Rhys' *Wide Sargasso Sea*) who followed her husband from Europe to the plantation house she was born to manage and "guard," to the woman in servitude who, defiled by her race and her class, was born to silently sweep and clean the corners of her keeper's (the white, European homesteader's) "hearth" as well as to fulfill the sexual functions deemed improper for the dependent and submissive wife whom she shadowed, women in the Caribbean were each and all subject to the stereotypes devised to justify the oppression and suppression of women's sexual automomy and individual identities. In fact, we can easily see how similar the histories of women in both places, in the United States and in the Caribbean, are by comparing the motifs in the literature which emerged from both during the nineteenth and early twentieth centuries.

"Madwomen" are a dominant presence in the literature by Caribbean women writers of the twentieth century. In her article, "Interior Schisms Dramatised: The Treatment of the 'Mad' Woman in the Work of Some Female Caribbean Novelists," Evelyn O'Callaghan presents a compelling list of Caribbean women authors who have used "the idea of the madwoman in the West Indian novel as social metaphor" (90). She cites Rhys' *Wide Sargasso Sea,* Warner-Vieyra's *As the Sorcerer Said,* Edgell's *Beka Lamb,* Brodber's *Jane and Louisa Will Soon Come Home,* Marshall's *Praisesong for the Widow,* Schwartz-Bart's *The Bridge of Beyond,* Patrick-Jones' *Jou'vert Morning* and Hodge's *Crick-Crack Monkey.* This revisionist use of the same figure to communicate the disenfranchisement of women in "post"-colonial Caribbean society suggests that the effect of European socialization must be taken seriously when considering the multiple features of Caribbean literature. When we refer to the Caribbean as polyphonous as well as creolized, we must not only pay attention to the African features of each society located in the Caribbean basin but also to the ways in which European cultures have marked the evolution of Caribbean ideologies; this effect is undeniable when one considers the status of gender relations. Franco-Caribbean women writers like Magloire also used the Victorian literary models exposed by Gilbert and Gubar in order to further use the novel genre as a voice box for their political and social views.

In charting the emergence of feminist thought in Haiti, it is possible to see that Haitian women's response to sexual oppression had much to do with the maintenance of the Napoleonic code which emerged in the same year in which Haiti declared its independence (1804). Women writers of the nineteenth century such as George Sand, of course, also objected to the limitations the code imposed on women in their literature. Writes Naomi Schor:

> Sand's feminist trilogy, and notably *Lélia,* attests to a profound crisis in the gender-power relations in post-Restoration France. The law that binds Sand's female protagonist is not some great, universal law of human desire; it is the Napoleonic code (proclaimed in 1804), which deprived women of their rights and fixed them in their (inferior) sexual roles, according them the same legal status as minors and madmen. (658)

Even before the emergence of the discourse of "hysteria," then, women were considered a breed, or "race" apart. The law relegated them to the status, as Smith-Rosenberg has put it, of "child-woman," a creature denied her independence and represented as a burden to the state. Sand struggled to present a female protagonist in her fiction who would reflect a new social vision of emancipation for women and of equality between the sexes. Thus Sand wrote: "There is no true association in the love between the sexes, because the woman's role is that of the child and the hour of emancipation never rings for her" (Sand qtd. Schor 659–660). In Caribbean fiction, disatisfaction with oppressive gender roles finds its expression in the motif of flight as a result of social confinement.

As Elizabeth Wilson writes in her essay "'Le Voyage et l'espace clos' —Island and Journey as Metaphor: Aspects of Woman's Experience in the Works of Francophone Caribbean Women Novelists," "the quest in [Caribbean] women's writing usually ends in withdrawal and isolation and/or flight and evasion, rather than confrontation. Central to the depiction of this quest are the metaphors of the journey and the closed space." Further, she notes, "[s]elf-knowledge often leads to destruction of self" (45). The perennial motif of the journey is transformed, as Wilson writes, into one of alienation rather than revelation and, I suggest, always in some way encoded as a feature of *culture-lacune.* For Wilson, this "interruption" finds its articulation in the symbolism of the island, by which "[l'Antillaise] is an island, cut off, stranded with no life-lines" (47). The Francophone Caribbean woman escapes her alienation through the written text, through the actualization of identity in language, the world of words shaping a new reality within the inviolable space of the imagination, of the mind. Writes Wilson of the female protagonists of a number of Francophone women's works: "their only effective liberation [is] implicit in the act of writing, explicitly portrayed in several works as the means to achieve relief through a symbolic reunion with the self, with other women, and the mother (land) from which they have been exiled" (46).

Consequently, in Magloire's equation of the written text with the body, her character's journey is by definition one of alienation. For the most part, it takes place internally, in opposition to male control, and manifests itself in the form of the development of Claudine's sexuality. "Folie," that is, madness, is defined as Claudine's search for "true" love. Rather than acting as a panacea for her lack of fulfillment, her eventual affair with a married man is truly madness. Claudine comes to recognize this reality as she evaluates the lives of her female "friends," who, for the most part, have made unhappy marriages. Claudine devotes much textual space to the women of the middle class in order to demonstrate that their unhappiness mirrors her own. One woman, Ginnette, marries to maintain her class privilege, and another, Alice, puts off having children until she can push her husband to seek higher aspirations. For this latter woman, says Claudine, "the essential function of a husband is to keep the money flowing home."[8] A third woman is married to an unfaithful husband and bears the cross of this infidelity like a martyr by continuing to be faithful herself. Claudine, however, believes that fidelity is a gift that once bestowed must be deserved (33). The only woman for whom Claudine has an ounce of respect is the twenty-year-old Maud, an artist's model and a working-class woman, who is permitted access to the inner sanctum of the women of the bourgeoisie through her objectification in art. Claudine participates in this objectification by desiring Maud for her beauty and for what she defines as

unchaste sexuality. "She has a splendid body," says she. "I have more respect for a woman who uses her body to fulfill her own whim than for
these wives who are so proud of their faithfulness but who, in fact, are sell-
ing themselves to their husbands."[9] Positing that marriage should be
equated to prostitution and thus that it contributes to women's social degra-
dation, Claudine exempts herself from the obligation to abide by the conventional rules of the marriage contract; in so doing, Claudine bestows
upon herself the privilege of desire that is otherwise reserved for males
within the novel.

Maud thus becomes both her double, the side of her own identity that
does not find its full expression either textually or sexually, and her "other,"
the object of her desires: Claudine seeks to embody the *marabout*. In a
brief bid to satisfy her desire, but at the suggestion of André, her boyfriend,
Claudine attempts a lesbian relationship with Maud. It is, of course, a point
of irony that Claudine's exploration of her object of desire should be insti-
gated by the suggestion of a man who has little interest in her aside from a
purely sexual one; André is never once concerned with Claudine's struggle
to achieve selfhood. For him, sexuality is a static component of identity and
he interprets Claudine's "frigidity" as a marker of sexual confusion (hence
his suggestion that she must be a lesbian) rather than as an expression of
her lack of fulfillment in a world that demands her erasure both as a
woman and as an artist. Claudine's erotic escapade is foiled because she
feels no passion or desire in her sexual relations with Maud; nonetheless,
as she attempts to please Maud sexually she experiences a rare moment of
selflessness, an emotion which she experiences with neither André nor with
Hans, her final paramour. Revealing the extent to which she is prevented
access to her own agency, Maud remains acted upon but never acting in
this scene, as in the next in which Claudine voyeuristically watches Maud
and André's friend, Jean, make love; he too is unable to fulfill Maud sexually and Claudine is disappointed. Even her voyeurism does not enable her
to access the sexuality represented by Maud's black, female *marabout*
body, which remains a closed book to all the characters in the novel. As
Lionnet suggests (in her analysis of works by Condé and Warner-Vieyra)
"the body has therefore . . . a double function, namely, to represent the real
and to mediate the possible" ("Inscriptions" 34). In this sense, then, Maud's
body can be understood as serving such a double function: as a woman of
the working class she invokes the possible "real" at the same time as she is
made to represent the stereotyped Haitian woman (such as Durand's
choucoune), whose only purpose is to be a vessel for sexual gratification.

Had Claudine been able to transform her erotic interest in Maud into a productive union meant to empower both women against their disenfranchisement, then Maud's status as the textual inscription of the *marabout* woman here would have, indeed, been revolutionary. As it stands, Magloire stops short of making such a union possible, suggesting that both women are unable to transcend the limitations of their roles as women within the Haitian class/caste system.

Claudine and Maud are representative of a generation of Haitian women who cannot negotiate their positions at the crossroads of various polarized identities: between blackness and whiteness, privilege and poverty, femalehood and malehood. What Magloire suggests in *Le mal de vivre* is that women in Haiti experience their oppression not only as a function of their *Haitiennité* but also as a function of their sexualization within overdetermined class, sex, and racial categories. Haitian women writers such as Magloire are thus involved in the articulation of a heterogeneous Caribbean literature of hybridity, which Lionnet, referring to Francophone "postcolonial" literature, has described as a "mongrelization or *métissage* of cultural forms [that create] hybrid identities, and interrelated, if not overlapping, spaces" ("Logiques métisses" 101). The concept of *métissage* is extremely powerful in that it problematizes the notion of the bipolarization of cultures into positive and negative spheres (First and Third Worlds, for instance) and confirms that "even before colonial times, the interrelations of cultures was the norm" (Lionnet, "Logiques métisses" 106). In this analysis, I want to push the concept of *métissage* beyond its racial or ethnic connotations to encompass a hybridity within a "unified" culture, a nation-state such as Haiti, in which the multiple levels of social existence are brought together in one or more characters and expressed through them as the *métissage* not only of race/culture but also of class and sexuality. It is for this reason that Claudine's attempt to formulate and articulate her identity in the Haitian context encompasses, without resolution, the exploration of alternatives to rigid sex roles.

Ultimately, Claudine's search for self-expression and self-fulfillment through what is in the end the story of the passage of her body through a male-defined society is curtailed by those whom she chooses as lovers. Her boyfriend, André, himself a painter, responds to Claudine's articulation of her desires in the following manner: "Claudine, you are too romantic. Novels are one thing and life is another. Look at all your friends who married for love. What do they have to show for it? They're pathetic!"[10] André, of course, is unaware of the ways in which the meaning Claudine derives from literature informs her attempt to construct an identity. She is not so much enraptured by the idea of "true love" as she is by the possibility of attaining a sense of her own worth, of confronting the passions she has only experienced vicariously through her reading. For Claudine, there is no separation between life and art since she experiences the one through the other. She does, however, fear that she has lost her desires to the world of art, as she comments: "The sensual feelings I experience are provoked only by an erotic image in a movie or by a description of a love scene in a novel."[11] Thus, Claudine continues to search in vain for the trigger that will unleash her sexuality, which until now she has avoided confronting in much the same way as she has evaded nineteenth-century ideals of marriage and motherhood—through solitude.

Because she rejects the respectability of marriage, choosing instead to live alone, Magloire's defiant Claudine is an "anomaly" (11) in the Haitian context. Claudine calls her bungalow, surrounded by its trees filled with birds and its garden, a "dream realized" (11). In fact, it is in the space of her garden that Claudine comes closest to finding her identity. She interrupts her writing "to look at the trees, their leaves rustling in the breeze or a bird fluttering from branch to branch."[12] It is in this state that Claudine believes herself to have found wisdom, only to have it wrenched from her at the thought of her aloneness, as well as presumably at the thought of confronting a blank page she has failed to imbue with her spirit. At such times, she says, "often the emptiness of my life grips me painfully."[13]

Ironically, then, Claudine's ability to come alive in her "natural" surroundings suggests that it is in an association between herself and the Haitian landscape that she will ultimately find her identity. Yet, this cannot come to pass at present because the association she draws between herself and the natural world continues to bind her to the stereotypes she herself adopts, for example, in her relationship with Maud—stereotypes that equate land and woman by figuring both in terms of fertility/fecundity and rape/objectification. Embracing these stereotypes, Claudine is unable to effect the liberation of her imagination from the space of her mother's closet and the encroaching walls of her childhood attic that would enable her to create a new sense of landscape, and, by extension, a new definition of Haitian nation-woman-hood. This negotiation of time and space isolates Magloire's protagonist and prevents her from being able to relate fully either to the physical landscape that surrounds her or to the landscape of the novel that demands her full attention. Magloire thus shows that Claudine actively interrupts her own narrative, and, in so doing, demonstrates that the text of her character's life can never be completed. Claudine chooses to abandon her writing and, as she does so, her body becomes her only tool of communication. There is a shift in the novel, then, from an exploration of the possibilities of sexual liberation through storytelling to the textualization of sexuality. Claudine no longer dreams through the novel; instead, she fulfills her role as a character within its confines and becomes all that she most despises. Magloire's Claudine demonstrates that for women whose lives are defined primarily by privilege, symbolic unions to the Haitian landscape will remain unfulfilled precisely because the "motherland" for which they yearn is held captive by an overtly patriarchal social order.

As a result, Claudine is continuously intent on the need to "justifier [son] existence" (12). She cannot justify her existence as André can through his painting, because, as a Haitian woman, she has had no models (artistic or otherwise) to follow. She is a scandal, as she lives what she calls a little life of egoism (12). Unable to withstand the social pressures entailed by such a life, she declares that "a true love would give meaning to my life."[14] In attempting to find herself in a (male) double, Claudine forecloses the possibility of self-discovery and self-fulfillment. Her life is eventually defined by Hans, a married man for whom she says "I could die or kill."[15] At the end of the novel, Claudine loses all self-respect as she runs out into the rain, half-naked, feet floundering in the mud, to beg Hans to stay with her instead of returning to his wife. In this image, we are brought full circle to the novel's opening lines: Claudine is no longer using the landscape she had hoped to tame as a symbol of her despair; instead, she becomes subject to its viscissitudes. "My life is a dead-end," she says. "I suffer endlessly but I love my pain. I do not want to heal."[16] Claudine's masochism is symptomatic of her despair; her pain is replacement for the emptiness that defined the contours of her life before her affair with Hans, who finally betrays her in order to appease his wife. As a single woman, Claudine is, like Maud, a woman without status. Claudine cannot recover from Hans' betrayal and she does indeed become "mad": "All morning I walk through the city hallucinated with the hope of finding him alone at last. In the evening, I wait for him. I must hope at all cost that I will get him back because without this hope I will have nothing left. I would rather die."[17] Her final act of transgression, her affair with Hans, is subverted as she becomes the "other," the woman whose existence outside of marriage strips her of class identification and makes of her a target for sexual aggression.

In *Le mal de vivre,* the return to "home" can only be enacted through the male figure. Self-knowledge results in self-destruction precisely because female identity cannot be fulfilled through the phallogocentric social and symbolic order. Claudine abandons her search for self because she has internalized the oppression of Haitian women and has found no plausible alternative expressions of female identity in the world around her. She is a symbol of *métissage* gone awry as she transgresses class, race, and sexual lines only to refuse to renounce the very privilege that allows her the mobility to explore the various aspects of her identity. That privilege, in fact, makes her blind to the fact that she does indeed have access to a Haitian identity that need not be male; this identity is represented by Maud whom she rejects on the basis of her class but whom she also cherishes, ironically, because of the color of her skin.

Through Claudine, Magloire dramatically redefines the phrase *léspoua fè viv,* for her protagonist clings to a hope that can only lead to her ultimate destruction. Claudine's need for male approval and acceptance is at the heart of her alienation from her identity as an artist and as a Haitian woman; failing to rearticulate her world in these terms she falls into the abyss of invisibility.

Searching for the Mother/Goddess

In Edwidge Danticat's *Breath, Eyes, Memory,* Haitian women are represented through images drawn from folk traditions. The subtext of the story of three generations of the Caco family involves a careful subversion of Haitian tropes of identity. Danticat uses the symbol of the *marassa,* the cult of twins in *vodou,* to highlight the divisions that are created between women who have been brought up to deny their sexuality as well as each other. In invoking *vodou* traditions, she strives, moreover, to disassociate them from their prevalent use as tools of state control during the Duvalier years of terror. Danticat also makes use of the principles of *palé andaki,* a practice of code switching particular to Haitian creole, to underscore the complex dimensions of Haitian women's survival in varied social contexts. Danticat thus engages the challenge of Haiti's cultural doubleness in order to emphasize the need to reformulate the traditional Caribbean novel genre to reflect the particularities of Haitian women's lives.

In *Breath, Eyes, Memory,* narrative acts ironically as a metaphor for the absence of writ social existence; in this way, the physical text becomes the manifestation of the social forces at work in Haiti over the span of three generations of Haitian women. It also provides a vital link to indigenous languages while using the vehicle of literary production to supply the context for female liberation. The Cacos of Danticat's novel are a family of women from the working classes who struggle both to maintain continuity from one generation to the next, and to reshape through education the fate of the younger generation, represented by the narrator and protagonist, Sophie. Throughout the novel, education, and, more specifically, literacy, are posited as the only means to salvation; ironically, access to literacy is connected to a life of exile, to a move from valley to city for the older generation within Haiti, from Haiti to the United States for the younger. Resisting this movement, the older generations, represented in part by Sophie's grandmother, cling to their sense of Haiti's "glory days," an invisible African past that is textualized in the novel through the oral folk tales the older generations tell to the younger ones. It is through the thematization of secrecy that the damage resulting from generational disruption is unveiled. The language of the ancestors, which grows increasingly difficult to access, is the key to each woman's freedom.

Sophie is alienated from her natural mother by the latter's memory of the rape of which she is a product, an act that is duplicated by her mother who abuses her sexually in adolescence under the guise of protecting her from future harm. Martine, who wants to make sure that Sophie remains sexually "whole," persists in describing her acts of sexual abuse in terms of a spiritual "twinning" of souls. Presented as a ritual enacted between mother and daughter through the generations, the "testing" that scars Sophie for life is a product of the suppression of female sexuality and the codification of women's bodies as vessels for male gratification in marriage. The Cacos perpetuate this ritual, although none of the women in the family has ever married, in what Danticat terms a "virginity cult."

It is because she has internalized the ideology of female inferiority that Sophie's mother is capable of abusing her daughter. Taught to despise the female body for itself and to covet it only as a means by which to acquire a male mate, Sophie's mother commits incest against her daughter, rationalizing her behavior as necessary to her daughter's survival. Social worker and therapist E. Sue Blume notes in *Secret Survivors* that it is rarer for women to incest their children than it is for men. She writes: "Incest often manifests itself in a manner consistent with gender socialization: for a man, the abuse is generally overtly and directly sexual; for a woman, it may be more emotional, more focused on relationship and bonding, or perhaps manifested through care of the child's body, her primary domain" (7). The incest motif overwhelmingly present in the literature by women of the African diaspora—in the works of Toni Morrison, Alice Walker, Joan Riley,

Maya Angelou, to name the most notable—clearly demonstrates that Danticat's portrayal of incest between mother and daughter should not be taken as evidence that Haitian women are any more apt than other individuals to commit acts of incest against their daughters and that men are hapless bystanders to such abuse. Rather, Danticat demonstrates (as do the aforementioned women writers) through this aspect of her text the *extent to which the subjugation of women* has led to one mother's sexual oppression of her own daughter. The effect of this subjugation is that the mother believes that she is taking "care of the child's body" when she is in fact subjecting it to very abuse from which she is hoping to save it.

After having been raised for most of her early life by her mother's sister, Tante Atie, in Haiti, Sophie is summoned to New York by her mother. The community rejoices at what appears to be a "natural" turn of events, the reclamation of a daughter by her mother. As grandmother Ifé says to Sophie: "You must never forget this. . . . Your mother is your first friend" (24). Sophie, however, knows her mother only as an absence; she reacts to her dislocation by withdrawing from the world which until this time had seemed so familiar, so unchangeable. When she is told that she will have to leave Haiti for her mother's New York, she says: "I could not eat the bowl of food that Tante Atie laid in front of me. I only kept wishing that everyone would disappear" (14). Only later do we learn that her inability to eat the bowl of food is symptomatic of what will become a cycle of bodily abuse; once she is in the United States—a place her mother describes to her as a sort of paradise—Sophie becomes bulimic.

For Sophie, the United States is not a garden of Eden; instead, it is a place in which she hungers for the comfort of her true mother, Tante Atie, whom she honors in a poem as a brilliant, delicate, yet nonetheless hardy, yellow daffodil. That image is connected to Erzulie who is the "Goddess of Love, the divinity of the dream. . . . [t]o Haitian women, the goddess . . . signifies escape from a life in which women carry a greater share of work and suffering" (Steber 110). Thus Sophie recalls:

> As a child, the mother I had imagined for myself was like Erzulie, the lavish Virgin Mother. She was the healer of all women and the desire of all men. She had gorgeous dresses in satin, silk, and lace, necklaces, pendants, earrings, bracelets, anklets, and lots and lots of French perfume. She never had to work for anything because the rainbow and the stars did her work for her. Even though she was far away, she was always with me. I could always count on her, like one counts on the sun coming out at dawn. (59)

Sophie's mother can never be Erzulie, who is herself most often imaged as a mulatta of the upper classes (Desmangles 132), and whose power—defined as both erotic and sexual—is derived from these combined class and race distinctions. She nonetheless seeks Erzulie's elusive powers, attempting to transcend Haitian barriers of class, race, and color by exiling herself to the United States, where she appears to find love with Marc Chevalier, a lawyer and a member of the Haitian elite. "In Haiti," she explains, "it would not be possible for someone like Marc to love someone like me. He is from a very upstanding family. His grandfather was a French man" (59). Marc idolizes Erzulie and decorates his home with small busts of her image (56); it would appear that Sophie's mother has begun to access Erzulie's world. Danticat, however, quickly undermines the association of the mother with Erzulie.

In *The Faces of the Gods,* Leslie Desmangles writes that "[i]n combination with Damballah, Ezili guarantees the flow of human generations," and that "[s]he is believed to have given birth to the first human beings after Bondye [the supreme Being] created the world" (131–132). Erzulie, or, as Desmangles writes, Ezili, is the mother of us all, that is, of all Haitians, male and female; as such, she is all-powerful and all-controlling. Her power over men is legendary, as is her power over other *vodou loas* [gods] (Desmangles 133). She is often shown wearing a crown or a halo, "a symbol of her transcendent power and of her radiating beauty" (Desmangles 144). It is crucial to note that Erzulie's power is defined in terms of her relationships, primarily to male deities and human male subjects: she is concubine to all but subjugated to none; she is beyond containment. As much as she seeks to transcend temporality by emulating Erzulie, Sophie's mother is bound to self-negating mores of womanhood embedded in nineteenth-century ideals; for this reason, Sophie is the painful memory of what she perceives to be her failure as a woman.

Sophie's mother never comes to term with the fact that the man who raped her in her late teens robbed her of her sexual autonomy; she perceives herself as "damaged," incapable, in fact, of being Erzulie, because she is no longer "virginal," or "chaste," a status the Caco women associate with social mobility. It is through marriage that freedom from poverty, and endless toil, can be achieved; marriage, however, is an institution that, historically, has been socially constructed in such a way as to benefit men and deny women their autonomy. Thus, Danticat's protagonist recalls the story of a man who bleeds his young wife to death in order to be able to produce the soiled, bloody sheets of their first marriage night: "At the grave site, her husband drank his blood-spotted goat milk and cried like a child" (155). On the surface, it seems as if Sophie is being led away from such a tragic fate. In the United States, she will be freed from the constraints of class that attend marriage in Haiti; she will gain an education and no man will be able to reject her as one Mr. Augustin rejected her Tante Atie because of her illiteracy. That possibility, however, is as elusive as Erzulie's loyalties, for Sophie knows only what she is in the process of losing. As she leaves Haiti behind, she imagines the friend/twin she has never had: "Maybe if I had a really good friend my eyes would have clung to hers as we were driven away" (31). Sophie has no point of contact, no shared sight, with another human being who can complete for her her sense of self. Identity, Danticat appears to say, is inextricably linked with community, and the image of the twin, the true friend, is the vehicle for communal (re)identification.

Vodou and the Exploitation of Women's Sexuality

In *vodou* culture, the *marassas* are endowed with the power of the gods. Twins are *mystères* (mysteries), who, since they can never be deciphered, must be held in high esteem and revered. As Alfred Métreaux writes: "Some even contend that the twins are more powerful than the *loas*. They are invoked and saluted at the beginning of the [*vodou*] ceremony, directly after Legba."[18] This is no small thing, for Legba is the sun god, the keeper of the gates; he is thus associated with Christ and, as the "guardian of universal and individual destiny" (Desmangles 110), with St. Peter as well. Twins are believed to "share a soul": "Should one die, the living twin must put aside a bit of all food he [sic] eats, or a small part of any gift given him [sic], for the other" (Herskovits 204). Sophie's inability to eat, then, can be understood as having been caused by her separation from the unknown twin, the best friend she wishes she had had in Haiti. On the other hand, because she has been deadened by her loss of family, Sophie can in some sense be regarded as the twin who has died. Her "living twin" on this reading would be the Haitian landscape to which she had last looked to for comfort in her departure from Haiti; it stores away its resources while awaiting her return. Sophie's mother, however, insists on figuring herself as her daughter's *marassa*. The image of her mother as her *marassa* only serves to terrorize Sophie and alienate her from her identity, which becomes both sexualized and demonized in its association (by the mother) with *vodou*.

In the United States, when Sophie has her first love affair, clandestine and innocent, with an older man, Joseph, her mother suspects her of ill-doing; this is the occasion for Sophie's first "test." Characteristically, Sophie prays to the "Virgin Mother" Mary/Erzulie while her mother tells her a story about the *marassas,* "two inseparable lovers . . . the same person duplicated in two" (84). At first, the story seems to be a warning to Sophie to resist her desire for sexual union with a man. Her mother says: "When you love someone, you want him to be closer to you than your *Marassa.* Closer than your shadow. You want him to be your soul. The more you are alike, the easier this becomes." In the story, then, the union betwen man and woman is presented as a bond that can only be a pale imitation of the union between the *marassa,* who are described as reflections of oneself: "When one looked in the mirror, the other walked behind the glass to mimic her." The story, as does the testing, ends chillingly as Sophie's mother tells her:

> The love between a mother and daughter is deeper than the sea. You
> would leave me for an old man who you didn't know the year before.
> You and I we could be like *Marassas.* You are giving up a lifetime
> with me. Do you understand? There are secrets you cannot keep. (85)

Secrecy is central to the image of Haiti created by Danticat, suggesting that holding on to a sense of renewed options is a narrow, almost non-existent possibility. Secrecy, in the above passage, refers to Sophie's inability to keep her body to herself: it is positioned as her mother's reflection and is consequently not her own. But the truly unkeepable secret is the act of abuse itself, which Sophie attempts to exorcise through the only thing she feels she can still control: food.

Sophie's bulimia is a manifestation of her sexual abuse. As E. Sue Blume explains, eating disorders are manifestations of the ways in which women who have been abused attempt to regain control over their bodies; ironically, these attempts at regaining control perpetuate the cycle of abuse. Blume writes: "Most men can achieve mastery in the real world, but many women can exercise total control only over their own bodies. Additionally, rigid social expectations define women through their appearance. Body size relates to power, sexuality, attention, self-worth, social status and the aftereffects of incest" (151). Unlike anorexics, who try to rid their bodies of the sex characteristics they feel (consciously or unconsciously) have led to their victimization, bulimics attempt to *maintain* the sex characteristics they feel they must possess in order to achieve a "perfection" which will

put a stop to their abuse (Blume 152–153). Sophie becomes the prototypical sexual abuse survivor described by Blume as she attempts to control her
body—which remains the only socially sanctioned site for her rebellion—
precisely because it has fallen beyond her control. She binges and purges in
an effort to cleanse herself of her violation.

Sophie's eating disorder will not, however, erase the abuse she has
suffered. Through the "testing," Sophie loses her mother a second time and
instead of becoming her twin becomes her victim. She clings to an elusive
image of perfection, of Erzulie, which neither she nor her mother can attain. Like Nadine Magloire's protagonist Claudine in *Le mal de vivre,*
Sophie cannot reclaim her identity because her *Haitiennité* demands that
she deny her desires as well as her need for sexual autonomy. This implicit
denial of self, as I will demonstrate below, leads Danticat to reject those
cultural markers most associated with Haitian Afrocentricity, such as *vodou*
and matriarchal family structure, because they signify oppression rather
than liberation; *this is not to say that, in so doing, she abandons what those
markers represent.* Rather, Danticat shows that in order to reclaim the landscape of the female body and of Haiti, both must be redefined. Thus, the
novel introduces at its start a set of seeming dichotomies that will be re-
shaped and reimaged as the plot advances: mother versus daughter, food
versus starvation, language versus silence, ritual versus violation, *marassa*
versus life partner. Each of these seeming dualities reflect the rigid sex
roles Haitian women are taught to desire, even though they defy those social sanctions through their very acts of daily survival.

As Ira P. Lowenthal points out in his essay "Labor, Sexuality and the
Conjugal Contract," Haitian women of the rural working classes appear to
have some power equity due to the fact that many are market women (han-
dling booths at the market, money, trade) while their male counterparts
work the fields. Lowenthal writes: "men make gardens for someone and
that someone is invariably a woman. . . . she is a socially recognized spouse
of the man. The control of produce, then, as opposed to production itself,
falls to women—as men's gardens mature" (18). Lowenthal points out that
this seeming inversion of sex roles does not guarantee women's economic
autonomy. Instead, it suggests a potential that is never realized because
male and female sex roles are maintained in such a way as to prevent an
equal division of labor. Women continue to have to sustain the home even
as they manage the commerce: "domestic labor is overwelmingly the responsibility of women and . . . [w]hen men cry out, as they sometimes

do—especially when actually faced with the unsavory prospect—that they 'can't live without a woman'. . . . it is to these basic domestic services provided by women that they primarily refer" (20). Put more bluntly, in Haiti, as in other parts of the Caribbean, even though a quasi-matriarchal system seems to be in place, it is one "that represses women" (Kurlansky 135): "women are stuck running the household, and if they are tough and strong it is because their children would starve if they weren't" (Kurlansky 134). The Caco women thus represent the sort of matriarchal family formation that has been celebrated in many Caribbean women's writings (most notably in Audre Lorde's *Zami* and Michelle Cliff's *Abeng*, both semi-autobiographical novels), but which, in most Haitian contexts, is one born both out of necessity and out of the legacy of African social formations where quasi-matriarchal societies did indeed flourish and empower women.[19]

In the Caribbean context, where identity resides at the crossroads of creolization or *métissage*, matriarchal society is a product of a disrupted society (or societies). Sexuality takes on a striking importance in a repressive matriarchal society for it is the ultimate site of women's subjugation and is, by extension, the site of possible empowerment. As Lowenthal explains,

> [f]emale sexuality is here revealed to be a woman's most important *economic* resource comparable in terms of its value to a relatively large tract of land. Indeed, when discussing their relations with men, adult women are likely to refer to their own genitals as *interèm* (my assets), *lajan-m* (my money), or *manmanlajan-m* (my capital), in addition to *tèm* (my land). The underlying notion here is of a resource that can be made to work to produce wealth, like land or capital, or that can be exchanged for desired goods and services, like money. (22)

Lowenthal insists, however, that, just as women wield full control over the goods balanced precariously in weaved baskets upon their heads for sale at market, they have full control of the ways in which their bodies are exchanged or marketed. Yet, if women did, in point of fact, have full control over their bodies and their sexuality, one would expect that they would be endowed with power in whatever social strata in which they were born; this, of course, is not the case. Thus, when women attempt to control their sexual interactions with men, they do so precisely because social and sexual power is taken out of their hands from birth: theirs is an unrelenting struggle.

Danticat's very carefully exposes this truism as one would expose a frame of film to light. The result is not often clear or pleasing to the eye, but it reveals part of what has been obscured by inadequate representations of the difficulties faced by women in Haiti and elsewhere. Haitian women are not immune to what Catharine MacKinnon has called the "body count [of] women's collective experience in America," by which girls are taught to suppress their own ambitions in order to fulfill the sexual needs of men (23). As Danticat shows, even in a family in which men do not "exist," the threat of sexual violence and subjugation remains a reality too immediate to be ignored.

Learning the Mother Tongue

In many ways, the novel's true heroine is Tante Atie who gains a sense of self and identity only as she grows older. Rejected by a suitor, Augustin, because of her illiteracy, Atie's social role becomes that of care-taker to her aging mother, Ifé. Nonetheless, Atie rebels against her position in the family, and when she has to give up her role as Sophie's surrogate mother-figure, she begins to construct for herself a new life. Her life is re-activated through her being taught to read and write by a market woman, Louise, with whom she develops a strong love relationship. Although both Atie and Ifé have worked diligently to give Sophie and her mother the means to escape the endless cycle of work, poverty, and exploitation, Ifé strongly resents Atie's newfound independence at the same time that she covets it. Through Atie, Danticat presents literacy as a metaphor for the fulfillment of identity and yet she also demonstrates that freedom for the Haitian woman cannot be achieved solely through education; she must also be able to control the passage of her body through a society that rejects her presence and demonizes her sexuality.

Atie defies social convention by severing her relationship to her mother (whom it is supposed she will take care of as she ages since Atie is yet "single") in order to have a primary relationship with Louise. Her relationship with Louise is, in fact, subtly coded as a lesbian love relationship. Although there is the merest hint that the two are not sexually involved, suggested through numerous scenes in which Louise leaves at sundown and in which the two only come togther at daylight, theirs is undoubtedly an erotic relationship. They embody the power of the erotic as theorized by Audre Lorde who writes:

> The erotic is a measure between the beginnings of our sense of self and the chaos of our strongest feelings. It is an internal sense of satisfaction to which, once we have experience it, we know we can aspire. For having experienced the fullness of this depth of feeling and recognizing its power, in honor and self-respect we can require no less of ourselves. (54)

This reflects Atie's experience with Louise as she grows in her "sense of self," escaping the strict confines of her role as dutiful daughter and becoming more literate in her own (woman's) language. Access, through education, to both the past and to the future provides an increasingly empowering double-sightedness imaged through the *twinning* of these two women. Louise's descriptions of her relationship with Atie imply as much. She says: "We are like milk and coffee, lips and tongue. We are two fingers on the same hand. Two eyes on the same head" (98). In the end, these two women are the true *marassas* of the novel. Danticat deftly and subtly inverts the linguistic terms with which relationships between women can be described in the Haitian context in a manner akin to that involved in *palé andaki* (as described more fully below), the process of code switching within creole (the equivalent, perhaps, to what Zora Neale Hurston has defined as "specifyin'" in Black English). Through this code switching, Danticat appears to reject the identifiable markers of *vodou* and to reformulate them in terms which are inclusive of its origins but that also encapsulate the exigencies of working-class and impoverished women. Creole is the mother tongue that links these two women to their Haitian identity, and, thus, to each other, through the process of literacy. Through creole, that literacy retains its oral roots.

Why should literacy be linked so explicitly to Haitian women's process of self-actualization? The languages in which we speak, write, and communicate are signifiers of the societies and/or cultures we live in. Haitians, male and female, have, since Haiti's tragic beginnings, been made to feel as if our ways of speaking are deficient. Creole, to this day, is often referred to as a "bastard" tongue, "denigrated as a lesser language of French" (Lawless 100), even though it has certainly always been the "dominant" language of the country despite efforts to enforce French as the language of the polished, accomplished, upper classes. For the last several decades, creole has been taught in the schools and used as the common language of the untutored in various literacy programs. It is a living language that is continuously changing; it accurately reflects a culture that is constantly in flux both socially and politically.

Cultural sociologist Ulrich Fleischmann notes in his article, "Language, Literacy, and Underdevelopment," that in rural Haiti, where the older Caco women live, creole culture distinguishes itself from those "recognized" in Western contexts in that it "cannot be considered as culturally integrated . . . for each member is in some way aware that his [sic] culture seen from a socially more elevated position appears as a 'lower variant' of the dominant culture." Haitians are acutely aware of the ways in which linguistic creolization is perceived to be a deviation, but they are also ardently opposed to assimilating.

Fleishmann describes oral creole as follows:

> [T]hough a nationwide intelligible form of Creole speech exists, there is a continuous change and generation of meanings in the narrow local context. Therefore, Creole speech can take on double and even multiple meanings. The information it conveys can vary considerable according to the social context. The diligent use of contradictory explicit and implicit references, for instance, is a highly esteemed art which Haitians call *palé andaki.* (109)

In effect, Danticat's novel is speaking *andaki* to those who are open to the possibilities of cultural doubleness. A litle more than halfway through the text, readers are made aware that they have been reading in another language. When Sophie's mother comes to Haiti to reclaim her daughter for a second time, Ifé and Atie complain about their use of English. "Oh that *cling-clang* talk," says Ifé, "It sounds like glass breaking" (162). What should, in effect, be broken in the reader's mind is the illusion that s/he has been reading an English text; the narrative reveals itself to be a masquerade, and the unevenness that is palpable in the passages of dialogue between the Caco women (between those who have stayed in Haiti and those who have emigrated) can be seen as evidence that the text is in fact a creole one.[20]

Danticat's Atie becomes the translator of the camouflaged text, a translator to rival the Dahomean god Eshu, the trickster figure who has become the focus of some phallocentric, Afrocentric criticism, such as in Henry Louis Gates' *The Signifying Monkey.* Like the poeticized women of Dahomey in Audre Lorde's poetry collection, *The Black Unicorn,* Atie embodies a marginalized ancient African *woman-identified* culture in which "[b]earing two drums on my head I speak/ whatever language is needed/ to sharpen the knives of my tongue" (Lorde 11). Atie's language is one of covert resistance as she appropriates the French language through creole translations when she learns to read and write and as she appropriates the image of the *marassa* to constitute her own Haitian female identity.

As she becomes literate, Atie creates a new language in order to write down her thoughts in her notebook; Louise "calls them poems" (103). At times, Atie reads to the family from her notebook; one of her most significant creations is an adaptation of a French poem, which remains unidentified in the novel, given to her by Louise. Her poem serves a dual function—one can assume, first, that it is in creole, and secondly, it tells the same story as that of the young husband who kills his young bride because he wants to prove her virginity, or purity, to the community. The important difference, of course, is that the story is now told in Atie's voice:

> She speaks in silent voices, my love.
> Like the cardinal bird, kissing its own image.
> *Li palé vwa mwin,*
> Flapping wings, fallen change
> Broken bottles, whistling snakes
> And boom bang drums.
> She speaks in silent voices, my love.
> I drink her blood with milk
> And when the pleasure peaks, my love leaves. (134–135)

The line Danticat leaves untranslated suggests the interconnectedness of like spirits: she speaks my voice, thus, she is my voice. And since Atie's tongue is creole, it can never be entirely translated, nor does her love attempt that transmutation. The last two lines of the poem echo the traditional tale except that Atie has taken the place of the male hero; she occupies his position but is not male-identified.

This latter distinction leads us to the key element of Atie and Louise's relationship: the partings that figure so prominently in the text are metaphors for the non-acceptance of their union in their community, which denies that women can choose one another as their primary sources of emotional and erotic support. This societal rejection is verbalized by Atie's mother, Ifé, who continously opposes the relationship, saying "Louise causes trouble" (137) and "the gods will punish me for Atie's ways" (167). But Atie defies her mother and the community: "After her reading, she and

Louise strolled into the night, like silhouettes on a picture postcard" (135). And after Louise hears that one of her fellow market workers has been killed, Danticat chooses to reveal the women's closeness in an overtly erotic image: "Their faces were so close that their lips could meet if they both turned at the same time" (138). Their lips "could meet" but do not; what keeps the women from "turning" at the same time is the overt mysogyny of Haitian society that Danticat exposes in the shattering of Martine (Sophie's mother) and Sophie's own life; their lives are kept out of view, and silenced. The many departures that occur in the novel symbolize, like the last line of Atie's poem, these women's stifled desires. Their partings culminate in Louise's emigration to the United States; she leaves without saying goodbye to Atie, an event that surprises Sophie (171). Atie, however, speaks the same language as Louise: there is no need for the articulation of goodbyes, for she knows already the loss she is about to experience: "I will miss her like my own second skin" (145). For Atie and Louise, options are few. They are denied all but each other, but cannot live for and with each other in Haitian society and expect to survive the consequences of that transgressive choice.

In the end, Nadine Magloire's *Le mal de vivre* and Edwidge Danticat's *Breath, Eyes, Memory* resist the romanticization of the Caribbean, and of Haiti specifically, as a culture within which the infinite play of meaning, of subjectivity, can be achieved through the recognition of cultural creolization and/or *métissage*. Magloire reveals the novel genre as inadequate for the textual representation of Haitian women's lives at the same time that she convincingly represents the social and psychological mores that prevent her protagonist from being able to express her own identity. Claudine occupies a position at the crossroads of cultures but is not enabled by that positionality; hybridity, then, can only become a useful force if it is used in the service of disrupting rather than maintaining social and class privilege. Magloire's novel reveals that Claudine's inability to survive is ultimately a function of her being a woman in Haiti; as a woman, she is denied most privileges, and it is for this reason that she clings so fiercely to those privileges that class alone can provide. Similarly, Danticat's Sophie is caught between her memories of happiness in Haiti among women immobilized by their illiteracy and her exile to the alienating U.S. landscape, which will alleviate the oppressions that attend female existence in Haiti. Danticat's use of *andaki* strategies of doubling within the novel form also underscores the need to reformulate the traditional Caribbean novel genre. It is up to us, as readers, to realize that both Magloire's and Danticat's heroines lose "le goût de vivre" because Haitian/North American culture has relegated them to the margins of a text they cannot forcibly rewrite. In that resounding silence, in the absence of textual representations of identity that reflect a vision of hope, we should hear the "cri du coeur [cry of the heart]"[21] of all Haitian women whose bodies are subject to endless commodification in art, in literature, in everyday domestic life. If we fail to do so, then perhaps not even their shapes upon the sea shores will be left behind; their magic will remain as yet unwritten.

CHAPTER 5

Malè pa gin klaksonn

THE POLITICS OF *CULTURE-LACUNE* IN THE WORKS OF MARIE CHAUVET AND ANNE-CHRISTINE D'ADESKY

━━ ≡✦≡ ━━

Apocalypse: n.f. fin du monde; apocalyptique: adj. Qui évoque la fin du monde, de terribles catastrophes.
—Le Robert micro-poche

Un temps viendra, il venait d'en avoir la révélation, où les mains des exploités s'animeront pour réclamer justice.

[A time will come, he had just had the revelation, when the hands of the exploited would come together to demand justice.]
—Marie Chauvet, *Les rapaces*

If we do not now dare everything, the fulfillment of that prophecy, re-created from the Bible in song by a slave, is upon us: God gave Noah the rainbow sign, No more water, the fire next time.
—James Baldwin, *The Fire Next Time*

$\mathcal{S}$he is falling forward, very slowly, and faces ranging from light to darkest browns dance before her eyes. For a moment, she cannot tell what has happened. The faces are distorted with some emotion she cannot decipher as she feels her body cut through the air, her arms flailing in front of her without her control. They could be angry, those faces, or sad, or sorry for something they have done to her.

What *has* happened? The question murmurs through Solange's head endlessly as she attempts to mouth the words. She cannot even feel the pull of her lips as they try to shape each sound. She is falling slowly forward. This much she realizes. She recognizes the yellowing stones of the piazza; but now there is another color staining them. A red color, like the blood seeping from the cut throats of slaughtered cattle. Her blood? Now there is nothing before her but a blinding whiteness. Solange's mind panics, out of fear, out of desperation. And the pain begins.

Solange reaches out for her mother but her hands fall only on torn pieces of fabric, warm flesh. She is surrounded by strangers. She cannot breathe. Such pain. . . . She tries to remember her mother's touch, all the times she had sat Solange on the kitchen table to cleanse cuts on her knees with some soap water or a cloth soaked in *clairin,* moonshine.

Her mother's hands are rough from field work. They are gnarled like the branches of an old tree; each of her knuckles protrudes as if it were an unnatural growth. Her mother's hands look like an elderly woman's yet she is not old, barely thirty. Solange thinks of her mother's hands as having lived many lives because they struggle so to work all day, to put food on the table, to spread ointments on the cuts and scrapes Solange never seems to stop having. Now that she is going to school, Solange tries hard to stay out of trouble. It is a hard thing to do, what with this matter of running, always running—away from *macoutes,* secret police, people you cannot even label or recognize who want to do you harm because they can gain something out of it. Your life could be worth nothing more than a meal, a pack of cigarettes, a broken promise.

Promises. Solange promised her mother she would not stay long under the lamps of the piazza. She promised she would study hard and then return home. She can no longer feel her hands, her arms, legs, the muscles in her face. There is simply great pain and great fear. Will no one help her? Suddenly, the pain lifts. Then she realizes that it is only her body that has been lifted. It is her mother come to rescue her, to make her keep her word. Solange is glad her mother has come but she cannot thank her; she cannot think. Soon, she will feel nothing, not even her mother's arms around her body.

. . . a mother's cry rising with the twilight of a day which is never new, but simply repeated. The last breath of a daughter. The unexpected disruption of silence: the release of a bullet into soft flesh, into a mother's heart. The death of a child. This is what the end of the world feels like.

Apocalyptic Rhetoric at Century's End: Whose World, Whose End?

Every end of century brings with it images of doom, discussions of the coming of the world's end, predictions of how the world will ultimately fall to pieces. With the advent of nuclear arms, an end that appeared to be far in the future has come to seem imminent and is a belief reflected in everyday images of popular culture which suggest that the world in which we live is gravitating toward destruction. This sense of imminent disaster has also been taken up—most notably in the mid-eighties—in academic discourses intent on deciphering the knowability of human existence (past and future); this discourse has come to be known as apocalyptic rhetoric. Apocalyptic: meaning, evoking the end of the world or terrible catastrophies. Stephen O'Leary notes in his recent study *Arguing the Apocalypse: A Theory of Millenial Rhetoric* that rhetoric (the art of persuasion in speech and writing), "since it is explicitly concerned with the relationship of texts and audiences . . . enables the critic to view apocalypse as both literary text and social movement, and to incorporate insights from sociology, psychology, history, theology, and literary criticism without being bound by the limitations of these fields" (195); thus, the apocalyptic speaker/writer has a culturally and historically defined view of the world garnered from a variety of fields of study that she or he conveys coherently to her or his audience, thereby producing what can be examined and understood as a cohesive social phenomenon.

Why should apocalyptic rhetoric be in any way relevant to the question of Haitian women's identity, to Haiti in particular, or to any country of the Third World? In my opinion, it is essential to confront this phenomenon, the rhetoric of apocalypse, for it presents us with yet another form of neocolonial thought that suppresses a crucial facet of global reality—again, the exploitation of the South by the North. It is a rhetoric which reveals the ways in which neocolonial ideologies have themselves constructed the cultural lacunae, gaps or disruptions, inherent in those cultures that have suffered through the process of colonization. I am suggesting, then, that it is the necessity of undermining discourses which annihilate as they seek (paradoxically) to undo an imagined and unrealized global annihilation that is at the center of Haitian women writer's political strategies of resistance. Seen in this light, just as Haitian women's literature can be understood as confronting the textualized stereotypes of Haitians (as they did at the end of the U.S. Occupation)—whereby neocolonial forces sought to claim that Haiti could, somehow, destabilize and annihilate U.S. hegemony—as well as the sexualization and social limitations imposed upon Haitian women from within the culture itself by virtue of their sex and/or class—whereby women are positioned as the locus of cultural disintegration—their works can also be seen as actively participating in the unveiling of the ways in which the modern discourse of apocalypse also serves to denigrate as well as to constrict the aspirations of Third World inhabitants. They achieve the latter by revealing that the Third World is undergoing its own forms of apocalypse, which in the Haitian context is most notably imaged through the terror of the Duvalier regime. Thus, when we speak of the apocalypse in the West, we must first address two interlocking, crucial questions: Whose world? And, whose end?

By and large, apocalyptic rhetoric in the West has been unable to conceive of the world as "global village," that is, as a vast terrain occupied by very different, albeit interconnected, bodies of people who adhere to a variety of beliefs about the world around them. Apocalyptic rhetoric, as it seeks to predict the outcome of the struggle between good and evil from within a Judeo-Christian frame or predict "the logos of the farthest or last things" (O'Leary 195), cannot divorce its unitary vision of the world from its racialization. In other words, those who are considered "inferior" on the global scale because of the combined factors of their racial, ethnic, geographical and economic categorizations are either understood to embody or perpetuate the cataclysmic evil fatalists brace themselves against, or are discounted as actors in the world altogether. The Third World, then, is once again relegated to the bottom of the human scale even in matters of global annihilation, as if it plays no "real" role in the world's affairs. More crucial, however, is that in this disenfranchisement of the Third World from global affairs through apocalyptic rhetoric, the First World absolves itself of responsibility with respect to its relationship with that "othered" global community; in doing so, it fails to see the evidence before it, that is, that for the Third World and its inhabitants, the apocalypse is already underway.

Muriel Grimaldi and Patrick Chapelle, in their *Apocalypse: Mode d'emploi [Apocalypse: A User's Guide]*, argue that "[l]e Sud a le couteau sous la gorge [the South has a knife held against its throat]" (310). They come to this conclusion by examining the "development" strategies employed by the First World with regard to the Third World. Grimaldi and Chapelle write:

> In positioning themselves as guardians of the liberal temple, international institutions thus advocate all in one breath the limitation of the State's intervention, the slashing of social budgets and salaries, the unrestricted admission of foreign investors and the diffusion of a homogenized, Western model of consumption of which the "lavish manifestations" and sumptuous expenses are the sinister results in many countries of the Third World.[1]

At the mercy of an economic system beyond its immediate control, the Third World is forced to survive, paradoxically, through its exploitation. Haiti stands as a case in point.

The U.S. Agency for International Development (USAID), which has for decades overseen and financed Haiti's economic development,[2] has put into motion a plan to make Haiti competitive in the world market. According to it, "Haiti's greatest international comparative advantage [is] its hardworking, low-cost labor force" (Dewind & Kinley, 124); on this basis, it has proceeded to encourage an export-based economy. As it has done so, USAID has actively opposed union organizations that have demanded minimum wage increases and fair labor conditions, thereby preventing the very outcome they were mandated to ensure—Haiti's economic growth. The New York-based National Labor Committee, which monitors labor practices in Latin America and the Caribbean, notes that while Haitian workers were paid, on average, 23 U.S. cents a day in the early nineties, they were forced to attach labels in children's clothing contracted to Sears that "proudly advertised . . . [they] had been printed on recycled paper." The environmentally friendly label, meant to appeal to a mass market of concerned global citizens, does not reveal the role it plays in destroying the lives of Haitians; the U.S. consumer believes s/he is helping the world when s/he is contributing to its erosion. The NLC continues: "In 1992 *despite the OAS international embargo,* U.S. apparel firms and retailers . . . imported *$67,629,000*-worth of clothing sewn in Haiti" (my emphasis, Ridgeway 138). Not only that—a 56 percent decline in wages from 1983 to 1991 "coincided with a virtual doubling of Haitian apparel exports to the U.S." (Ridgeway 141). Thus, the Third World lives by dying, supplying (sometimes literally, as has been the case for Haitians whose blood was harvested for export to U.S. blood banks) the First World with its lifeblood. The apocalypse the North imagines as far off, or attempts to prepare itself for, is that which it inflicts upon the South; the apocalypse, as Grimaldi and Chapelle suggest, is already of this world.

Why has this definition of apocalypse not been given credence? Why is it that the ills of the Third World are so blatantly ignored? It is quite simply in the interest of the First World to perpetuate a rhetoric through which the Third World is represented as not only responsible for global patterns that are beyond its control but also as embodying the "evils" of the world; in this way, they are seen as an infantile shadow of the "real" world, that is, of the First World. The early twentieth-century travel literature that served to substantiate claims of European might or imperial superiority (such as

William Seabrook's *The Magic Island* or John H. Craige's *Black Bagdad*) exemplifies such a fostering of a now deeply ingrained perception of Third World inhabitants as marginal.

In his essay, "No Apocalypse, Not Now," Jacques Derrida points to nuclear criticism in particular as having ushered into being a state of global crisis in the First World through literature itself, the textual representation of an imagined, futuristic world end. The "nuclear age," Derrida contends, is one marked by a "critical zeal" which "would seek in the stockpile of history (in short, in history itself, which in this case would have this blinding search as its function) the wherewithal to neutralize invention, to translate the unknown into a known, to metaphorize, allegorize, domesticate the terror, to circumvent . . . the inescapable catastrophe, the undeviating precipitation toward remainderless cataclysm" (21). The implicit reliance on a linear and Western (for it is the West, the First World, that Derrida presumes to speak to, with, and for) history, by turn, guides the apocalyptic critic toward an understanding and explication of an unknowable future. That "revelation" is, as Derrida points out, fictive; it can never be true to an event which has not yet occurred and which would seem to lie somewhere beyond the grasp of the imagination. The revelation of non-revelation that Derrida seeks to expose throughout his essay exposes the very limitations of at least one strain of apocalyptic thinking. The cataclysms recorded in apocalyptic writings are of a nature that continuously pre-empts the possibility of absolute closure, of absolute annihilation. For Derrida, then, nuclear criticism is kept alive through the paradox of its announcement of an absolute end.

Interestingly, the industry of literature itself becomes indivisible from apocalyptic rhetoric; Derrida compares literature and literary criticism as the products of "stockpiling, of building up an objective archive" (25). Concurrently, this stockpile (of ostensibly historical data tracing the path of the West through time, its speed through time) is made realizable by its own "fictive or fabulous referent" (26-27). Hence, literature and nuclear criticism go hand in hand, for "literature gives us to think *the totality* of that which, like literature and henceforth in it, is exposed to the same threat, constituted by the same structure of historical fictionality, producing and then harboring its own referent" (27). This close alliance of literature with the nuclear age, with apocalyptic thinking, brings Derrida to the brink of totalization and, by extension, to an implicit collusion with the destruction of archives not referenced by his own criticism of the limits of the nuclear age. For, if nuclear criticism takes nuclear war to be "according to a structuring hypothesis, a fantasy or phantasm . . . the total destruction of the archive, if not of the human habitat, it becomes the absolute referent, the horizon and the condition of all the others" (28). What concerns me here is that even Derrida's rigorous and far-reaching deconstruction of this hypothesis places the Western literary tradition at the center of the conflict over what is known and what remains the imagined unknowable.

Derrida allows that "nonliterary memory" may escape the fate of this fabulousness, but what of a memory which is both literary and nonliterary, that is, both oral and literary, both textual and extratextual? The argument that nuclear war (or a similar apocalypse) is the absolute referent can only be true for those scribes (i.e., the creators of the archive) who adopt nuclear was as that absolute; I would argue that in Third World resistance literature we find another sort of scribe, a Third World scribe whose resistance is, in part, effected through an acknowledgment that an unreclaimable repository, an archive without history, without textual trace, has already been destroyed en masse. This is especially true for women in the Third World whose silence and apoliticization is assumed and thereby imposed, negating the recognition of all and any texts they might produce. For the Third World women scribe, then, apocalypse is not beyond imaging; it has already occurred. Recognizing that in the age of texts (and hypertexts) that those who have the power of the word have the power of the world, she seeks to bring to life that which has otherwise been buried or destroyed, to make her texts living entities.

Ideology, that which produces textuality in the first place, can take on features of the apocalyptic when it asserts itself as the guardian of a particular strain of thought, as absolute. The North, with its claims to moral, economic, and racial superiority, has in effect used ideology as a tool by which to secure supremacy over the South. In so doing, the North (or the West) textualizes the future of the world in light of its own heady claims to "truth" and "absolute knowledge" and in terms that absolve it of global awareness. Thus, when Derrida concludes that the final war will not be "in the name of" but that "that name in the name of which war would take place would be the name of nothing" he unwittingly silences or mutes the Third World scribe. Within this discourse, the Third World scribe can no longer attempt to wrestle the First World scribe for the power of the word— the true word which brings about transformation dialogistically as Paulo Freire would suggest—for it (the word) will suddenly no longer exist.

This discourse is strikingly similar to the rhetoric, which I discussed earlier, that is employed by mainstream Western feminists, a rhetoric that in dogmatically assuming the truth of anti-essentialism prevents the Third World woman from affirming her corporeal experience and hence, from using her lived experience in the service of her feminist politics. Apocalyptic rhetoric similarly denies the Third World scribe the means by which to affirm and describe the cataclysms the Third World suffers contemporaneously. Those who have the power of the word also have the power of the world; truth or absolute knowledge cannot emerge because the messenger is effectively dismissed. The Third World does not have an investment in the "nuclear" age because it has already been divested of its interest in that age; in other words, the Third World has been stripped of any ability to be an active participant in the "nuclear" age and the cataclysmic end it has engendered in the apocalyptic imagination, even though it provides the First World with the raw resources and labor necessary for its technological advance and might.

Views of the apocalyptic in the Third World context, if present at all, are utopic rather than dystopic, affirming a sense of the world's continuity. John May, in his study of apocalypse in the American literary tradition, claims that "primitive peoples" have no myths of "future cataclysm" since they see the world as regenerating itself cyclically. He concludes, however, that "[t]here is a millenialism . . . developing among contemporary primitives that is built upon cataclysm and the expectation of a new age; and all of these myths are understandably antiwhite and antichristian, representing a revolt against the failure of missionaries to live their religion" (6). May's reductive understanding of non-Judeo-Christian belief systems leads to the subordination of non-apocalytic, or pseudo-apocalyptic, visions of the world; what May ignores is that when apocalyptic beliefs appear to surface in indigenous people's communities, the focus is on *revelation* rather than annihilation, a distinction that leads me to believe that there is an implicit denial of apocalypse amongst indigenous peoples in favor of a faith in future justice. Interpretations such as May's thus insist upon the Western definition of the apocalyptic as a singular "truth." Haiti, however, stands as a classic case of a country in which a vast web of non-Judeo-Christian beliefs have been sustained through *vodou*—an indigenous religion despite the fusion of some aspects of African animist beliefs with Christian ones.

The "apocalyptic," in the large sense of the word, is circumvented in *vodou* by a firm belief in the regeneration of the world. In conformity with ancient animist beliefs of various African societies, believers in *vodou* do not see death of any kind as an end in and of itself but as the gateway to a new birth, to a higher state of being (Desmangles 61). This belief became especially important under colonialism as it enabled the colonized to make sense of a world in which their terms of existence lay beyond individual and communal control. Writes Leslie Desmangles: "Poverty becomes a means of salvation; illness, a source of divine power; and death is . . . transformed into life itself" (61). Haitians thus projected a utopic rather than dystopic sense of the world in order to resist and overcome oppression. Desmangles contends that in one important respect, Haitian *vodou* can be perceived as having absorbed Judeo-Christian millenarianism—Ogou ceremonies, in which Ogou, the Nigerian god of war, is invoked, are, he claims, millenarian in character because they recreate a past event in order to illuminate the present (151). The event these ceremonies recall is that of the Revolution.

By recalling the ancestral heroes of this salient moment in Haitian history—Boukman, L'Ouverture, Dessalines, or Christophe—*vodou* practitioners are able to affirm a significant moment of liberation in Haitian history. Desmangles interprets this ritual as millenarian because it appears to invoke the Judeo-Christian pattern of death and rebirth. He writes: "Ogou's manifestations as Boukman, Dessalines, and Christophe represent the death and resurrection of his devotees at every Vodou ceremony in his honor" (153). Though it is possible to interpret the Ogou ceremony as a process of "apocalypse" followed by "revelation" it seems to be unnecessary to do so. The ritualistic reenactment of the Revolution suggests that Haitian independence has been stripped away and that it must be regained. Furthermore, the repetition of the ceremony invokes a sense of the cyclic and a hope in the animist belief of continuous rebirth. It gains both political and cultural currency in its use of the historical rather than the mythical: the religious, the ritualistic, thus acquires revolutionary potential. Desmangles himself notes that this adaptation of African beliefs in the "New World" reflects a "*disengagement* of Christian millenarianism from its theological context" (emphasis mine) and reconstructs Haiti's revolution in order to articulate "a desire for freedom from political and religious suppression" (152). There is no doubt that this metamorphosis could only have resulted from the collision of disparate cultures under imperialist colonialism but it is yet another matter to conclude that the subsequent synthesis is definable only, or primarily, through the frame of reference of a Judeo-Christian ethos. By continually repeating and resurrecting the specter of insurrection and revolution in *vodou* ceremonies, Haitians defy the Western sense of the apocalyptic (implying even that they will cause the "apocalypse" of their oppressors, at least within Haiti) and express a deep faith in the never-ending.

My purpose in this chapter is to address the ways in which Haitian women writers have conveyed and/or defied the apocalyptic in their works. I believe that Haitians' first encounter with apocalypse, like that of all enslaved Africans, occurred in the Middle Passage; that encounter, paired with European imperialist powers, shaped a Haitian culture which existed both at the mercy of and in resistance to colonialism. Thus, in true *vodou* fashion, Haitian culture was born as West African ethnic groups were dismantled and/or utterly destroyed in the process of enslavement. Though Haiti freed itself from the yoke of slavery in the early 1800s, it did not achieve freedom from the ideology that has kept Haitians in a state of oppression since the late 1400s. With the emergence of the *noiristes* in the decades that followed the U.S. Occupation of Haiti, that ideology, which defined Haitian culture as a bastardization of French culture, was to become one that could not be understood in terms of dichotomies such as those of oppressor/oppressed, white/black, elite/peasant, North/South. The Duvalier regime and its legacy, as I will show, has contributed to the very real presence of the apocalyptic in the Third World at present.

Both Marie Chauvet's *Les rapaces* (1986) and Anne-christine d'Adesky's *Under the Bone* (1994) exhume the true terrors of the Duvalier regime as well as examine their military roots in the period during the 1915–1934 U.S. Occupation of Haiti. Both novels reveal that the combination of global economics and Duvalierism has resulted in the deterioration of social cohesion and the complete dehumanization of a people. That deterioration/dehumanization can be seen in nothing less than apocalyptic terms since it not only marks the near annihilation of a rich culture but also has the effect of forcing a beleaguered nation to find a means by which to unify itself and resist its own looming end. In this context, Haitian women are particularly at risk, since their right to unification is abrogated at every turn by a politicized culture that demands their servitude and imposes upon them a cult of silence.

Paradoxically, however, both Chauvet and d'Adesky suggest that it is through this silence that revolutionary potential can be garnered. In both novels, then, I find the theorem of *culture-lacune* instantiated in the suggestion of the possibility of revolution emanating from within, that is, from the realm of the subconscious, from the realm of dreams—dreams that, when acted upon in the name of a greater good, serve to empower women collectively, and ultimately, the entire culture itself. In Chauvet's novel, women are imaged as the suppressed, often mute, consciousness of the society while in d'Adesky's novel, women attempt to overcome silence through dreams that reconnect them to one another and that reimbue them with a sense of hope about the world, even as the society about them denies their oppression.

In her essay "'In Dreams Begin Responsibilities': Moral Imagination and Peace Action," clinical psychologist Mary Watkins makes a useful connection between the literary imagination and the possibilities of the subconscious for my analysis here. She claims that the imagination evokes the emotional as it "brings to life the particular" (72). It is a tool through which possibilities are explored and approached, though not in tangible form. In other words, the imagination brings us closer to the unimaginable but not necessarily into conscious fields of knowledge. Within this gap lies a dilemma, the individual decision to make of the imagination a tool for transformation or to regard it only as an idle psychological process. Watkins writes that "for the imagining to be moral . . . it must have another component, and that is action." She contends further that "we can use imagination's capacity for sympathy either as a stimulus for moral action or in the pursuit of self-interest" (75). This is true in any context but of crucial importance in the Third World, for there the choice to act morally or immorally based on one's own consciousness has immediate, visible, and often lethal consequences; clearly, in Haiti, the imagination, especially the role of the literary imagination, has played a tremendous part in transforming the ideological ground of the culture.

Watkins claims further that "images do not necessarily have intrinsic moral value" but "[h]ow we respond to them, act or refrain from action with regard to them, is crucial. Responsibilities can begin in a person's dreams and images, but they cannot be fulfilled there" (75). How do we progress from dream images to action, and more specifically, to moral action? Watkins suggests that moral action (that is, morally good action) results from dialogue with oneself, from effecting a negotiation amongst one's inner voices so as to transcend the barriers that any one of those voices might create to one's ability to act. For example, an inner voice of fear should be heard alongside one of assurance; if one can effect a dialogue between the part of oneself that is afraid and the part of oneself that is not, then the personal and/or cultural conflicts one experiences can be more readily solved. Without dialogue, there is simply stasis, an amoral stalemate, an inability to act.

In both novels, the world of the subconscious is made to appear more "real" than that which can be documented or textualized. Chauvet and d'Adesky thus engage the destructive power of apocalyptic rhetoric by inverting its codes; the imagination in both novels serves as the outlet for regeneration rather than desperation. The imagined is the realm of possibility rather than that of finality. Dreams are part of a better world, for the worse calamities have already taken place. In other words, since Haitians are already living through apocalypse, the "endtime" cannot be understood in terms of finality; rather, that potential "endtime" is understood as an opening out from annihilation, as a sign of hope for better things. That hope can only be kept alive through a hypertextuality that is not simply archival but ancestral, defying all sense of time, of linearity. It assumes a call for an ideological revolution that rests on the imagination for its actualization.

Haiti at World's End: The Apocalyptic Nature of Duvalierism

In the Haitian context, the Western concept of apocalypse has bread only disaster. Aside from the economic exploitation of Haiti, which in the last century has been enforced by the United States, the transformation of Haiti from an occupied nation-state to a totalitarian one is unique in that that process took on apocalyptic proportions. Haitian culture, forever altered by the U.S. Occupation, was further eroded by institutionalized violence perpetrated across class and color lines by military and paramilitary forces. The terror unleashed by Duvalier and his followers (both willing and coerced) appears to be almost unimaginable; it is the very nature of that violence, its quality of phantasm, that gives rise to my belief that Haitians are living through an apocalypse.

Historians unanimously agree that Duvalier *père* created a vast, intricate, unprecedented network of violence in Haiti. Michel S. Laguerre notes that Duvalier rose to power by exploiting the ideology of *indigénisme* that had arisen during the U.S. Occupation. An offshoot of that movement, the tenets of which were articulated in part by François Duvalier, was *noirisme*. Writes Laguerre: "in the 1940s [Duvalier] extolled the idea of the need for the country to empower itself through its reconciliation with its native cultural institutions and practices" (106). James Ferguson notes further that Duvalier's rise was made possible by the political climate of the country in the '40s: "Two autocratic mulatto regimes and increasing U.S. influence had served to frustrate and intensify the black nationalism which had emerged during the occupation" (31). Duvalier, a U.S. trained physician, garnered political and social power by espousing this Black nationalist philosophy. But unlike the former movement, *noirisme* limited its ideological parameters to the question of power; that is, according to *noirisme,* the middle and lower classes, whose racial and cultural profile was perceived to be more African than European, had a moral claim to "state power" (Trouillot 131). *Noiristes* did not, as Michel Trouillot points out, support the idea, as did *indigénistes,* that "no culture was superior, either in *savoir-faire* or *savoir-vivre*" (132); rather, it claimed the power of the people and, in so doing, usurped it.

Duvalier was ushered into power on September 22, 1957, a date that, as James Ferguson notes, marks Haiti's "first exercise in universal suffrage" (36–37). Those who voted on that day could not, however, cast private ballots, although women could for the first time vote alongside men. Duvalier had managed to create an image of himself as a social reformer (he also published a literary journal called *Griot* in which nationalists debated the direction Haiti should take), as a "man of the people," during the late 1940s and early 1950s. By the time of the elections, it had become clear that his course had not so much shifted as it had solidified into a plan of absolute authoritarian control. He exerted that control through the body of the army. "Duvalier," writes Trouillot, "ultimately owed his power to the army, which supervised the voting process and exercised a veto power over the presidency" (136). That army, of course, had been formed by the United States in 1915, and Duvalier appeared to model his own military administration on that of the Occupation.

Pierre Raymond Dumas suggests that armed forces in Haiti came to play the role they did under Duvalier as a result of the neocolonial nature of their inception in 1915: "the army [was] created with the goal of helping the Occupant to maintain the public peace by combatting all national resistance."[3] That Duvalier exploited this model of military administration is known—to what extent he exploited it is not because of the lack of documentation that resulted from what Trouillot calls the practice of "*kansoférisme*" or an "iron-pants" politics, through which press censorship was again instituted in order to mask the criminal activities of the government. Duvalier's regime was markedly different from the Occupation, however, in that class lines (or the line between oppressor and oppressed) were never clearly drawn on the basis of race; rather, they were drawn according to nuances of color and economic status in a variety of combinations. There was one clear line, however, and that was the one between Duvalier and the *en-*

tire population of Haiti. Here we should again reflect seriously on the implications of Duvalier's assertion that he stood for the Haitian flag and that any enemy of Duvalier's was in effect an enemy of the people. Through this rhetorical conflation of his own being with the nation, Duvalier implied that he would not tolerate any form of dissent, and indeed, he did not. He enforced a supression of dissent cataclysmic in its proportions. Writes Ferguson: "Duvalierism was in practice a form of institutionalized state terrorism; it also entailed massive corruption and a process of continual extortion" (46). But it was more than this. Michael S. Hooper, executive director of the New York-based National Coalition for Haitian Refugees, notes that in 1963, the International Commission of Jurists publicly declared:

> In the world today there are many authoritarian regimes. Many have at least the merit of being based on an ideology, but the tyranny that oppresses Haiti has not even this saving grace. A few men have come to power by force and stayed in power by terror. They seem to have only one aim, to bleed for their own gain, one of the most wretched countries in the world. (283–284)

That "bleeding" was achieved with the help of the United States, which, as I noted above, not only financed the Duvalier government but refused to denounce its flagrant disregard for human rights. The terror Haitians lived, then, was compounded by the lack of international response to their plight. The failure of the world to come to the aid of Haitians was not unprecedented—during the Occupation, the *caco* revolts, "[u]nlike the peasant resistance movements led by Augusto César Sandino in Nicaragua and the Gavilleros in the Dominican Republic . . . received no international support from either Latin America or other parts of the world" (Bellegarde-Smith 82). Trapped on the western tip of the island, Haiti suffered through an apocalypse, one unheeded (for the reasons enumerated above) by the First World community residing beyond the stifling world of Duvalierism.

The reason Duvalier's reign of terror took on cataclysmic proportions was that anyone, regardless of race, sex, class, age, or political affiliation, could become its victim. Michel Trouillot's analysis of the regime is the most succinct I have come across to date. He suggests that Duvalier's power rested upon "the extent of its social base" (153), a base that was maintained through what Trouillot calls "auto-neutralization." He defines the tactic as one that involved "increasing a group's access to political, economic, and ideological resources just enough so that the number of individuals in the group that aimed for new privileges became large enough to block the emergence of mass opposition" (156). In other words, Duvalier controlled the vast population of Haiti by having it control itself; Duvalier's policy was not, then, as David Nicholls contends, a "policy of non-interference" (11). More specifically, State control "systematically violated the codes governing the use of force by the state" (Trouillot 166) in four particular ways. Whereas past State violence had been directed against political adversaries, the Duvalier State 1) targeted "individuals beyond the socially accepted range for victims of state violence," including children, the elderly, and families of suspected political adversaries; 2) utilized the "torture-rape to acquaintance-rape to marriage" of women as a tool of political leverage;[4] 3) disregarded "rank and status in civil society"; and 4) "used violence against groups that could not be defined in political terms," such as villages, sports teams, etc. (Trouillot 167–168). It was not possible, under these conditions, for Haitians to unite around any point of commonality, be that a commonality of a familial, social, or religious nature, since not only were recognizably distinct social formations—such as the village, the town, a neighborhood, a *vodou* cult—that should have had no fear of being interfered with being arbitrarily killed, they were also being infiltrated by army/*macoutes* personnel whose aim was to wreak disunification amongst the members of those groups who remained. As horrific and pervasive as these methods were, they were implemented in subtle ways exemplary of the proverb *malè pa gin klaksonn* (disasters arrive without warning). The regime seemingly took shape overnight, breeding terror as the days of Duvalier's presidency-for-life accrued, without an end in sight.

La Culture-lacune: Cultural Resistance

In her book *Les rapaces* (*The Vultures*), Marie Chauvet[5] attacks the insidiousness of Duvalierism head-on. The novel, which is impossible to date accurately—it would seem from the events it recounts that it was written after 1971 but before the early eighties when it was posthumously published—unveils the psychology that informed Duvalier's methods of military control and demonstrates the ways in which individuals at all levels of the class hierarchy were coerced into taking part in the state's reign of terror. In this, the novel differs from Chauvet's avowed masterpiece, *Amour, colère, folie,* in which the novelist focused directly on the terror of the torture suffered by women under Duvalier. Passages from *Amour, colère, folie* like the following shocked readers (readers who were aware of such cruelty but pretended otherwise) so much so that Chauvet was forced to live in exile after the novel's publication:

> It seems that they've crippled her. Have you seen her? I'm still wait-
> ing for things to calm down. Eugénie Duclan has seen her. Secretly,
> but she saw her. She has nothing left, there. . . . It must be terrible.
> She told Eugénie that she saw her flesh fly in pieces as Calédu
> flogged her, flat on her back, legs open, kept down in that position
> by four prisoners, four dirty beggars to whom he then surrendered
> her. . . . I'm seventy-five years old. . . . never have I felt so much hor-
> ror and malediction hover over this city like today.[6]

These images of violence against women function on two interrelated levels: first, they defy the notion that Haitian women experienced torture any
less than Haitian men under the Duvalier regime. Secondly, they underscore the fact that there undoubtedly remain more stories to be told, terrors
at once beyond the scope of the imagination and endured by those who did
not survive to tell their stories themselves or to pass their stories on to
someone who could have then told those stories on their behalf.

In *Les rapaces,* Chauvet shifts the ground of her own revolutionary
discourse above by analyzing the nature of Haitian consciousness itself in
these years. She examines how the national consciousness of Duvalierism
severed Haitians from one another and she renders her central female characters, Anne and Adélia, moral voices in an otherwise politically and culturally corrupt state. The novel thus operates less on the historiographic
level of its predecessor than it does on the symbolic level; the novel in fact
demonstrates that the (phallogocentric) symbolic order cannot be trusted,
that the written or spoken word cannot free Haitians if it serves and nurtures the self-hatred that fosters the rule of a few. It must therefore be
reconfigured to mirror the real experiences of Haitian women and men.

The novel opens with the death of François Duvalier, and relates how
several members of the underclass react to witnessing his funeral ceremonies. One elderly man remarks with bitterness that their lot in life is inescapable since "God" has not seen fit to rectify the injustices under which
they all live. Another agrees: "Well said. . . . this is why we, we the poor,
cry out: long live the chief! whomever he may be!"[7] Yet another man,
physically deformed from some unknown ailment, notes the tragedy of
their impossible situation—an insurmountable hypocrisy: "For instance,
one day you will die. . . . if you die, they will throw your body into a hole

and no one, not even us, will ever know anything about it."[8] All three men are conscious of the fact that even the death of Duvalier will not alter the conditions of their existence. One comments: "They say in the mountains . . . that everything was settled before the death of the chief. The reins of power—he passed them on to his own."[9] Most important is that they not only acknowledge their political impotence but voice knowledge of the ways in which Duvalier destroyed the elite without ever bringing about change that would effectively free the massive underclass from its impoverishment.

Chauvet poignantly images the dilemma of being aware of yet powerless in the face of State control in the symbol of a black cat owned by a *macoute* named Lorius, a former "bread seller" (25), who has risen from poverty by taking a job as a military officer. She describes the cat as follows: "Raised in comfort, gorged like all the pets of the rich, he stole with pleasure anything which came within his reach."[10] The cat is like his owner: greedy, merciless. And he, like his owner, becomes the object of reprisals until the day he realizes that his life is intertwined with that of Lorius', who is finally carted away to prison by his enemies within the army. Like the impoverished men who speak in the opening pages of the text, the cat realizes his predicament in the power dynamics wielded by the State. Unlike these men, however, he has the luxury of being able to change: "His indifference persisted until the moment when he understood that their destinies were closely bound, that he would in turn be at the mercy of his most cruel enemies."[11] Chauvet then describes how the cat is forced to leave the rich quarters in which he has lived and descends, out of terror and necessity, into the streets. He ultimately finds a home with a revolutionary writer and is fed by the very hands that were victimized by his former owner; when the writer is also killed by the army, the cat remains in the house, which is soon after occupied by Alcindor, Adélia's father, and his children—who have had to leave the mountains and their former lives to seek out a living in the city streets. The cat saves the youngest of the children from a rat but is finally killed by the family, who have nothing else to eat. They gorge themselves upon the only living thing among them that has shown them any kindness. In this twist of irony, Chauvet illustrates the very real and inescapable cycle of life in Haiti under a totalitarian regime; it is a "dog-eat-dog" world (or in this case, a "cat-eat-cat" world) in which it is impossible to completely distinguish the good from the bad, the moral from the immoral.

The poor in Chauvet's tale are painfully aware that Duvalier's call to

"Black power" was simply a smoke screen for his totalitarianism, one that he used to gain control over the poorest in the nation:

> Even if he is encased in this casket, interjected the old man thought-
> fully, even if he is lying there, it is fear which has made all the bour-
> geois of the country pour out from their homes. Those who have
> witnessed the disappearance of members of their family like those
> who were personally mistreated. I have seen many filing into the pal-
> ace. That chief there, well, he knew how to tame us. Proof-perfect:
> we are dying of misery. Well, and then they are ordering us: cry, Long
> live the chief! And all of us along with the bourgeois, everyone cries:
> Long live the chief![12]

The despair Chauvet invokes in these passages seems insurmountable precisely because of the element of fear, which, embodied by Duvalier, refuses
to die with him. Her text reflects an inescapable reality under a regime in
which, as Michael S. Hooper has written, "local actions are stymied or re-
pressed, talent and resources drained, and the result is a pervasive sense of
fatalism that all decisions are in the hands of the government" (289).
Chauvet's characters attempt to avoid this sense of fatalism as they search
for ways to overcome their oppression.

   Les rapaces exposes misconceptions about the "ignorance" of Haitian people as a whole. Chauvet avoids equating illiteracy or a lack of formal education with an absence of intellect or political awareness. Her text,
albeit fictional, aims to correct the work of historians such as David
Nicholls who declares (illustrating the fictionality of formal strategies of
history) that under Duvalier "the peasant *feels* that he belongs to the nation" and goes on to say: "I was in Haiti when 'Papa Doc' died, and there
was a genuine feeling of loss on the part of many ordinary Haitians, which,
considering how little had been done for them in fourteen years, is perhaps
a tribute to the propaganda of the government" (11); Nicholls, however,
does not, and perhaps cannot, distinguish those who would be "sad" to see
Duvalier die because they harbor another form of fear, that of losing their
power over the masses, from those who have been coerced into publicly ex-
pressing "sadness" because they are subject to that power. Ironically,
Nicholls follows his remarks about this lack of disillusionment amongst ordinary Haitians with the paradoxical statement that since Duvalier's death
"peasants in certain parts of the country are becoming more politically
active than they have been for some years" (11). He does not seem aware
that this activism, without which the events that took place in 1986 and

thereafter could not have taken place, is in effect evidence that *with* the death of Duvalier was born the possibility for an ideological revolution, a lifting of sorts of the iron-clad suppression that had made of the people a fearful and voiceless mass; to a large extent, then, the propaganda of the government had indeed failed. Chauvet also suggests in the passages I have quoted above from *Les rapaces* that political activism was not so much a new facet of "peasant" life but rather that it had resurfaced after having been forced underground as a result of Duvalier's use of widespread violence.

Fear is shown to transcend all class barriers in Chauvet's last novel, and seemingly, those of morality as well. Even as the men in the streets discuss how they have not benefited from Duvalier's "redistribution" of wealth or from the ascent of a small portion of the "black" underclasses, one admits that were it not for the fact that he had lost a hand as a cane cutter, he would enter the army in order to escape state violence. Similarly, as Alcindor increasingly struggles to feed his children after the loss of his wife and his father's lands, he recognizes that his children, who have become beggars to sustain the family, have learned to lie in order to save themselves. Because of a military crackdown on the poor—one by which those who steal are placed under arrest as are those who are said to eat cats because they have nothing else to eat—both he and his children must lie to the "authorities" in order to avoid penalties. Alcindor concludes: "Fear was responsible. Fear that blinds your eyes to skin-crawling crimes. Fear that seals your lips. Fear that makes you hang your head *to appear indifferent and resigned* when your insides and your blood are boiling over within you out of rage and revolt" (my emphasis).[13] Fear, then, serves as a tool of ideological oppression at the same time that it offers the means by which many survive; through it, the oppressed are able to *mask* rage and harbor feelings of revolt. This, in essence, is the crux of my concept of *culture-lacune,* a path toward survival which on the surface appears to support and even accept the status quo while it ultimately defies it, rages against it.

Clearly, Chauvet wants to demonstrate that the Haitian army recruited both the hopeful and the hapless, the corrupt and the incorruptible, who entered its folds either for gain or for the purposes of survival. Significantly, her characters are modeled after people not from the city but rather after people from the countryside who appear more cognizant of their cultural roots. It is the elders here who are able to see that their world is crumbling not only from the effects of physical violence but also from the effects of physical and psychological disintegration caused by poverty. One

elderly man observes: "Yes, the young desert the fields. . . . they tempt
them down there with guns and money."[14] They know that fear plays a part
in the minds of the young, as do greed and ambition. One *vodou* priest declares: "Ambition is a sickness, brother. . . . it will spread and climb into
the mountains and take over the entire country."[15] During a ceremony, the
houngan begs the believers to "*kembè fèm* [stay strong]" by clinging both
to each other and to their native land: "Rope! Rope! Rope! he cried, bind
yourselves together with rope to these mountains because the vultures will
come all the way here to take from your mouths your daily bread."[16] There
is a deep irony in these words, which allude to those of the *Pater Noster;*
Duvalier's propaganda machine appropriated the most traditional of Catholic texts and inserted in them his name and his philosophy. Hence schoolchildren were made to recite a Duvalierist version of the *Pater Noster,* one
in which God was replaced by Duvalier himself, implying that *faith* was
due to him alone. It was nearly impossible, then, to make public displays of
dissent politically, socially, or religiously.

   Chauvet's revolutionary characters attempt the impossible by stead-
fastly adhering to a belief in freedom of expression; most are youthful students turned writers but the most revolutionary are the women, Anne and
Adélia, who act as the novel's driving moral force. Anne is the daughter of
a Duvalierist minister coerced into supporting the government; Adélia is
Alcindor's blind, eldest daughter. Without her father's knowledge, Anne
gets involved with a revolutionary youth group. One of her friends is a
writer, who, like Chauvet, is intent on exposing the ills of the regime. The
writer is killed by the army and Anne returns to his house to retrieve his
manuscript. At the house, she encounters Adélia and her family. Overcome
with compassion for them, she vows not to denounce them to the police.
She remains long enough to discover, along with the family, both the manuscript and the corpse of her friend buried in the yard. With this discovery,
Adélia echoes the words of the *houngan* quoted above:

> "What is it?" Adelia asks, turning the white orbs of her eyes towards
> the yard. "I feel something, father, something like danger. Within me,
> everything is bound together like the knot in a rope. I feel spirits. It
> smells like blood."[17]

Literally, Adélia smells the blood of the slain man; Chauvet uses this image
to convey the character's sense of the need for unity among Haitians. In
death, the writer is bound to the Haitian landscape—to the very land taken
away from Alcindor and his family and from other farmers like him; the

novelist's words will transcend the moment of their writing and illuminate the consciousness of a whole country, of all classes. As Anne confirms, "When the people in a country are well-informed, the leaders can no longer mislead them. For, if the leaders deceive the people, the people will revolt and hold them accountable."[18] Revelation will only occur after the silence is broken, that is, when dialogue is activated either through conversations between individuals or between texts and readers.

Anne attempts to activate both kinds of dialogue by trying to publish the writer's manuscript and by vowing to help Adélia; she promises to help Alcindor and his family by giving them money, providing the children with an education, and, most importantly, by providing medical aid to restore Adélia's sight. Tragically, Anne is killed by the military along with Alcindor before she can fulfill any of her promises. In this case, there is no failure to act, no moral lapse on the part of the main characters. Their actions are thwarted by the corruption that surrounds them: Anne dies; Adélia remains blind. But it is their ability to see beyond the scope of their own lives that creates the potential for a profound transformation on the part of the Duvalierists.

This potential is realized at the end of the novel in the transformation of Anne's father. When Anne disappears, he comes to the realization that she has probably either been imprisoned or killed by the very government he works for, and formulates a plan to vindicate his daughter, a plan that includes publishing the manuscript she salvaged: "If Anne returns," he vows, "I will support her cause. I will spend my fortune to repair the damage I have caused my country. I swear to it. May this book be published and may all the other vultures follow behind me."[19] Even when the hope that she might return is dashed by the discovery of her corpse, her father still remains faithful to his word; he avenges her death and takes in Alcindor's children, thereby fulfilling both his daughter's promises and Adélia's hopes. Justice is brought about through an ideological shift that is effected by the two women's transgression of class boundaries. Anne's political insight is matched only by Adélia's; in their pairing, Chauvet achieves what Haitian women writers like Mme. Virgile Valcin could only hint at, a communal, empowered female Haitian consciousness. Still, the transformation brought about by the pairing of these two women is achieved at the expense of one of the women's lives. The state violence to which Anne falls victim, Chauvet suggests, will only end once the moral rectitude she embodies becomes an integral part of the *national* consciousness.

The Archives of the Imaginary: The Power of the Subconscious

Though *Under the Bone* is set six months after the coup of 1986, d'Adesky, like Chauvet, reveals the tenacity of the ideology of Duvalierism. Her main character, Leslie Doyle, an American human rights activist, encounters a Haitian man on the plane bringing them both to Haiti who tells her that "The players are different . . . but the game remains the same. I tried to tell them . . . but they don't want to know. . . . Duvalier was only the head of the animal—la bête. The real monster was all those people who did his dirty work, all of those who anticipated, who accepted, who kept their silence" (27). It becomes clear that that complicity is supported by the U.S. government, which claims that state terror has left Haiti along with Duvalier *fils*. The U.S. Embassy refuses to denounce state violence (80), and the ambassador speaks of Haitians to Leslie as if they were children: "I mean, quite simply, they don't distinguish fact from rumor. . . . you'd think the whole country was one big prison. You'd think Baby Doc was still running the show" (310). He elaborates: "Terror. . . . it's easy to throw the word around, but it's a lot of malarkey. You have to be very organized to carry out a campaign of terror. This army and what exists of this government are not organized. What you're witnessing is a lack of good policing. But it's not overtly political; it's civil in nature. There's an important difference" (311). The ambassador's rationale is not logical given that the policing of Haiti came about through the implementation of widespread civil and political *discord*. His way of thinking, however, makes it possible for the U.S. government to continue its activities in Haiti unperturbed; it also makes it possible for the U.S. government to declare Haitian refugees in the aftermath of the coup economic rather than political victims, effectively disregarding decades of exploitation and thirty years of totalitarianism.

D'Adesky confronts the Duvalierian use of coercion to control the masses by showing how some women were made to play the role of oppressor at the same time as others were subjected to violent treatment; she also shows that some men involved in acts of terror attempted to undo their wrongs. For example, she speaks of Madame Max, the notorious female *Tonton macoute* who headed that secret police force for years in actuality, and who, in the novel, is described as "a woman of modest means . . . said to have personally overseen the torture sessions of Fort Dimanche" (98). In another passage, Emmanuel, a priest searching for activists who have disappeared in the Haitian nights, receives the confession of a *macoute:*

"'Notre Doc, qui règne dans le Palais National à vie. . . . Our Doc, who dwells in the National Palace for life.' Yes, we had to pretend to worship him, but we didn't, we hated him. No one understands that. They judge us. But we were afraid. He treated us like animals too" (50). The man goes on to reveal that his task was that of picking up the dead, victims of state terror, but he disavows allegiance to the regime: "not for a moment, the entire time I worked for the government—I was never a Duvalierist" (51). He harbors guilt, however, for betraying Haitians; he explains further that he not only claimed the bodies, but stole from the corpses: "If it wasn't me, it would have been someone else, Pe. Not that it excuses me, but it's true. . . . And if the others hadn't done it, I wouldn't have had the idea. I followed their example. I acted like a child, right?" (53). The penitent breaks his code of silence as his guilt eats away at his conscience: he admits that he has stolen from the dead both to feed his family and out of greed. But his brave act of speech, his confession, reveals that his actions were driven by his identification with a collectivity, by his identification with a group unable to curb its desires, or to place limits on its anti-humanistic acts. The man's revelations speak to the existence of a conspiracy of silence, a cycle of vice, which his confession does not bring to an end, spoken as it is, in secret, in the darkness of the confessional box. D'Adesky complicates the idea of the need for un-silencing by suggesting here that it is not simply the act of speech that provides a solution to mistrust between individuals or between social or political classes, but *the quality of the dialogue* itself.

D'Adesky grapples with the theme of silence in the novel through her protagonist, whose reason for going to Haiti is to "research an oral history project about women who had been imprisoned under the Duvaliers" (23). Leslie Doyle soon discovers that her task will be hampered not only by the lack of trust in and between individuals within various social strata, but also by the fact that "there isn't much that's written down" (69). Leslie must rely, as must the other activists in the novel, on word-of-mouth and the annals of memory. For instance, in one of the many dream sequences that occur as the novel unfolds, a *vodou* ceremony is held to comfort a grieving widow whose husband has been slain by the army; that comfort is transmitted through a secret collectivity: "The crowd bathes in the collective memory of others who have died, in the long history of their own struggle" (223). This is a collectivity that Leslie distrusts, not because the society itself is constituted through conflict and contradiction, but because her own identity as an American places her in the position of an outsider—a position she accepts with difficulty.

Thus, when her driver, Clemard, gives her information about secret underground prisons that lead to the palace, Leslie is doubtful:

> Everybody knows. Collective truth. Better than proof in Clemard's eyes. His was the teledjol—street gossip—mentality. She was a non-believer, she wanted hard evidence. He understood it was part of her job, the only truth accepted by outsiders. But the truth is, he would argue to Leslie, everybody knows. (239)

Clemard's definition of "truth," which does not rely on archival documents to be substantiated but on the powers of the mind, of memory, hence, on acts of imagination, flies in the face of Western notions of the quantifiable. But in the Haitian context, memory, even when incomplete, even when false, takes the place of the official records. This fact is clearly exposed in a play written by Gerard, Leslie's friend and a human rights lawyer, in which a woman stands accused in a Haitian court of law of stealing.

Gerard's play invokes the role of memory with the key witness for the prosecution who has changed his name from Plus-Perfect to Imperfect. He declares: "I am no longer the man I was" (295). The lies he tells in court are thus adjusted accordingly to fit his name, to change the nature of his memory from that which is more than true to that which is untrue. The past is no longer real; it becomes the fodder of an imagination that masks itself as reality while reality goes forth into the future, unaccounted for and unrecorded. The court witnesses are paid to lie by government officials in order to convict the woman. Paradoxically, the most revealing words of Gerard's play are spoken by the judge of the court. His response to the objections of the defense lawyer encapsulates the mindset of the totalitarian state brought into being by Duvalier: "In any case, Counselor, deceit, like truth, is a matter of *interpretation*. Since I am the only one who can establish the facts, I am the only one who can judge deceit. Do I make myself clear?" (my emphasis, 294). These words could have been spoken by Duvalier himself. Again, *those who have the power of the word, have the power of the world.* The Duvalier regime, buoyed by the military and strenuous propaganda that made freethinking (hence freedom) a crime against the state, duplicated, in microcosm, the North-South relationship that destroyed Haiti's economic solvency.

Dreams thus act as conduits for home in d'Adesky's *Under the Bone.*

Through them, the female characters in the novel are provided with an outlet which allows them a freedom not provided for in their social surroundings. The subversion of Duvalierism is enacted from within the parameters
of the imagination. Dreams, then, provide the main characters with the opportunity to confront their own sets of beliefs as well as to imagine themselves in the place of another in order to shed claims to ignorance which in
turn lead to self-absolutions of responsibility. Leslie's dreams act as foils to
those of one of the imprisoned women, Elyse, whose experiences she is
seeking to document. Leslie's dreams cannot, in fact, exist without the
tragic lives of the women whom she researches. This irony turns on the basic principle of North-South dependency. Elyse, who suffers the worse effects of Third World exploitation, is one of the many whose lives support
the First World, which is itself obliquely embodied in Leslie's liberal humanism. For Elyse, dreams are a guiding force while for Leslie they
present an enigma she does not recognize as integral to her sense of self.
The protagonist's inability to delve into the subconscious—her own as well
as that of the men and women she comes to know in Haiti—thus prevents
her from being of any help to female victims of human rights violations.

Leslie's dreams are provoked not by her own life experience but by
her research—the words and images of women violated by the army. Interestingly, d'Adesky's allusions to this violence are oblique; violence against
men, on the other hand is explicitly rendered—since the story is primarily
told from Leslie's point of view, this suggests that she cannot see the effects
of violence against women even when presented with documentation. One
of the only passages that provides readers with a glimpse of the violence
suffered by women is a description of photographs passed on from a Dominican photographer, José, to Leslie through the intermediary of their mu-
tual friend, Gerard:

> The pictures showed a shallow grave with the remains of several bod-
> ies in a state of severe decomposition. They had been buried fully
> dressed. There were also close-ups of the women's clothing. On the
> back, José had written: *Artibonite: Mai 1981*. There were other pho-
> tographs as well: of different prisoners; individual shots of several
> older women and young girls; and one picture of a group of women,
> hands behind their backs, a soldier aiming his gun at them:
> *Duvalierville: Juillet 1983*. The last set of pictures were small pho-
> tographs, all of women's bodies, lying where they had fallen: in a
> gutter, in a courtyard, shot in a bedroom. . . . *Port-au-Prince: 3
> Novembre 1985, Victimes Inconnues.* (142)

Leslie's initial response to these photographs is to dream of coming to the rescue of these unknown women. She dreams in particular of one woman, Marie-Thérèse Dubossy, whose voice she has on audiotape describing her ordeal in a state prison.

On the tape, Marie-Thérèse tells of how she was kept in a clinic so that the government could claim that they "had no political prisoners" (149). When she revolts against her incarceration, the infirmary staff inflicts a violent beating: "they beat me and told me to stop causing problems. They tied my hands to the bed and beat me all around my head. . . . When they beat me I started to bleed in one eye and I couldn't see well. There was a sickness in my eyes after that called conjunctivitis. They brought the doctor to see me and he said I needed some ampoules of medicine" (150). She never receives the medicine and is blinded.

Leslie provides images to accompany Marie-Thérèse's voice in her dream. The voice is transformed into the image of a power unleashed: "a flurry of high-pitched sounds like machine-gun fire, followed by silence, then another rapid eruption. Bursts like flame . . . smoke following each reply" (142). And Leslie imagines herself propelled into the role of savior by the woman's break with silence:

> Leslie had an image of herself, face pressed against the window of the infirmary, looking in. The woman was dressed in a green hospital gown and sat on a steel cot in the corner. She saw her own tape recorder on the desk by the bed. Then she was standing at the entrance to the infirmary. . . . Something had happened. She had forgotten the ampoules. She opened her bag and found the thin glass vials filled with the precious liquid. They contained the aqueous humor to cure the woman's eyes. (142)

Leslie enters the infirmary with a priest and a lawyer, symbols of the omnipotent Catholic church and the corrupt legal system that cannot be outdone; she offers the women the vials of medicine only to drop them and watch them shatter upon the ground. Leslie's dream reveals that though she may bear good intentions, she remains—as she sees herself—an outsider peering into lives, contradictions, she does not understand. It is her failure to transcend her outsider identity that prevents Leslie from succeeding in her attempts to help others.

Although Leslie contends that her work in Haiti is meant to be "a kind of collaboration" (171), her use of language, like the images in her dream, betrays an *inability to collaborate*. In her dream, she becomes the questioning voice of the interviewer, then an immovable bystander "nailed to the ground" (144). In another instance, Leslie cannot connect her dream life with the voices she hears on her witness tapes. Leslie hears but she does not see. Significantly, d'Adesky uses sight imagery to convey her character's limitations. She writes: "her eyes had been sealed shut and she felt they could remain so forever. Sealed in heat, like an Egyptian mummy's, her dreams ossified. There was a trace of something disturbing, something important, if only she could recall it" (234). In contrast to Elyse, who ventures through her consciousness "analyzing the dream for clues . . . certain there is something important in the dream" (197), Leslie's subconscious is literally funereal; unable to connect with herself, she preempts the possibility of connecting with others, especially women. She imagines Elyse Voltaire's and Marie-Thérèse Dubossy's beaten bodies but cannot assimilate their pain; those images are immediately followed with disturbingly placid visions of blue sky. D'Adesky writes of Leslie: "the sky was so lovely she wanted to paint the landscape; the deep blue soothed her somehow" (235). She sees this same sky when she is finally allowed entry into a state prison, where she encounters Elyse Voltaire and an elderly, blind woman: "the woman turned the corner and was gone. The guard had pushed open the gate; Leslie saw blue sky" (d'Adesky 335). Leslie's sense of the world is Western in the extreme: she sees Haiti through utopic eyes—it may hide secrets but the country is never more terrible than her imagination permits it to be. Thus, when she finally tells someone that she suspects the blind woman in the jail whom she did not stop to help was Marie-Thérèse Dubossy, she rationalizes her behavior: "I keep thinking about what a coincidence it was. That tape you gave me, with Marie-Thérèse Dubossy's testimony, and seeing this woman with those eyes. I keep fantasizing that it's somehow her" (361). Unlike Anne's socialist vision in *Les rapaces,* Leslie's fantasies fall outside moral bounds because she cannot transform her desire to be a witness for Haitian women into action.

In contradistinction, Elyse's dreams give her a sense of hope and personal power that enables her to overcome a momentary inability to act. Her most significant dream occurs when she is still in prison and despairing over the fate of her husband, Ignatius. She shares her cell with a Dominican prostitute significantly named Luz—light. Leslie's dream occurs after Luz risks herself to come to the defense of young girls, students, who are being harassed by their male jailers. The soldiers permit Luz to rescue one of the girls but "not before laughing, pinching, fondling her." Elyse "wanted to cry out" (197) but her knowledge of the consequences of objecting to the jailers' treatment prevents her from speaking. Elyse is not yet ready to risk all even as she stands stripped of her human rights. Elyse's only recourse is a retreat to her imagination; a "sea voyage, the one she plays over and over in her mind" in which she is guided by Metres Agwe, goddess of the water and protector of children, through a rainy tempest. In her dream, Grann, her dying grandmother, is fused with Metres Agwe, and Elyse understands that she is being sent an important message. She travels through her dream as would a faithful believer in the supernatural, as would a believer in the idea that one's ancestors—both dead and alive—can speak through one's dreams, and tries to decipher that message. She asks, "Is this a vision of her own future or the future of the world without her?" (197). She hears the sound of singing birds, of the carnival bands, and believes she has understood the dream: "The stream will lead to the city of the dead, will flow into the street and blend with the red rain, the flood that will carry her family away. But why? And when?" (198). For her, the vision of Metres Agwe is a foreboding of her own death, and the demise of her entire family, including that of the child she carries within her, already dead in her womb.

Elyse anchors her understanding of the dream in her knowledge of past state terrors. For example, she recalls Duvalierist violence against students when she sees herself as a student being guided by her grandmother to school. They encounter other schoolchildren performing and experiencing a *vodou* possession. The children in her dream are combatting the injustices that they cannot combat in their actual lives; it is thus difficult for Elyse to imagine that the dream makes anything more than a negative prediction. She continues to question its ominous tone: "Is this a funeral procession? Elyse aks the queen, Metres Agwe. My funeral?" (200). The dream ends with her vision of a temple whose walls are "studded with fragments of mirrors and colored glass," of *seau d'eau,* "a waterfall baptizing the Apostles," and of Jesus with "a giant, divine eye, the hazel color of the child's eye, Metres Agwe, the same color as Grann's" (200–201). The all-seeing eye represents a coming together of the earthbound, the ancestral, and the supernatural, and points to the formation of a new Haitian identity.

D'Adesky revises here the idea of twinship that informs the concept of the *marassa* in Haitian mythology. Maya Deren has written that the "Haitian myth [of twinship] has gone beyond the concept of Marassa of the same sex, as metaphysical reflection, and Marassa of opposite sexes, as progenitive differentiation" to take on a third meaning, represented by that which is generated from a holistic fusion. Deren adds that "it is the affirmation of cosmic unity as opposed to dualism which results from the effort to make of segmentation a total separation. . . . The apex of the triangle of the Marassa-Trois is a statement of the androgynous, cosmic whole" (40–41). But whereas Deren insists that the androgynous quality of the *marassa* is best understood as a union between male, female, and its issue (40), d'Adesky obliquely suggests that the *marassa* can be envisioned, albeit within an androgynous religious and cultural context of *vodouisants,* as a purely female force. In the dream, the eyes move from the temple to the factory setting, where women toil as seamstresses, suggesting further that female labor, female (in)sight, will lead to revelation, to empowering sources of knowledge. The dream ends with Elyse in song, spirited by her grandmother's presence.

In the final pages of the novel, Elyse's dream becomes reality. But it is not her grandmother who leads her forward; rather, it is Luz. Luz leads "her down toward the waterfall and the road" (370), away from the ashes of her village. Her family has disappeared and she understands that the dream was a sign from her grandmother about life beyond Elyse's immediate predicament. By reading the dream in a way that made it only a reflection of herself, Elyse could not see Luz; she literally could not see the light. Her faith in her vision, however, allows her to modify her interpretations, to extend her hand to Luz and allow the Dominican woman to lead her out of her darkness and into a space in which she is able to experience a concrete sense of hope. This gesture on the part of Luz is one that Elyse finally reciprocates: "We'll help each other," she says to Luz, "I'll help you" (370). The two are caught in a storm, the red rainfall of the dream, and emerge into a new day. They sit together by the sea and Elyse recognizes a layer of black stones upon the shore: "In my dream . . . these stones turned into eyes. They watched me escape" (371). Elyse turns her dream into a moral force by allowing her visions to inform her actions.

In their writings, Marie Chauvet and Anne-christine d'Adesky counter fatalism by demonstrating that the imagination, the subconscious, can serve as a source of hope; it need not only perpetuate oppression and class, gender, and/or racial divides. Prevented access to the means of affirming their own cultures and identities, inhabitants of the Third World fall prey to the imagination of the First World, which disassembles the former's humanity. The First World thus controls not only the "logos of the final end" but the logos of the first beginnings and of our present. Consequently, when philosophers contend that a nuclear world war is the only conceivable "end of world" scenario and, as writes Jacques Derrida, that

the "terrifying reality of the nuclear conflict can only be the signified referent never the real referent (present or past) of a discourse or a text" (23)
what results is a claim to semiotic omnipotence. Derrida's ability to textually define and delimit what the West perceives as the ultimate world ca-
lamity results from the fact that the West has not suffered the same degree
of oppression it has inflicted on other sectors of the world. Thus, the power
to define the grounds of human terror derives from a secure and absolute
position of privilege which denies that world calamities that have already
taken place are indeed calamities; this deliberate occlusion of the past—
what I would term ideological blindness—can only lead to its repetition.
Though we can reason that the cataclysm of nuclear war is "unreal" insofar
as it has not yet occurred on a global scale, we can nonetheless infer from
past global experience how it will affect very real human lives. Certainly
those who were callously murdered in (or physically suffered through) the
traffic of the slave trade, the Holocaust, the nuclear bombings of Nagasaki
and Hiroshima, and present-day war and/or neocolonialism, know the terror of absolute annihilation, what produces it and what it will take to prevent its repetition: remembrance and a decentralization of power on the
individual, regional, national, and global level. That the entire world has
not been wiped out by any of these events does not mean that such suffering is unimaginable; this is tantamount to saying that since every living
person has not died and has no firsthand knowledge of death, death does
not occur on a daily basis. Only those who feel themselves contained in a
cocoon of relative safety can afford to hypothesize about a distant future at
the expense of taking care of the present in light of past history. Haitian
women, who are acutely aware of having to live without the safety net of
economic and military might, cannot entertain a rhetoric of annihilation
that preempts—if I may make a final appeal to a rhetoric of morality—
justice, hope, and the possibility of terminating the cycle of exploitative
oppression.

    Chauvet and d'Adesky's Haitian female characters should not be un-
derstood as reductive symbols of life and/or regeneration; they are revolu-
tionaries who in the act of renouncing personal or economic privilege usher
into being a reinvigorated sense of the *plausibility* of Haitian women's collectivity, even in the face of its presumed absence. That collectivity's main
purpose is to regain the integrity of its own *logos* for the greater good.
Chauvet's Anne/Adélia and d'Adesky's Elyse/Leslie form two parts of the
whole of any human consciousness: they represent the struggles laying before us all, that is, our own power to bring about a transformative future at

the level of both our personal and social interactions. Our own politicized reflections can serve to problematize ideologies of exclusivity and hierarchy in ways that will enable us to act, that will enable us to create a dehierarchized, inclusive global economy that will provide not only Haitian women but all of the Third World with a forum in which their voices will be heard—true words transmitted between the heretofore divided.

Jou va, jou vien—m'pa di passé ça

—✦—

Writing in the feminine, And on a colored sky.
—Trinh T. Minh-ha, *Woman, Native, Other*

*I*t is a bright, cloudless Sunday morning and something in the air is telling me that it will be a peaceful day, here, in this country that has not known peace for decades. I am standing on a dust road in the hills above Pétion-Ville before a wall of colors as magnificent as a rainbow: row upon row of paintings have been strung up on a net. They sway, almost imperceptibly, beneath banana trees whose branches are curved with the weight of long-stemmed green fruits which will be taken down and sold at market any day now, someday soon.

Beads of sweat form a necklace around my neck. I wipe them away with one motion of my left hand, while with my right hand, I bring the camera up to my eye. The two hands act seemingly without knowledge of the other. My mind concentrates on the bunch of bananas overhanging the catch of paintings. My eye frames the blur of color. And there she is: Solange. Can it be? her? my only angel? There she is: walking across my field of vision, in her Sunday dress, all frills and light as air, dignified. The sound of metal folding upon metal: the shutter sounds the magnificent stopping of time. She has quickly walked away, quietly, like only angels can.

Later, when I will look at this picture, before I have even begun to imagine Solange, I will realize that whoever she is (or was, or can be) will never be told. Her story is her own. But here, her path and mine have crossed: our stories have intersected. And in this frame, she lives, without beginning and without end. She is forever stilled in this photograph.

I will set this picture of a little girl walking before unframed paintings side by side with a picture of a grown woman, head down, walking
past bright red graffiti painted on brick walls in Port-au-Prince. I will wonder what this woman thinks of the anti-American slogans: *Jimmy Carter fo
magouy* (Jimmy Carter go home?). I will wonder at the bent of her head. I
will remember taking this picture, camera shooting out of a moving car,
wanting to capture that dissent, the voicing of opposition (whatever the
source—wondering who and why). And I will look at that woman, a
woman I did not see walk through the frame I had constructed at the moment the shutter clicked shut and open. I will want to know her story. I will
not know her story.

It is when I put these pictures side by side that I see that these two
moments in time—a girl and a woman, walking—frame a story in themselves: a story of silence: a story of their untold lives, of so many forgotten
women in Haiti who survive on a daily basis the oppressions the world has
seen fit to lay across their shoulders. Perhaps the particular stories of these
two Haitian women overlap somewhere in these dirt roads, in dreams, in visions of hope. But perhaps they are both Solange: prototypical of all Haitian women: living beyond the history books that will not acknowledge
them: creating life from the ashes of invisibility: living beyond sight. At
least, this is my secret hope: this is what I think silently to myself, this is
the sum of my (in)sight as I attempt to bring her/their story to light:

> Solange is not real: she exists in my unconscious. Solange is too real:
> she exists in your mind and in your heart. Solange is the sun in the
> midst of despair: she exists. Solange is dignity personified: she is
> our moral conscience.

Frames of Reference

In September 1994, on the eve of the U.S. invasion of Haiti, Anne-
christine d'Adesky reported in the *Los Angeles Times* on the duplicity of
the U.S. government's policy on Haitian refugees. The U.S. government had
argued against providing sanctuary for Haitians since 1986, asserting that
Haitians were economic rather than political refugees, only to later claim
that "human rights abuses today are comparable to those of the notorious
François (Papa Doc) Duvalier regime" so as to legitimate its impending invasion. In the final sentences of her article, d'Adesky invokes the image of
a survivor of state violence—a woman whose arms had been "hacked off"

and left for dead. Her name is Alerte Balance. Balance is now a spokes-woman for Haitians and their calls for freedom. D'Adesky wonders at the woman's courage and laments her losses: "I imagine there are moments when her brain cannot accept her loss of limb . . . and she may suffer from phantom pains for decades" (M60). Though d'Adesky clings to a "hope for recovery," for her, Alerte Balance's arms are symbols of what can never be regained. She writes: "No miracle—no Aristide, no Clinton, no invasion—can give back what has been lost" (M6). Alerte Balance is, however, through her acts of speech, taking back a measure of what her assailants had attempted to take from her—self-respect, courage, humanity: in short, her life. It is with this political context in mind that I began work on this booklength study of Haitian women's literature.

Framing Silence is my effort to contribute to the un-silencing of Haitian women whose lives have been defined by fear. That fear is born not only through violence but through all possible forms of repression. In the novels I have analyzed here, Haitian women writers expose the source of those fears, putting an end to the silencing that has shaped their lives in order to give voice to their various oppressions. As the theorem of *culture-lacune* demonstrates, this framing impetus has the paradoxical implication of both mastering and making an ally of silence and of transforming static forms, themes, and styles into revolutionary ones.

In the process of uncovering such strategies of resistance, I have confronted not only my own fears—that of not finding the texts by Haitian women I was told time and again could not exist, of setting out to write from an explicitly, radical feminist point of view in a field openly hostile to admittedly Third World feminism as a political ideology, as methodology—but also have come to understand and affirm my own particular frame of reference as a Haitian woman. As I learned more about Haitian women's history by analyzing the writings of women writers from my home country, I came to realize that I had moved through the world without ever having felt *of* that world. I had traveled at a quick pace through years of higher education in the search for "truth" and "enlightenment." My enlightenment was acquired through the shock of being confronted with the virtual absence of representations of women, of people of African descent, of women of color, of Haitians and Haitian women specifically. I literally did not exist in the world of academia until I decided that my very being defied my academic exclusion and that of other "minority" groups. But even as I became more knowledgeable about the existence of literary works by women like myself circulating in the world today, I was not prepared for the discoveries the writing of this book would bring to me. Historical world events like World War I, for example, which had seemed so detached from my own existence, almost meaningless on a personal-cultural scale, suddenly acquired a relevance I had never known, never *felt,* until, as I wrote this text, I could interpret them from within the frame of Haitian history. It became suddenly clear why the United States had sought to curtail German interests in a country so close—too close—to its own shores, one year after the war had begun. This is one small example, but it accurately conveys how a sense of place is crucial to creating both the imaginary and textual archives that serve to release, as they reveal, counter-hegemonic discourses of revolt, insurgency, and cultural integrity.

The Haitian creole phrase *"jou va, jou vien, m'pa di passé ça"* means literally "day comes, day goes—I will say nothing more than that." In Haitian culture it signifies a higher understanding on the part of the speaker of the workings of a world in which injustices take place day in and day out. In other words, the days may go by, the speaker says, but, you will see, my day will come. In each of the novels I have analyzed from within a Haitian feminist methodological frame, it is clear that the writers themselves feel that their day has come; it is, however, yet another matter whether that day has come for the Haitian women they seek to represent in their writings. *To place oneself in time, to refuse one's exclusion from how the times are remembered*—this is ultimately the mandate of Haitian women writers and activists. In their words of witness, these women step out of frames that dispute the realities of their oppression to in turn step into frames that affirm all that has been denied, culturally and ideologically.

In all of the texts that have emerged from the pens of Haitian women writers literature serves a key function in making visible that which has been said not to exist. The writers thus make use of the principles of what I have defined as *culture-lacune* to bring Haitian women's realities into relief while also attempting to shield Haitian women from further harm. They "fill in the gap" missing from Haiti's landscape, in its cultural and political history, by re-creating that history from a variety of women's points of views. They also do so by using textual ellipses to highlight women's absence from a variety of narratives. At the same time, they fill in the *lacunes* of women's own consciousness (the gap in the body or that which is missing from a person) by providing the kernels of women's revolutionary potential through the annals of memory and of the imagination. The use of literature for this purpose harkens back to the 1920s and 1930s, when Haitian women of varying class backgrounds organized to resist aspects of the nationalistic ideology that emerged during the Occupation (from which women were continuously shut out) in order to put forth a feminist agenda. A foreboding sense of a loss of autonomous identity is thus reflected in women's literature of that era, especially in the novels of Mme. Virgile Valcin and Annie Desroy. These novels show how the neocolonial phantasms of all Haitians as "savages" that were derived from the stereotypes of Haitian women as one-dimensional mammies and/or *mambos* solidified Haitian women's social subordination during the U.S. Occupation.

The literature that has emerged since 1934 emphatically engages in the political struggle over ideology and self-representation begun by Haitian women during the Occupation. In novels written from the 1960s to the 1980s by Nadine Magloire, Ghislaine Charlier, Jan J. Dominique, and Marie Chauvet, the image of Haitian women as "earthmothers," and, ultimately, as traitors of Haitian culture, changes dramatically from the prototype imaged by Oswald Durand in his folksong "Choucoune" of 1883. In each of these novels, heroines contest the social order that holds them captive and attempt (although not always successfully) a re-visioning of their identities. The authors contest and reformulate the image of Durand's *marabout* in order to take control of how they are represented. Drawing on a folk image that itself attempted, post-Independence, to reformulate a sense of Haitian identity under siege (from the vestiges of French acculturation), the authors adopt a *créole* frame of reference that, on the surface, appears absent from works written primarily in French, and feminize it. In so doing, they obliquely reclaim the figure by granting her all the forbidden fruits of Haitian female emancipation: sexuality, self-expression, pride and autonomy. But, the reclaimed *marabout* woman—imaged in Annie Desroy's *Le joug* as Lamercie, as Maud in Magloire's *Le mal de vivre,* and as the *marassas* in Chauvet, Danticat and d'Adesky's novels—exists at the margins of society even as the desires and hopes of women whose class or social privilege effectively forecloses their revolutionary potential are bestowed upon her. And Anglophone texts written since the early 1990s, by Anne-christine d'Adesky and Edwidge Danticat in particular, make clear that the revisioning of Haitian women's identity is an ongoing process that has been further complicated by recent waves of emigration to the United States and by the U.S. military's "invasion" of Haiti under the guise of a peace-keeping mission in the fall of 1994.

Nonetheless, the *marabout* women within each text demonstrate that it is in the underlying ability to transgress not only social and class barriers, but ideological ones, that hope for Haitian women's socio-cultural emancipation remains. It is not clear, however, how the collective fusion that is suggested through each of these figures will be made reality in the face of the growing violence toward women in Haiti over the last several years and in the face of the as of yet undetermined effects of the present-day occupation of Haiti by foreign powers.

In 1993, Deborah Sontag, reporter for the *New York Times,* wrote an article entitled "Refugees from Rape" in which she described the physical and sexual abuse suffered by Haitian women within Haiti. Her examples dated back to 1991, during which time women were brutally used, mutilated, and raped as various political groups sought to control the reins of power within Haiti. During this period, Haitian women were fast becoming part of a growing group seeking asylum in the United States for a unique reason—"seeking asylum," as Sontag writes, "on the ground that they suffered different forms of political persecution because of their sex." Anne-Marie Coriolan, spokeswoman for SOPHA (*Solidarité fanm Aayisyen* [Haitian Women's Solidarity]), echoed Sontag's findings in a report appearing the following year in *Ms.* magazine. She stated that rape is "a means of terrifying women specifically and the population in general" in Haiti currently. In her article "Lives in the Balance," which appeared in the December 1994–January 1995 issue of *The New Yorker,* Amy Wilentz also wrote of pre-invasion violence against women: "Rape became a common form of political repression, [and] in at least two instances . . . mothers were forced to have sex with their sons in order to save the boys' lives" (100). These reports make clear that, given the extent to which the violence inflicted upon Haitian women goes unnoticed, it is incumbent upon us to make that violence discernible. As the neglect of women's literature attests, Haitian women's voices and calls for help have been continuously ignored or relegated to a lesser plane of importance for far too long.

We also know that between 1991 and 1994, the Haitian army organization named FRAPH (*Front pour l'avancement et le progrès Haitien* [Front for Haitian Advancement and Progress]), rumored to have been formed with the CIA, killed over 3,000 civilians (d'Adesky, *Tension* M6). Certainly, many more were injured. Although fewer and fewer reports about violence have appeared in the United States since the invasion, it is not clear whether or not it has truly abated as a result of the presence of the remaining U.S. and U.N. troops; when I returned to Haiti in the early weeks of August 1995, it was clear that killings continued to occur daily and that many individuals lived in fear even as they went about their daily business. Haiti continues to be a country under siege and its women continue to live a marginalized existence even as they toil daily in the streets of the major cities as market women or factory workers. It becomes difficult, I believe, when one has altered one's frame of reference to absorb the realities of Haitian women's lives going back to the time of the first occupation to have any hope in a bright future for Haitian women under the present circumstances. Today's occupation (or "intervention" as it is otherwise called) has replicated the terms of the first. As John Canham-Clyne and Worth Cooley-Prost report in their article "Haiti to the Haitians?," the United States will maintain economic control of the country through USAID even after the remaining troops have left (22). That control has made it impossible for Haiti to make its own advances for most of this century; Haiti is, in this context, to borrow Grimaldi and Chapelle's sentiments, being held hostage and its forgotten female population is being held hostage along with her.

In her song "Fear," Nigerian-English singer Sade Adu interprets the story of a woman waiting for a lover who may never return. I am listening to her words now, as I write the last pages of this text, the lyrics of her song seeming strangely (perhaps not so strangely) apropos. Sade sings of the fires of passion, of grieving a loss foretold. The drumbeats in the background are military in tone, akin to a death march—they could represent either the beating of a woman's heart or the slow and steady progress of a violent force beyond her immediate control. She seeks to defeat her own fear, of love, of loss. Fear—the emotion brings all of the senses into high relief, reveals a vision of the world drastically different from its surface appearance. Her voice quavering, Sade sings of a colored sky, a blue sky turned red by the force of her emotions. We know that the sky is a mirror for the blue of the world's oceans; similarly, it is a canvas on which we project our feelings and emotions—shaking our fists when it tears into rain, smiling when it graces us with a rainbow, making wishes upon falling stars when its blue turns to jet black. In Sade's song, the sky is not only the canvas for the expression of one woman's emotions; it is also a metaphor for the intermingling of passion and fear, one acting as the mirror of the other. "Fear" is emblematic of too many women's lives globally; it is especially emblematic of the lives of those women of African descent who realize that the regenerating world is held together by the scar tissue of their subsumed lived experience. Such women, unlike the utopic protagonist of d'Adesky's *Under the Bone,* know that the blue sky is a mythic blanket of solace beneath which they must toil, a screen against which the truth of their dispossession is projected. It frames the existence of Third World women and appears to make that existence as translucent as emotion, as invisible as air, without, however, denying its attendant terror—the violence of physical and ideological colonization. It is within this space that most Haitian women live; targeted as victims of overt and often violent oppression, they survive against justifiable fear, but when they have sung that fear, battled it, exposed it, their voices have been pushed to the side, ignored, labeled reactionary, and finally silenced altogether.

Haitian women writers have endeavored to testify to both the triumphs and sufferings of their class, but they have done so at great personal risk and in the face of unrelenting persecution. In the end, that persecution is beyond our immediate control but we challenge it and diminish its power through the common use of a revolutionary discourse of transgression, a dialectical subversion implicit in the creation of our *culture-lacune:* silence framed: textually, in language, and through storytelling what truths lay beneath the surface are acknowledged at the same time as they are not explicitly exposed.

The epigraph to this conclusion, Trinh T. Minh-ha's locution for Third World women who take part in both the scripting of women's lives and the creation of their own written selves, summarizes well the way in which Third World women have, of necessity, reconfigured the terms of their existence to assert individual and communal experiences textually, theoretically, the purpose of which writing is to (paraphrasing Trinh) exist simultaneously with the text in order to come alive within the frames of our own making: "Writing in the feminine. And on a colored sky" (28–29). Trinh's words, like the lyrics of Sade's song, fall on my ears like rainfall, like tear drops. We—women of the African diaspora and of the Third World—as Haitian women may mask ourselves with a veneer of blue, but beneath it there will always remain the red sky, the true contours of our lives.

Port-au-Prince: Her story yet to tell . . . *(Photo: M.J.A. Chancy)*

NOTES

Introduction

1. This occurred in 1955 in the pre-elections that ultimately brought Duvalier senior to the seat of power in 1956. Although the military subjected the participants in this election to similar forms of intimidation and, by all accounts, few were free to place a private vote, it remains the first voting situation in which women were able to cast their ballots and, at the lower levels of government, able to contribute to the political life of the country.
2. Although in the body of the work I provide excerpts from the Francophone texts in English translation to make for easier reading (and I have endeavored to produce translations that are as close as possible to the original in tenor), since most of this writing exists in French and is untranslated, I have also provided the excerpts in the original French in the endnotes so as to enable the reader to refer to them easily, as well as to preserve the reality of the bilingualism at work in my own text.
3. Selwyn Cudjoe articulated a similar position, prior to Harlow, in his 1980 text *Resistance and Caribbean Literature*. In it, he defined Caribbean literature as characterized by a politics of resistance whereby literature itself "becomes a process in which man [sic] is injected into his [sic] past world, and acts to come to grips with that past reality before he [sic] can come to terms with his [sic] present. To write is to historicize reality; that is to concretize the past" (69).
4. Charles's anthology is entitled *La poésie féminine d'Haïti (histoire et anthologie)* (Port-au-Prince: Choucoune, 1980). It is interesting to note the name of the publishing house in the context of my assertions below!
5. See Barbara Christian's essays, "The Race for Theory" and "Black Studies or Women's Studies." In the latter, she writes: "There are scholars, I hear, who produce feminist theory and there are those of us, I guess who practice feminist theory. Among the latter are usually listed women of color. Theory, in other words, occupies a different space from the study of the intersection of class/race/gender which the study of American women of color implies" (21). This statement, I contend, is as applicable to the discourse that surrounds the theo-

rizing by women of color in the "postcolonial" world which is also concerned with the intersection of various oppressions and/or identities.

6. It is impossible to provide an accurate count of Haitian women writers since so little work is being done in the area; nonetheless, it appears that the numbers cited by Frickey are on the rise, especially if one takes into account writers in exile. The discrepancy between female and male production, however, remains the same overall.

7. "dans une récente anthologie intitulée *Poésie vivante d'Haïti* . . . parmi 61 auteurs cités, on ne compte que 4 femmes" (Condé 81).

8. "à travers elle, il est possible de cerner l'image d'une collectivité et même, de vivre un moment avec elle. Le roman, s'il est le monde intime qu'un écrivain entrouvre, est aussi un témoignage social" (Condé 113).

9. "le caractère national d'une culture, d'une littérature, n'est pas fonction de la langue d'expression" (Huannou 105).

10. I should note here that the word *marabout* functions differently in the Haitian context than it does in the African context. In Haiti, the word denotes an "ethnic" or racial category, while, in Africa, it is the name given to a muslim holy man. I am indebted to Gay Wilentz for pointing out this important difference. This difference can also be seen as a productive one in light of the present study in that it is possible to think of the *marabout* woman found in the texts I analyze as the symbols of truth, as spiritual guides toward progress.

11. "le personnage qui parle dans le poème s'y représente cinq fois comme agent, dans la fonction grammaticale de sujet et dix fois comme victime, dans la fonction grammaticale d'objet" (Laroche 119).

12. "l'actuelle écriture en haïtien s'efforce de marroner l'écriture dominante en français par l'oraliture des dominés" (Laroche 112).

13. This Haitian song has been popularized in the Anglophone Americas more recently as "Yellowbird" by Harry Belafonte.

14. Since there continues to be much debate about the use of the words "white" and "black" to describe those of Caucasian and African heritage, I have made use of two variations throughout the text. Wherever the word "Black" appears capitalized, it is meant to convey a political community which defines itself by virtue of its African heritage diasporically; when the word "black" appears lowercased (as will be the case as well for the word "white"), it is meant to denote a construction of race that is not necessarily political in nature or an agreed upon demarcation by those it seeks to identify. Perhaps in the future, we will have better words by which to make human beings intelligible in a nonracial (that is, nonracist) and nonhierarchial context of difference(s).

15. It is interesting to note that Marie Chauvet's first novel, *Fille d'Haiti*, published in 1954, owes its raison d'être to Valcin's sentimental novels of this period; written in the same sentimental style, the novel explores the coming-of-age struggles of a young Haitian girl, Lotus, and her tragic love affair with a socialist, played out against the backdrop of the wake of Haitian nationalism.

CHAPTER 1 *Haitian Feminism*

1. Although some women acted as *macoutes,* they were always behind the scenes, hidden from view; they were certainly not as notoriously visible as were the male *macoutes.*

2. In her article "Women and the Law," Kristian Miccio discusses the concept of *femme couverte* and specifies that with it woman's "legal status was shaped by her relationship to men within the family—as one's wife or as one's daughter." In effect, marriage became, as Miccio writes, "a legal death" (139), for women and girls existed only through their legal objectification rather than as autonomous beings with rights equal to that of their male family members.

3. For reasons that will become plainly obvious in the following and subsequent chapters, I define the West here most strictly as the United States.

4. One must note here that, increasingly, this pattern of exclusion has been activated within the arena of lesbian studies where the efforts of women of color and Black lesbian feminists in particular have been largely ignored.

5. "Un peuple qui se divise en deux catégories d'individus vivant chacun de leur vie propre, d'un côté les hommes, de l'autre les femmes, sera toujours un peuple faible. Il nous faut arriver à une collaboration des deux sexes pour le bien du pays."

6. "La femme mariée ou non ne possède aucun droit politique; moins favorisée que ses frères illettrés, elle ne peut élire un député ou donner son opinion sur un texte abstrait. Certaines fonctions nécessitant la jouissance et l'exercice des droits politiques tels que juge, juré, notaire ne lui sont pas accessibles. Tel est le statut légal de la femme haïtienne" (Guillaume 18).

CHAPTER 2 *Emergence of Women's Literary Voices*

1. "[Valcin's] roman est . . . une tranche d'histoire contemporaine et le lecteur ne sera pas surpris de rencontrer au cours du récit une pointe de critique sur les hommes et les choses qui occupent l'attention publique dans la plus flagrante actualité" (Price-Mars ii).

2. Madeleine Gardiner notes also that Desroy's novel "was greeted with a stunning silence" (my translation, 4) at a time when men's novels—by Roumain, Laleau, Alexis—on similar topics were receiving excessive press.

3. "Et dans le cadre du révisionnisme critique réclamé à bon escient par le deuxième sexe, il importe de réexaminer les verdicts—négatifs ou chaleureux—portés sur toute femme auteur, car discrimination ou paternalisme masculin y jouent un rôle d'autant plus insidieux qu'il est souvent inconscient" (Feldman 35).

4. "Le cachet unique du *Joug* provient de ce qu'il se veut un carrefour d'échanges culturels" (Feldman 37).

5. It must be noted here that those who formed the ranks of the elite were often more or less regarded as lighter-skinned "mulattoes," though many, as Toussaint's rise attests, were also of the "darker" masses; their Eurocentrism should thus be considered not so much a function of skin-color as of the ideology attendant to power; I will return to this point in subsequent chapters.

6. The Dominican Republic, for example, was also invaded from 1914 until 1924, forever altering the course of the interconnected histories of the two countries.

7. This is an astonishing claim given that Jean Price-Mars' researched and informed text, *Ainsi parla l'Oncle (So Spoke the Uncle)*, appeared in the same year. Price-Mars, quite in opposition to Seabrook's memoir approach, opened his preface with the following words: "This entire book is an endeavor to integrate the popular Haitian thought into the discipline of traditional ethnography" (7). Seabrook makes no such claim in his own work; indeed, he could not. Price-Mars' text, on the other hand, was among the first to validate the African and syncretic aspects of Haitian culture with scientific and anthropological data.

8. Barbara Christian defines the "mammy" as follows: "She relates to the world as an all embracing figure, and she herself needs or demands little, her identity derived mainly from a nurturing source" (*Black Feminist Criticism* 2).

9. "Tu n'ignores pas qu'un certain Seabrook a écrit, problament sur commande, un livre intitulé *L'Ile Magique* où nous sommes pris à partie comme d'habitude le font ces aventuriers de la plume, avides d'un succès de scandale" (Desroy 111).

10. "Nous subissons le joug de notre ignorance, de nos passions, de nos superstitions, de nos préjugés. Ce sont toutes ces entraves qui paralysent notre évolution et nous livrent pieds et poings liés aux mains de l'étranger qui bénéficie de notre stupide désunion" (Desroy 112).

11. "Murray n'était plus l'être à qui la Civilisation avait forgé une âme raffinée et snob. Une envie irrésistible lui venait de se jeter au milieu de cette frénésie" (Desroy 131).

12. "Il faudrait pour votre évolution, affirmer votre personalité, c'est à dire ne jamais abandonner l'idée que vous êtes tous des nègres sans aucune distinction de nuances. Vous n'avez aucune tradition" (Desroy 142).

13. "Depuis quelque temps un grave débat s'est élevé dans notre monde intellectuel sur *la culture haitienne*. D'aucuns en nient l'existence ou la mettent en doute"; "Si, par définition, le folk-lore est la somme des croyances, superstitions, légendes, contes, chansons, devinettes, coutumes sur lesquelles repose la vie primitive d'un peuple et constitue les fondements de sa 'culture,' il n'est pas un pays qui possède un plus riche fond de traditions orales que le nôtre. Et ces traditions sont d'autant plus profondes et merveilleuses qu'elles remontent aux origines mêmes de la race" (Price-Mars, *Formation Ethnique*, 42–43).

14. "Être américains en Haïti, depuis 1915, c'est déposséder les paysans en établissant le régime du latifundia, c'est se déclarer experts aux appointments de quatre à cinq cents dollars; être américains, c'est rouler auto avec une vitesse vertigineuse, emprisonner le journaliste, se saouler, tuer le plus paisible haïtien et trouver quelqu'un pour déclarer que vous êtes "idiots", c'est se promener en pleine paix avec des machines-guns braquées sur de pauvres étudiants en grève; être américains enfin, c'est vivre d'abondance, mourir d'indigestion à côté de l'haïtien dont les tripes se sont rapetissées à force de privations" (Valcin 57).

15. "Pourquoi résisterait-il au désir de chanter le rhum et le clairin de cette petite île noire? d'écrire un livre sur elle?" (Valcin 58).
16. "Çé mystère nous servi, nou-minme, par permission Grand Maître. Moune qui guin Zombi, çé mauvé moune qui bésoin yo pou gadé hounfort, ou pou travail nan jadin. Nou pa nan ça, nou-minme" (Valcin 146).
17. In actuality, *vodou* went unrecognized for most of the nineteenth century. Dessalines, and especially King Christophe sought to legitimize Haiti in the eyes of European powers by making Catholicism the national religion (Desmangles 43); it was not until 1940 that *vodou* was actively condemned and the Christian churches (both Catholic and Protestant) launched campaigns to abolish the religion (Métraux 47).
18. Barbara Christian writes of the image of the mulatta in African-American literature: "the plight of the mulatta arose as reading material for the ears of white folks. . . . the existence of the mulatta, who combined the physical characteristics of both races denied their claim that blacks were not human while allowing them the argument that they were lifting up the race by lightening it" (*Black Feminist Criticism* 3).
19. "le coeur de la femme était un bibelot" (Valcin 40).
20. "Laurence, songez au bonheur d'un malheureux qui préfère troquer sa puissance de maître contre la docilité de l'esclave. Je suis votre esclave, non, moins que cela . . . votre chose. Je me traine à vos pieds. Chère Laurence!" (Valcin 109)
21. "Fou de rage, l'américain . . . tira son couteau et lui coupa la langue. Il cessa de parler, puisqu'il n'avait plus la langue, mais il se mit à rire" (Valcin 12).
22. "La loi du mariage? Mais, c'est une barbarie. On voit bien qu'elle a été faite par les hommes pour terroriser les femmes, pour faire d'elles d'éternelles mineures. Ne m'en parlez pas, oh! non" (Valcin 125).
23. Il est temps que le mariage ne fasse plus d'une femme libre, une opprimée. . . . Tenez, moi, grâce à ce mariage je suis une esclave que seul le divorce libérera" (Valcin 126).
24. "Elle voudrait avoir quelqu'un qui la protège, qui lui soit dévoué. . . . Elle se tourne encore vers le grand Christ d'argent qu'elle avait imploré naguère dans ses premiers jours d'angoisses, et murmure: "Mon Dieu protégez Eveline. Si je suis coupable envers Guy, ne punissez que moi" (Valcin 205).
25. "Elle dort. On eût dit une déesse, à la voir ainsi, la tête rejetée en arrière, ornée d'un touffe de jasmins sauvages. . . . Ses deux nattes blondes comme deux rubans jaune-pâle tombent négligeamment sur ses épaules nues. Elle dort profondément dans une pose inconsciemment lascive et naturellement séduisante. Un sourire erre sur sa lèvre rose. Tout se tait, c'est la nuit, une nuit ouatée de mystère" (Valcin 129).
26. "On ne vous le dit pas que vous êtes exquise/Dans toutes les chansons et dans touts les sonnets,/On célèbre toujours quelque pâle marquise,/Vous êtes excitante, on n'en parle jamais" (Valcin 66).
27. "Ai-je l'air de Vénus avec ce teint pâli?/Vous vous croyez déjà blonde comme Cybelle,/Mais le miroir se tait parce qu'il est poli" (Valcin 69).
28. "Eh bien! moi, j'ai par trop chanté la femme blanche,/. . . . Je m'en vais

t'ériger—à charge de revanche—/Une statue avec le bronze de ta peau" (Valcin 67).

29. "J'aime tant ses silences sacrés où l'on parle à l'âme de son âme" (Valcin 211).

30. "Ne comparons pas 1934 à 1803. Deux dates historiques, oui, mais combien différentes l'une de l'autre. 1804: proclamation glorieuse de l'Indépendance d'Haïti après des luttes incessantes par des citoyens jaunes et noirs de la petite île opprimée par les Français! 1934, hélas!; libération . . . évacuation pacifique d'Haïti . . . grâce aux *besoins de la politique* du Président des Etats-Unis . . . et, ô ironie! . . . deuxième Indépendance" (Valcin 214).

31. "le préjugé de couleur, existe-t-il en Haïti entre les naturels mêmes du pays?" (Valcin 67)

32. "la grandeur d'une nation se mesure à la persistance de ses souvenirs" (Valcin 73).

33. "une nuit rose, hésitante apeurée, éperdue, une nuit qui s'avançait et qui s'arrêtait, vaincue et triomphante" (Valcin 174).

34. Madeline Gardiner, in her own study of four Haitian women writers (Desroy is not among them), claims that Desroy's women are too flighty and hedonistic to be representative of the Haitian woman (5). It is my contention that the novel, though falling short of presenting a strong Haitian female character, demonstrates *why* Haitian women have not been accurately represented in Haitian literature in this time period.

35. "tenant des deux mains son ventre, tandis que le sang s'échappait d'elle et tombait en flaques" (Desroy 93).

36. "Qu'on l'enlève . . . si elle crève ce sera une de ces maudites négresses de moins" (Desroy 94).

37. "De toute cette scène que Murray venait de raconter, ce qu'il n'avait point vu, *ce qu'il ne pouvait pas voir,* c'était deux petites filles qui se tenaient par les mains, toute endimanchées; leurs jambes décharnées brinqueballaient dans des chaussures trop larges" (Desroy 96, my emphasis).

38. "Pauvres épaves, déjà ballottées par la vie; deshéritées, qui ne savaient pas encore ce que c'est que d'être orphelin" (Desroy 98).

39. The text of "Choucoune" reads in part: "Choucoune, c'est une marabout: Ses yeux brillent comme des chandelles/ Elle a des seins droits" (Laroche 116).

40. "une jolie négresse, taille cambrée, seins droits, robe bariolée de fleurs vives" (Desroy 30).

41. "Tu as un idéal de beauté qui est le type caucasique. Attends d'être familiarisée avec les créoles, et tu me diras si tu n'en trouves pas de très jolies. . . . Regarde le corps de Lamercie. Quelle ligne! Nue, elle tenterait l'artiste le plus difficile. Et cela sans massage, sans sport. Elle est 'nature'" (Desroy 60).

42. "Elle est magnifique. . . . Oh! Arabella, rarement j'ai vu une plus jolie femme, quel galbe! Le mari ne doit pas s'embêter." (Desroy 61).

43. "Elles affectent un air:—toujours cigarette aux lèvres, mine marmoréenne, moue méprisante, l'air trop grande dame pour être de vraies dames" (Desroy 39).

44. "Le préjugé de couleur, c'est l'américaine qui l'entretient" (Desroy 39).

45. "ce que nous ne pouvons empêcher, il faut bien le subir" (Desroy 42).
46. "Malgré elle[,] sa haine d'haitienne jaillissait contre l'Occupant, dont les agissements portaient des êtres jeunes à se subalterniser presque afin de pouvoir vivre" (Desroy 207).
47. "Comme pour un dernier salut, le Phare au loin alluma ses feux. /Puis tout disparut./Lentement le paquebot s'enfonça dans l'obscurité que la/lueur des premiéres étoiles n'éclairait pas encore" (Desroy 222).

CHAPTER 3   *Ghislaine Charlier and Jan J. Dominique*

1. "du plus loin qu'elle se souvienne, elle a toujours écrit."
2. "parce qu'elle aime le faire, parce qu'elle en a besoin."
3. "Ce portrait ornait la maison de ses proches en Haïti et elle décida qu'il ornerait la page couverture de son roman."
4. "débutée en Haïti, [la rédaction] a été continuée à Paris et à New York et s'est terminée à Montréal."
5. This theme of flight is not unique to Haitian women's experience. Women writers of the Anglo-Caribbean also articulate this sense of continuous exile. Trinidadian writer Dionne Brand, for example, writes in *Bread Out of Stone:* "A long time ago I think I fled this place because flight is as strong as return; the same, often. One is not the end of the other or the beginning of the next, and often when we go back all we can think of is flight. And in flight" (65).
6. "s'il m'avait demandé de le suivre, je n'aurais peut-être pas dit non, ce qui montre bien que je n'étais pas destinée à être une victime de l'oppression" (Charlier 96).
7. "Ogé périt, victime de son aveuglement. Il ne savait pas, ce ce que nous avons appris depuis, ce qui cause toutes les révoltes, à savoir que l'oppresseur ne comprend qu'un langage: celui de la force" (Charlier 106).
8. "D'humeur gaie, paisible, il acceptait les prévenances avec bonne grâce et remerciait avec délicatesse. Lorsqu'il rendait service, ce qu'il faisit fréquemment, il s'arrangeait toujours pour paraître l'obligé" (Charlier 74).
9. "ce que pourrait devenir un quarteron foncé et pauvre dans cette société de blancs" (Charlier 75).
10. "Nous reprenions goût à la vie. Dans nos âmes en peine, la douleur se calmait et nous nous réjouissions d'avoir enfin obtenu l'égalité" (Charlier 168).
11. I should note here that the plot of Charlier's text also bears striking resemblance to Marie Chauvet's novel, *La danse sur le Volcan* of 1957, which focuses on the the life-story of an *affranchie* named Minette who progressively abandons the privileges of her class in order to work for the emancipation of the slaves of Saint-Domingue. It differs significantly, however, in its textualization of the plot in postmodern stylistics and its thematic concern with memory as the locus of historicization.
12. "Les hommes dont je te parle furent plus grands que les héros antiques. Ils durent reconquérir un bien beaucoup plus précieux que la plus belle des mortelles . . . la liberté" (Charlier 14).

13. "un mémoire rédigé par un colon de Jérémie dans lequel celui-ci proposait de libérer les esclaves en leur distribuant les terres vacantes pour en faire des paysans" (Charlier 106).
14. "dans une vieille malle ayant appartenu à Madame Théophile Noel, née Zulma Laraque par son parent Octave Petit" (Charlier 106).
15. "Peut-être avait-il eu la tête tranchée? Ou bien, tombé aux mains des royalistes, avait-il péri dans l'enfer du NOUVEL AMOUR" (Charlier 160–161).
16. "il était politique d'avoir à Saint-Domingue, une alliée dans la classe montante" (Charlier 183).
17. "blancs sont rentrés en ville en portant triomphalement des têtes de mulâtres au bout de leurs baïonnettes; se faisaient précéder d'une pique sur laquelle ils avaient fiché un enfant de couleur encore vivant" (Charlier 113).
18. "s'il en a, subissent les derniers outrages" (Charlier 114).
19. "une provençale grande et forte, toujours armée d'un sabre et de pistolets, la tête chargée de plumes rouges, les épaules nues couvertes des ses longs cheveux noirs" (Charlier 136).
20. "Les femmes qui entourent Mme Martin s'emparent de lui et un sapeur lui tranche la tête. Ses membres coupés, jetés ça et là, sa tête fut portée par toute la ville au bout d'un piquet, pendant que Mme. Martin lui ayant d'un coup de couteau, tranché les parties génitales, les emporte chez elle en triomphe" (Charlier 137).
21. "J'ai envie de détruire les pages déjà écrites, elles sont insatisfaisantes, elles ne montrent pas ce que je sens, pense, vis" (Dominique 29).
22. "Je suis bâillonnée. Je me bâillonne; je voudrais, je veux enlever ce bâillon mais il tient bon, je le sens qui emprisonne mes doigts comme souvent il me ferme la bouche" (Dominique 9).
23. "on ne sait jamais à qui on a affaire" (Dominique 11).
24. "Je ne dois plus avoir peur mais trouver un moyen de ne plus mettre les masques. Toujours les masques. Il ne s'agit pas de faire attention, de ne pas en dire trop, il faut au contraire que je dise trop, trouver le moyen de transmettre cet ordre à mes doigts, c'est une question de survie, je n'en peux plus de me taire. Je sais que je parle, seule, à voix haute parfois, plus souvent au fond de moi, mais j'ai besoin d'écrire ce texte, tant pis pour la prudence, il y aura toujours quelqu'un pour m'empêcher de commettre les erreurs impardonnables, si j'arrive réellement à perdre mes habitudes d'auto-censure" (Dominique 11).
25. "Je dois écrire pour qui ne manque pas de lectures" (Dominique 12).
26. "Le premier geste de malaise. La première manifestation de cette différence qui n'arrêtera jamais de hurler dans sa tête" (Dominique 18).
27. I will return to the role of the army in my final chapter.
28. "la révolte devant cet homme lui parlant d'héritage. Cet homme disant qu'elle était son fils" (Dominique 20).
29. "elle se pense sans nom, elle n'a plus de nom" (Dominique 54).
30. "Si elle rit de tout, même si elle se moque parfois des souvenirs, elle ne parlera jamais de ce banc d'écolière où elle s'est blottie, tremblante, avec dans les oreilles, sans arrêt, le bruit des balles qui ne ricochaient pas" (Dominique 55).
31. "Je crie mon silence pour apprendre à parler" (Dominique 57).

32. "il n'existe jamais de tout-bon ou tout méchant" (Dominique 34).
33. "Oser insulter votre drapeau. Vous présenter à demi nus, pieds nus, pour montrer votre hostilité" (Dominique 74).
34. "La majorité des gens de notre pays vont pieds nus, faute de chaussures. Est-ce une insulte au drapeau?" (Dominique 70).
35. "Comme d'habitude, tout avait commencé par un bruit connu que la mémoire se refusait à identifier" (Dominique 70).
36. "Mais au second passage, il y le regard de l'autre. Elle sourit et l'autre regarde cette enfant-élève cachée à l'ombre des tireurs. L'autre regarde, horrifié, et elle prend peur. L'autre qui, une fraction de seconde, a pu guider le regard des hommes embusqués sur le balcon de la maison. Elle s'aplatit encore plus et écoute le silence soudain des fusils" (Dominique 72).
37. "Votre compagnon essaie quelques fois de vous parler, vous aussi. A travers des mots, des gestes, vous lui montrez votre plaisir. Il vous conduit ensuite à la grande place: arbres feuillus, fontaine, bancs à l'ombre, vous découvrez une autre ville. . . . vous . . . oubliez l'anomalie de votre tourisme devant ces jardins parfumés au camélia et au jasmin" (Dominique 65).
38. "j'essaie de fuir pour rentrer chez moi" (Dominique 75).
39. "Ils me croyaient indifférente quand je ne manifestais ni surprise horrifiée ni écoeurement aux récits des matraquages policiers, des interrogatoires-annuaire-téléphonique-épais-sur-la-tête-pour-éviter-les-recours-en-justice-des-victimes-à-cause-des-traces-de-coups, des activités illégales de la police" (Dominique 98).
40. "la violence . . . est toujours exercée contre le plus faible"; "l'insolence, l'assurance, la riposte facile, la tête levée, ce que méritaient des policiers qui doivent respecter mes droits, respecter une loi" (Dominique 98).
41. "[Il] n'a pas été mon premier amant, je n'ai pas eu de premier amant; Steve était ma réponse" (Dominique 99).
42. "Pourquoi les femmes devraient-elles toujours être celles qui donnent sans rien recevoir en retour? Seule la tradition les y oblige et je refuse ce genre de tradition" (Dominique 117).
43. "j[e leur] ai fait confiance très vite: ils prononçaient des mots qui répondaient à ma quête. . . . je me promettais d'aller retrouver les hommes au grand courage. Et je les ai rencontrés . . . sentant la distance avec ceux qui parlaient en mon nom tout en me refusant la parole" (Dominique 120).
44. "Je continuais à photographier Liza comme si quelque part en moi je craignais de ne plus pouvoir, une seconde fois, partir avec elle au bout du monde. Quelque part en moi je savais déjà, puisque le mariage, qui m'avait offert ces jours de congés, était le prélude au Retour" (Dominique 136).
45. "livres de femmes, conversations de femmes sur les matelas posés par terre, projets de femmes" (Dominique 140).
46. "les yeux grands ouverts je regardais vivre ma soeur siamoise" (Dominique 140).
47. "Je n'arrivais pas à me sentir choqué de voir ces deux filles, joue contre joue, se balancer lentement. Martine semblait émue, je sentais son corps nous dire 'elle a voulu danser avec moi, tant pis pour vous si vous refusez de comprendre'" (Dominique 142).

48. "Je ne voulais pas comprendre quand elle me disait la vie d'une femme et, sentant ma crainte, elle devinait que j'essayais de refuser les phrases offertes" (Dominique 147).
49. "J'ai di 'pourquoi?,' elle répondit dans un éclat de rire 'pourquoi pas?!' Je n'avais plus envie de savoir. J'avais retrouvé ma peur et, malgré elle, je m'entendais rire. De sa tendresse inattendue, de la chaleur de sa peau, de sentir ses tentatives de contrôle quand le désir la rendait trop vulnérable. . . . Je fermais les yeux et elle me tendait la main" (Dominique 150).
50. "il a utilisé mes rêves, a parlé de notre rage, il a pris le droit de vouloir mon corps à cause de la folie commune"; "il n'a rien vu en elle de ces hurlements, n'a rien compris de la souffrance muette, car il ne regardait que ses seins" (Dominique 161).
51. "Je ne saurais te parler des femmes, mais plutôt te dire mes femmes, celles qui remplissent mon coeur et ma vie, celles qui, complices, respectent ma force et soutiennent mes pas trébuchants, celles qui copinent, celles qui partagent, celles qui maternent et qui me veulent sage, celles folles qui protègent mes éclats de rire, mes femmes-merveilles que je porte accrochées à mon coeur" (Dominique 170).
52. "Je n'arrive pas encore à te dire Liza, je ne peux que te promettre un autre voyage, un autre continent, pour rencontrer Liza. Arriverai-je à bien te raconter Lucie?" (Dominique 171).
53. "Je me suis dirigée vers elle, lui ai tendu la main qu'elle a attrapée d'un air moqueur et je l'ai fait descendre lentement" (Dominique 173).
54. "je découvrais tout à coup la présence des femmes dans ma vie. Pas simplement une femme avec qui le lien était devenu très fort, pas seulement Julia ou Liza, mais les femmes pour tout" (Dominique 172).
55. "Paul existe, Lili m'échappe encore" (Dominique 179).

CHAPTER 4   *Nadine Magloire and Edwidge Danticat*

1. "'une petite pluie fine strie l'air de raies blêmes'" (Magloire 7).
2. "On se croit parmi les élus et puis on découvre un jour qu'on est tout compte fait destiné à un vie médiocre puisque c'est cette vie-là qu'on a en lot. . . . Q'importe que je me sois sentie faite pour de grandes choses. Je mène une existence insignifiante" (Magloire 7).
3. "Toussaint Louverture avait bien raison"; "C'est avec le fouet qu'il faudrait obliger ce peuple à travailler en attendant qu'il apprenne la dignité humaine" (Magloire 48).
4. "C'est absurde de les avoir invitées puisqu'elles m'ennuient, mais le mal est fait. Nous parlerons des futilités habituelles. Le confort matériel, les toilettes, les ragots. Il semble qu'il n'y ait rien d'autre qui puisse passionner les femmes haïtiennes" (Magloire 36).
5. "Les livres, la musique, voilà mon univers. Mon refuge contre l'angoisse de mon néant" (Magloire 9).
6. "j'ai découvert le roman et je m'y suis jetée passionnément. D'une certaine manière je retrouvais le monde enchanté de mon enfance, mais un monde

adapté à mon nouvel état d'âme. Le roman c'était une féerie pour adulte" (Magloire 28).

7. "C'est étrange. Chaque fois que quelque chose me fait envie je le découvre en rêve dans ce cabinet" (Magloire 27).

8. "la fonction essentielle du mari c'est de faire affluer l'argent à la maison" (Magloire 30).

9. "[E]lle a un corps splendide"; "J'estime davantage une fille qui use de son corps au gré de son caprice que ces épouses si fières de leur fidélité mais qui, en fait, se vendent à leur mari" (Magloire 34).

10. "Tu es trop romanesque, Claudine. Le roman c'est une chose et la vie une autre. Vois toutes tes amies qui ont fait des mariages d'amour. Qu'est-ce qu'il en reste maintenant? C'est lamentable tous ces couples" (Magloire 62–63).

11. "Les seules sensations que j'éprouve ne sont jamais provoquées que par une image érotique au cinéma ou la description d'une scène d'amour dans un roman" (Magloire 28).

12. "pour regarder les feuilles des arbres frémir sous la brise ou un oiseau qui voltige d'une branche à l'autre" (Magloire 18).

13. "souvent le vide de ma vie m'étreint péniblement" (Magloire 18).

14. "un grand amour donnerait un sens à ma vie" (Magloire 14).

15. "je pourrais mourir ou tuer" (Magloire 87).

16. "Ma vie est sans issue"; "Je souffre sans cesse mais j'aime mon mal. Je ne veux pas guérir" (Magloire 89).

17. "Toute la matinée je marche en ville comme une hallucinée dans l'espoir de le rencontrer enfin seul. Le soir je l'attends. Je dois espérer à tout prix que je le retrouverai parce que sans cet espoir il ne me resterait plus rien. J'aime mieux mourir" (Magloire 103).

18. "D'aucuns prétendent même que les *marassa* sont plus puissants que les *loa*. Ils sont invoqués et salués au début d'une cérémonie, tout de suite après Legba" (Métraux 129).

19. Here, the reader is referred to Ifi Amadiume's *Male Daughters Female Husbands* (London: Zed Books Limited, 1986).

20. In many respects, the uneven language in the novel can be ascribed to the fact that it was published when Danticat was twenty-five years of age. I am suggesting, however, that there is a level of complexity in the narrative that has more to do with the author's own bilingualism and identity as a displaced Haitian woman herself.

21. This refers to Haitian poet Marie-Alice Théard's collection of poetry, *Cri du Coeur,* published in Port-au-Prince in 1986.

CHAPTER 5   *Marie Chauvet and Anne-christine d'Adesky*

1. "Se voulant les gardiennes du temple libéral, les institutions internationales prêchent ainsi dans la foulée la limitation de l'intervention de l'État, la réduction des budgets sociaux et des salaires, l'accueil sans restriction des firmes étrangères et la diffusion d'un modèle de consommation homogénéisé, occidentalisé dont les "effets de démonstration" et les dépenses somptuaires

sont les sinistres reflets dans beaucoup de pays du tiers monde" (Grimaldi and Chapelle 306).

2. James Ridgeway notes that the research of Josh DeWind and David H. Kinley III reveals the USAID's bankrolling of the Haitian government in amounts ranging from $58.3 million in 1975 to $100 million annually. He explains further that "the Haitian government did not carry out the [US]AID projects, and, for its part, [US]AID did nothing to promote change in the power structure" (123); they did so to nurture "a web of international alliances" rather than to alleviate poverty or human rights abuses.

3. "elle [l'armée] est créé dans le but d'aider l'Occupant à maintenir la paix publique en combattant toute résistance nationale" (Dumas 65).

4. I am in disagreement here with Trouillot when he states that "[w]omanhood, which had traditionally afforded partial protection from the state, now became a disadvantage" because that partial protection could only have been extended systematically to the upper crust of the society that benefited from legal protections; in other words, those women whose womanhood would have been "protected" can only feasibly be conceived of as having belonged to the moneyed 10 percent of the Haitian population.

5. Although the manuscript of *Les Rapaces* was published posthumously by Marie Chauvet's family under her "maiden" name Vieux, given the circumstances under which the text finally appeared—Chauvet's family refused to have her works translated and bought back all unsold copies of the book that sent her into exile (*Amour, colère, folie*)—I have chosen to restore the name that she used all of her writing life.

6. "Il paraît qu'ils l'ont estropiée. Tu l'as vue? J'attends encore que les choses se tassent. Eugénie Duclan, elle, l'a vue. En cachette, mais elle l'a vue. Elle n'a plus rien, là. . . . Ça doit être terrible. Elle a raconté à Eugénie avoir vu sa chair voler en éclats tandis que Calédu la cravachait, couchée sur le dos, les jambes ouvertes, maintenue dans cette position par quatre prisonniers, quatre mendiants pouilleux à qui il l'a ensuite livrée. . . . J'ai soixante-quinze ans. . . . jamais je n'ai senti comme aujourd'hui planer autant l'horreur et la malédiction sur cette ville" (Chauvet 42).

7. "Bien parlé. . . . c'est pourquoi nous crions, nous, les pauvres: vive le chef! quel qu'il soit!" (Chauvet 12)

8. "Ainsi toi, tu vas mourir. . . . si tu meurs, on jettera ton corps dans un trou et personne, pas même nous, n'en saura jamais rien" (Chauvet 12).

9. "On dit dans les mornes . . . que tout a été réglé avant la mort du chef. Les rênes du pouvoir, il les a passées aux siens" (Chauvet 13).

10. "Elevé dans la jouissance, gavé comme toute bête de riches, il avait volé avec plaisir tout ce qui lui était tombé sous la patte" (Chauvet 23).

11. "Son indifférence persista jusqu'au moment où il comprit que leur destin était si étroitement lié, qu'il se trouvait livré à son tour sans défense à ses plus cruels ennemis" (Chauvet 27).

12. "Même s'il est enfermé dans ce cercueil, plaça alors le vieillard, sentencieusement, même s'il est couché là, la peur aura fait sortir de leur maison tous les bourgeois de ce pays. Ceux qui ont vu disparaître des membres de leur famille

comme ceux qui ont été personnellement maltraités. J'en ai vu beaucoup défiler dans ce palais. Ce chef-là, eh bien, il a su comment nous dompter. La preuve: nous mourrons de misère. Bon, et alors on nous ordonne: criez, vive le chef! Et nous tous et les bourgeois avec nous, tout le monde crie: vive le chef!" (Chauvet 14)

13. "La peur était responsable. La peur qui vous clôt les yeux sur des crimes crapuleux. La peur qui vous scelle les lèvres. La peur qui vous fait baisser la tête *pour paraître indifférent et résigné* quand les tripes et le sang bouillonnent au fond de vous de rage et de révolte" (Chauvet 67; my emphasis).

14. "Oui, les jeunes désertent les champs. . . . on les tente en bas avec des armes et de l'argent" (Chauvet 69).

15. "L'ambition est une maladie, frère. . . . elle se propagera et montera sur les mornes et elle envahira le pays tout entier" (Chauvet 69).

16. "Les cordes! Les cordes! Les cordes! hurlait-il, liez-vous par des cordes à ces mornes parce que les rapaces viendront jusqu'ici pour vous enlever de la bouche le pain de chaque jour" (Chauvet 71).

17. "Qu'est-ce qu'il y a? interrogea Adélia, en tournant ses yeux blancs vers la cour. Je sens quelque chose, papa, quelque chose comme un danger. En dedans de moi tout est amarré comme par un noeud de corde. Je sens des présences. C'est comme un odeur de sang" (Chauvet 76).

18. "Quand dans un pays tout le peuple est éclairé, les chefs ne peuvent plus le tromper. Car si les chefs le trompent, le peuple se révolte et réclame des comptes" (Chauvet 89).

19. "Si Anne revient, j'épaulerai la cause qu'elle défend. Je dépenserai ma fortune à réparer le mal que j'ai fait à mon pays. J'en fais le serment. Que ce livre soit publié et qu'à ma suite marchent tous les autres rapaces" (Chauvet 113).

WORKS CITED

Primary Sources

Charlier, Ghislaine Rey. *Mémoire d'une affranchie*. Montréal: Lemeac, 1989.
Chauvet, Marie (Vieux). *Les rapaces*. Port-au-Prince: Deschamps, 1986.
d'Adesky, Anne-christine. *Under the Bone*. New York: Farrar, Straus, Giroux, 1994.
Danticat, Edwidge. *Breath, Eyes, Memory*. New York: Soho, 1994.
Desroy, Annie. *Le joug*. Port-au-Prince: Imprimerie Modèle, 1934.
Dominique, Jan J. *Mémoire d'une amnésique*. Port-au-Prince: Deschamps, 1984.
Magloire, Nadine. *Le mal de vivre*. Port-au-Prince: Verseau, 1967.
Valcin, Mme. Virgile [also known as Cléante Desgraves]. *La blanche négresse*. Port-au-Prince: n.p., 1934.

Secondary Sources

Abbott, Elizabeth. *Haiti: The Duvaliers and Their Legacy*. New York: McGraw-Hill, 1988.
Anzaldúa, Gloría. *Borderlands/La Frontera: The New Mestiza*. San Francisco: Spinsters/Aunt Lute, 1987.
Bellegarde-Smith, Patrick. *Haiti: The Breached Citadel*. Boulder, CO: Westview Press, 1990.
————. "Haitian Social Thought: A Bibliographical Survey." *Inter-American Review of Bibliography* 32.3–4: 330–337.
Benitez-Rojo, Antonio. *The Repeating Island: The Caribbean and the Post-modern Perspective*. Durham, NC: Duke University Press, 1992.
Blume, E. Sue. *Secret Survivors*. New York: Ballantine, 1990.
Bouchereau, Madeleine. *Haïti et ses femmes*. Port-au-Prince: Presses Libres, 1957.
Brand, Dionne. "Just Rain, Bacolet." *Bread Out of Stone*. Toronto: Coach House, 1994.
————. *No Language is Neutral*. Toronto: Coach House, 1992
Campbell, Elaine. "The Unpublished Short Stories of Phyllis Shand Allfrey." *Caribbean Women Writers*. Ed. Selwyn R. Cudjoe. Wellesley, MA: Calaloux Publications, 1990.

Canham-Clyne, John and Worth Cooley-Prost. "Haiti to the Haitians?" *The Progressive* Sept. 1995: 22–25.

Charles, Carolle. "Gender and Politics in Contemporary Haiti: The Duvalierist State, Transnationalism, and the Emergence of a New Feminism (1980–1990)." *Feminist Studies* 21.1 (1995): 135–164.

Chauvet, Marie. *Amour, colère, folie.* Paris: Gallimard, 1968.

Christian, Barbara. *Black Feminist Criticism: Perspectives on Black Women Writers.* New York: Pergamon Press, 1985.

———. "Black Studies or Women's Studies." *Women's Studies* 17 (1989): 17–23.

———. "The Race for Theory." *Feminist Studies* 14:1 (1988): 67–79.

Condé, Maryse. *La parole des femmes: Essai sur des romancières des Antilles de langue française.* Paris: L'Harmattan, 1979.

Coste, Didier. *Narrative as Communication.* Minneapolis: University of Minnesota Press, 1989.

Cudjoe, Selwyn. *Resistance and Caribbean Literature.* Athens: Ohio State University Press, 1980.

d'Adesky, Anne-christine. "The Nightmare That Is Haiti: Gunshots in the Quiet of Night." *Los Angeles Times* 18 Sept. 1994: M1, M6.

———. "As Tension Swirls in Haiti, Just What Is the U.S. Role?" *Los Angeles Times* 9 Oct. 1994: M1, M6.

Dash, Michael. "Through the Looking Glass: Haitian-American Relations in the Literature of the Occupation." *Komparatistische Hefte* 9–10 (1984): 41–56.

Dayan, Joan. "Vodun, or the Voice of the Gods." *Raritan* 10.3 (1991): 32–57.

Deren, Maya. *Divine Horsemen.* New York: Chelsea House, 1970.

Derrida, Jacques. "No Apocalypse, Not Now (Full Speed Ahead, Seven Missiles, Seven Missives)." *diacritics* 14.2 (1984): 20–31.

DeShazer, Mary K. *A Poetics of Resistance: Women Writing in El Salvador, South Africa, and the United States.* Ann Arbor: University of Michigan Press, 1994.

Desmangles, Leslie G. *The Faces of the Gods.* Chapel Hill: University of North Carolina Press, 1992.

DeWind, Josh and David H. Kinley III. "'Export-Led' Development." *The Haiti Files: Decoding the Crisis.* Ed. James Ridgeway. Washington, DC: Essential Books/Azul Editions, 1994.

Dumas, Pierre-Raymond. *Haiti: Une armée dans la mêlée.* Port-au-Prince: Bibliothèque Nationale d'Haiti, 1994.

Farmer, Paul. *The Uses of Haiti.* Monroe, ME: Common Courage, 1994.

Feldman, Yvette Tardieu. "Une romancière Haitienne méconnue: Annie Desroy (1893–1948)." *Conjonction* 124 (August 1974): 33–57.

"Feminism and the Current Crisis in Haiti." *oob* 24.3 (1994): 8, 16.

Ferguson, James. *Papa Doc, Baby Doc: Haiti and the Duvaliers.* New York: Basil Blackwell, 1987.

Fitzgerald, F. Scott. *The Great Gatsby.* In *Three Great American Novels.* New York: Charles Scribner's Sons, 1959.

Fleischmann, Ulrich. "Language, Literacy, and Underdevelopment." *Haiti—Today and Tomorrow.* Ed. Charles R. Foster and Albert Valdman. Lanham, MD: University Press of America, 1984.

Ford-Smith, Honor. *Lion-Heart Gal.* Toronto: Sister Vision, 1987.

Fraser, Nancy and Linda J. Nicholson. *Feminism/Postmodernism.* New York and London: Routledge, 1990.

Freire, Paulo. *Pedagogy of the Oppressed.* Trans. Myra Bergiman Ramos. New York: Continuum, 1994.

Gardiner, Madeleine. *Visages de femmes, portraits d'écrivains.* Port-au-Prince: Deschamps, 1981.

Gilbert, Sandra M. and Susan Gubar. *The Madwoman in the Attic.* New Haven, CT: Yale University Press, 1979.

Gillis, John R. "Memory and Identity: The History of a Relationship." *Commemorations: The Politics of National Identity.* Ed. John R. Gillis. Princeton, NJ: Princeton University Press, 1994.

Gilman, Sander. "Black Bodies, White Bodies: Toward an Iconography of Female Sexuality in Late Nineteenth-Century Art, Medicine, and Literature." *Critical Inquiry* 12.1 (1985): 204–242.

Glass, Charles. "Invasion of the Hypocrites." *The Spectator* 273.8670 (1994): 11–12.

Gouraige, Adrienne. "Littérature Haïtienne: Le rôle des femmes dans la société chez deux romancières." *Revue francophone de Louisiane.* 4.1 (1989): 30–38.

Gouraige, Ghislain. *Histoire de la littérature Haïtienne.* Port-au-Prince: Imprimerie Théodore, 1960.

Gregory, Steven. "Voodoo, Ethnography, and the American Occupation of Haiti: William B. Seabrook's *The Magic Island.*" *Essays in Honor of Stanley Diamond: The Politics of Culture and Creativity—A Critique of Civilization.* Vol. 2. Ed. Christine Ward Gailey. Gainesville: University Press of Florida, 1992.

Grimaldi, Muriel and Patrick Chapelle. *Apocalypse: Mode d'emploi.* Paris: Presses de la Renaissance, 1993.

Guillaume, Denyse. "Le statut légal de la femme." *Voix des femmes* Dec. 1939-Jan. 1940: 18.

"Haiti: Attacks on Women Intensify." *Ms.* 5.1 (1994): 12.

Harlow, Barbara. *Resistance Literature.* New York and London: Methuen, 1987.

Harrison, Lawrence E. "Voodoo Politics." *The Atlantic Monthly.* June 1993: 101–107.

Healy, David. *Gunboat Diplomacy: The U.S. Navy in Haiti, 1915–1916.* Madison: University of Wisconsin Press, 1976.

Heinl, Robert D., Jr., and Nancy G. Heinl. *Written in Blood: The Story of the Haitian People, 1492–1971.* Boston: Houghton Mifflin, 1978.

Herskovits, Melville. *Life in a Haitian Valley.* New York: Alfred A. Knopf, 1937.

Hoffman, Léon-François. "The Originality of the Haitian Novel." *Caribbean Review* 8.1 (1974): 44–50.

hooks, bell. *Yearning: Race, Gender, and Cultural Politics.* Boston: South End Press, 1990.

Hooper, Michael S. "The Politization of Human Rights in Haiti." *Haiti—Today and Tomorrow.* Ed. Charles R. Foster and Albert Valdman. Lanham, MD: University Press of America, 1984.

Huannou, Adrien. *La question des littératures nationales.* Paris: CEDA, 1989.

Hutcheon, Linda. *The Politics of Postmodernism.* London: Routledge, 1990.

Irwin-Zrecka, Iwona. *Frames of Remembrance: The Dynamics of Collective Memory.* New Brunswick, NJ: Transaction, 1994.

James, C.L.R. *The Black Jacobins.* New York: Vintage, 1963.

Kurlansky, Mark. *A Continent of Islands: Searching for the Caribbean Destiny.* Reading, MA: Addison-Wesley, 1992.

Laguerre, Michel S. *The Military and Society in Haiti.* Knoxville: University of Tennessee Press, 1993.

Lamour, Adeline. "Allocution." *Quand la Faculté de Droit commémore le centenaire de sa fondation, 1860–1960.* Port-au-Prince: Imprimerie de l'Etat, 1961.

Laroche, Maximilien. "La littérature en Haïtien." *La littérature Haitienne.* Montréal: Lemeac, 1981.

Lawless, Robert. *Haiti's Bad Press.* Rochester, VT: Schenkman, 1992.

Lionnet, Françoise. "Geographies of Pain: Captive Bodies and Violent Acts in the Fictions of Myriam Warner-Vieyra, Gayl Jones, and Bessie Head." *Callaloo* 16.1 (1993): 132–152.

———. "Inscriptions of Exile: The Body's Knowledge and the Myth of Authenticity." *Callaloo* 15.1 (1992): 30–40.

———. "'Logiques métisses': Cultural Appropriation and Postcolonial Representations." *College Literature* 19.3 (1992): 100–120.

Loomba, Ania. "Overworlding the `Third World.'" *Colonial Discourse and Post-Colonial Theory.* Ed. Patrick Williams and Laura Chrisman. New York: Columbia University Press, 1994.

Lorde, Audre. "Dahomey." *The Black Unicorn.* New York: Norton & Co. 1978.

———. "The Power of the Erotic." *Sister/Outsider.* New York: Crossing Press, 1984.

Lowenthal, Ira P. "Labor, Sexuality and the Conjugal Contract." *Haiti—Today and Tomorrow.* Ed. Charles R. Foster and Albert Valdman. Lanham, MD: University Press of America, 1984.

Mackinnon, Catharine A. *Feminism Unmodified: Discourses on Life and Law.* Cambridge, MA: Harvard University Press, 1987.

May, John R. *Toward a New Earth: Apocalypse in the American Novel.* Notre Dame and London: University of Notre Dame Press, 1972.

Métraux, Alfred. *Le vaudou Haïtien.* Paris: Gallimard, 1958.

Metzger-Théard, Héloise. "Une visite aux pauvres." *Voix des Femmes* 6.47 (1940): 5.

Miccio, Kristian. "Women and the Law." *Women: Images and Realities.* Ed. Kesselman et al. Mountain View, CA: Mayfield Publishing, 1995.

Miller, Errol. "Primary Education and Literacy in the Caribbean." *Caribbean Affairs* (1990): 66–103.

Modleski, Tania. "Postmortem on Postfeminism." *Feminism Without Women.* New York and London: Routledge, 1991.

Mohanty, Chandra Talpade. "Under Western Eyes: Feminist Scholarship and Colonial Discourses." *Colonial Discourse and Post-Colonial Theory.* Ed. Patrick Williams and Laura Chrisman. New York: Columbia University Press, 1994.

Nicholls, David. "Caste, Class and Colour in Haiti." *Caribbean Social Relations.* Ed. Bori S. Clarke. Monograph Series No. 8 Liverpool: Center for Latin American Studies, 1978.

Nora, Pierre. "Between Memory and History: Les Lieux de Mémoire." *History and Memory in African-American Culture.* Ed. Geneviève Fabre and Robert O'Meally. New York: Oxford, 1994.

O'Callaghan, Evelyn. "Interior Schisms Dramatised: The Treatment of the 'Mad' Woman in the Work of Some Female Caribbean Novelists." *Caribbean Women Writers.* Ed. Selwyn R. Cudjoe. Wellesley, MA: Calaloux Publications, 1990.

O'Leary, Stephen D. *Arguing the Apocalypse: A Theory of Millenial Rhetoric.* New York: Oxford University Press, 1994.

Ott, Thomas O. *The Haitian Revolution 1789–1804.* Knoxville: University of Tennessee Press, 1973.

Pamphile, Léon D. "The NAACP and the American Occupation of Haiti." *Phylon* 48.1 (1986): 91–99.

Paravisini-Gebert, Lizabeth and Barbara Webb. "On the Threshold of Becoming Caribbean Women Writers." *Cimarron* (Spring 1988): 106–131.

Plummer, Brenda Gayle. *Haïti and the United States: The Psychological Moment.* Athens: University of Georgia Press, 1992.

Pompilus, Pradel et les Frères de l'Instruction Chrétienne. *Manuel illustré d'histoire de littérature Haïtienne.* Port-au-Prince: Deschamps, 1961.

Price-Mars, Jean. *Formation ethnique: Folklore et culture du peuple Haitien.* Port-au-Prince: Valcin, 1939.

———. *So Spoke the Uncle.* Trans. Magdaline W. Shannon. Washington, DC: Three Continents Press, 1983.

Quinn, Roseanne L. "'I should learn to see the truth as great men have seen it': Male Mentoring and Sexual Harassment in Higher Education." *Feminist Teacher* 7 (1992): 20–25.

Rey, Ghislaine. *Anthologie du roman Haïtien 1859–1946.* Sherbrooke: Naaman, 1982.

Rich, Adrienne. "Compulsory Heterosexuality and Lesbian Existence (1980)." *Blood, Bread, and Poetry.* New York: W. W. Norton, 1986.

Ridgeway, James. *The Haiti Files: Decoding the Crisis.* Washington, DC: Essential Books/Azul Editions, 1994.

Riley, Denise. *Am I That Name?: Feminism and the Category of "Women" in History.* Minneapolis: University of Minnesota Press, 1988.

Rochemont, Weber Augustin. *Du féminisme national.* Port-au-Prince: Belizaire, 1950.

Rosbottom, Ronald C. "The Novel and Gender Difference." *A New History of French Literature.* Ed. Denis Hollier. Cambridge, MA: Harvard University Press, 1989 (1994).

Saldívar, José David. *The Dialectics of Our America.* Durham, NC: Duke University Press, 1991.

Schor, Naomi. "The Scandal of Realism." *A New History of French Literature.* Ed. Denis Hollier. Cambridge, MA: Harvard University Press, 1994.

Seabrook, W. B. *The Magic Island.* New York: Harcourt, Brace & Co., 1929.

Shelton, Marie-Denise. "Haitian Women's Fiction." *Callaloo* 15.3 (1992): 770–777.

Spivak, Gayatri Chakravorty. "Can the Subaltern Speak?" *Colonial Discourse and Post-Colonial Theory.* Ed. Patrick Williams and Laura Chrisman. New York: Columbia University Press, 1994.

Suleri, Sara. "Woman Skin Deep: Feminism and the Postcolonial Condition." *Colonial Discourse and Post-Colonial Theory.* Ed. Patrick Williams and Laura Chrisman. New York: Columbia University Press, 1994.

Sylvain, Madeleine G. "Congrès féminin pour la paix." *Voix des Femmes* 6.45 (1940): 2.

Théard, Marie-Alice. *Cri du Coeur.* Port-au-Prince: n.p., 1989.

Trinh, T. Minh-ha. *Woman, Native, Other.* Bloomington: Indiana, 1990.

Trouillot, Michel-Rolph. *Haiti: State Against Nation—The Origins and Legacy of Duvalierism.* New York: Monthly Review, 1990.

Truth, Sojourner. "Ain't I A Woman?" *Feminist Issues.* Ed. Sheila Ruth. Mountain View, CA: Mayfield Publishing, 1994.

Watkins, Mary. "'In Dreams Begin Responsibilities': Moral Imagination and Peace Action." *Facing Apocalypse.* Ed. Valerie Andrews et al. Dallas: Spring Publications, 1987.

Wilentz, Amy. "Lives in the Balance." *The New Yorker* 26 Dec. 1994: 92–105.

Wilson, Elizabeth. "'Le voyage et l'espace clos'—Island and Journey as Metaphor: Aspects of Woman's Experience in the Works of Francophone Caribbean Women Novelists." *Out of the Kumbla.* Ed. Carole Boyce Davies and Elaine Savory Fido. Trenton, NJ: Africa World Press, 1990.

INDEX

ABOUT THE AUTHOR

𝓜yriam J. A. Chancy, Assistant Professor of English at Vanderbilt University, is a Haitian scholar and writer born in Port-au-Prince, Haiti and raised in Canada. Her critical and creative work has appeared in a number of journals and anthologies, including *Fireweed* and *By, For, and About: Feminist Cultural Politics*. She is also the author of *In Search of Safe Spaces: Afro-Caribbean Women Writers in Exile*, forthcoming from Temple University Press.